"十二五"普通高等教育本科国家级规划教材

U0645778

语言学导论

An Introduction
to Linguistics

文　旭　主编

北京师范大学出版集团
BEIJING NORMAL UNIVERSITY PUBLISHING GROUP
北京师范大学出版社

图书在版编目（CIP）数据

语言学导论/文旭主编．—北京：北京师范大学
出版社，2012.2（2024.7重印）
　ISBN 978-7-303-14116-6

　Ⅰ．语…　Ⅱ.①文…　Ⅲ.①语言学–高等学校–教材
Ⅳ.①H0

　中国版本图书馆CIP数据核字（2012）第018527号

图书意见反馈：gaozhifk@bnupg.com　010-58805079

出版发行：北京师范大学出版社　www.bnupg.com
　　　　　北京市西城区新街口外大街12-3号
　　　　　邮政编码：100088
印　　刷：北京虎彩文化传播有限公司
经　　销：全国新华书店
开　　本：787 mm×1092 mm　1/16
印　　张：15.25
字　　数：269千字
版　　次：2012年2月第1版
印　　次：2024年7月第12次印刷
定　　价：27.00元

策划编辑：王　强　　　　　责任编辑：王　强　于　乐
美术编辑：李向昕　　　　　装帧设计：李向昕
责任校对：陈　民　　　　　责任印制：马　洁

作者简介

　　文旭，博士，教授，博士生导师，西南大学外国语学院院长。北京师范大学博士，北京外国语大学博士后。先后在美国伊利诺伊大学、加州大学伯克利分校访学，研修认知语言学。教育部国家级人才特聘教授。全国翻译专业学位研究生教指委委员，教育部英语分指委委员。*Cognitive Linguistic Studies*(《认知语言学研究》)、*Asian-Pacific Journal of Second and Foreign Language Education*(《亚太二语与外语教育学刊》)、《语言、翻译与认知》(集刊)主编，《外语教学与研究》《中国外语》、《外语与外语教学》、*Review of Cognitive Linguistics*(《认知语言学评论》)、*Intercultural Pragmatics*(《跨文化语用学》)等国内外多种学术期刊编委。中国英汉语比较研究会认知翻译学专业委员会会长、认知语言学专业委员会副会长，中国逻辑学会语用学专业委员会副会长，重庆市外文学会会长。商务印书馆"中国认知语言学前沿丛书"主编，中国人民大学出版社"全人教育英语专业本科教材系列"总主编，清华大学出版社"新世界互动英语系列教材"总主编。主要研究领域为认知语言学、语用学、认知翻译学、外语教育学等。

前　言

　　语言是人类存在的家园，是人类思维和交际的工具，也是洞察人类心智最好的窗口。人类之所以为人类，就是因为人类掌握了语言这一特殊的工具，如《春秋穀梁传·僖公二十二年》中所言："人之所以为人者，言也。"哲学家伽达默尔甚至认为："谁拥有语言，谁就拥有世界。"我们很难想象，没有语言，人类社会将是什么样子。对语言进行系统而科学的研究，就是语言学。语言学是一门"领先的科学"（pilot science），是人文科学与自然科学之间的桥梁。哲学家卡西尔说："在整部科学史中也许没有一章比语言学这门科学的出现更令人神往。这门科学的重要性完全可以跟 17 世纪伽利略改变了我们关于物理世界的整个观念的新科学媲美。"

　　根据《普通高等学校本科外国语言文学类专业教学指南——英语类专业教学指南》的规定，"语言学导论"为专业核心课程，"旨在培养学生对人类语言的理性认识，提高学生的语言文化意识和思辨能力"。"语言学导论"是选修其他语言学专业方向课程的先决条件（如英语句法学、英语语义学、英语语用学等），也是选修其他综合文化素质课程的基础。由此可见，"语言学导论"课程在英语专业教学中具有举足轻重的地位。

　　本书是为西南大学国家级一流课程"语言学导论"编写的配套教材，既可作为英语专业语言学课程的教材，也可作为报考语言学硕士研究生的学生和语言学研究者的参考书。作为一部配套教材，其编写的主要目的是就人类语言本质的基本问题为学生提供一些解答，使学生了解或掌握语言学的基本知识，了解语言的本质、功能和机制，掌握语言的语音、词汇、语法、语义、语用规律，认识语言与社会、文化、心理、生理、生物、认知等之间的关系，并学会分析语料，了解如何进行语言及语言学研究，由此为进一步的语言学习或研究奠定基础。根据党的二十大报告精神，并基于以上编写目的，在本书的编写过程中，我们主要突出以下特点。

　　知识性强，涵盖面广："语言学导论"主要是介绍语言学的基础知识，因此涉及语言学的方方面面。本书不仅涵盖语言学的主要分支学科，如语音学、音系学、形态学、句法学、语义学，还介绍了语言学研究中的一些新兴的或重要的学科，如语用学、话语分析、文体学、心理语言学、认知语言学等。我们希望通过本书的学习，可以让读者对语言学的基本概念、整个蓝图以及语言学的发展史有一个大致的认识。

语言简单，趣味性强：由于语言学的许多概念十分抽象，为降低读者阅读和理解的难度，我们在本书的编写过程中尽量使用比较简单的语言，运用大量的例子，对一些概念和理论进行深入浅出的阐述，使复杂的问题简单化。我们特别注重用一种科学的、生动的方式引出一个抽象的概念，因此，本书通常都是用一个故事、笑话、问题或例子引入一个概念，这极大地增强了内容的可读性和趣味性，在教学上也更具可操作性。

内容新颖，有针对性：本书不囿于对语言学中一些重要概念和经典理论的介绍，还有针对性地讨论了语言学研究中一些比较时兴的课题，如认知语言学的隐喻和转喻理论、认知文体学、批评话语分析和多模态话语分析等。这样既可以使读者学习经典，又可以让他们把握前沿，从而有利于他们的进一步学习和研究。

此外，我们为每章的练习题都提供了参考答案，并且还适时地介绍了一些必要的答题技巧。每章最后的参考文献也很丰富，我们为读者推荐了大量的相关文献，以便他们的后续阅读。书中的重要术语都用黑体标出，便于读者的查阅。在中国高校外语慕课平台(https://moocs.unipus.cn/course/2626)和国家级精品课程平台(https://www.icourses.cn/sCourse/course_2514.html)上的课程网站，我们还提供了许多相应的补充练习和资料，便于老师教学，利于读者学习和交流。

本书是西南大学"语言学导论"课程组成员根据多年教学实践和个人研究兴趣合作完成的，是集体智慧的结晶，反映了团队的精神和力量。参加本书编写的人员有：文旭(第一章)、王颖(第二章)、夏云(第三章)、马军军(第四章)、杨炳钧(第五章)、唐瑞梁(第六章)、成军(第七章)、梁爽(第八章)、刘承宇(第九章)、杜世洪(第十章)、文旭和杨坤(第十一章)、褚修伟(第十二章)。最后由我统稿，并做了一些修改和补充。

本书在编写过程中得到了北京师范大学出版社王强先生的大力支持，杨坤教授也付出了辛勤的劳动。在此，对他们表示衷心的感谢！

虽然我们在编写过程中力求做到语言的简明性和表述的准确性，但由于水平有限，对某些概念和理论还讲得不够清楚和透彻，不当之处在所难免，请同行专家和广大读者不吝赐教，便于以后修订、补充和完善。

文 旭

2023 年 5 月

西南大学外国语学院

目　录

Chapter 1　Preliminaries

1.1　Introduction

Ask people to name the most consequential inventions of world history, and you'll hear a list probably including the wheel, the telephone, the atomic bomb, the first computing machine. What might be missing from the answers, overlooked, is human natural language. For language is an invention, a fantastically successful one. Judged on longevity and extent of modern daily use, it compares with the wheel.

Language comes so naturally to us that it is easy to forget what a strange and miraculous gift it is. The gift of language is the single human trait that marks us all genetically, setting us apart from the rest of life. All over the world we humans fashion our breath into hisses and hums and squeaks and pops and listen to others do the same. We do this, of course, not only because we like the sounds but because details of the sounds contain information about the intentions of the person making them.

There is a well-known story in the Bible that reflects the importance of language in human society. According to the Old Testament, mankind spoke only one language until Nimrod began to build a tower that was to reach heaven. To prevent the people of Earth from reaching His Heaven, God spread chaos and confusion amongst them. He scattered them throughout the Earth, and forced on them different languages so that they would be prevented from communicating with one another and building another Babel.

Language is what makes us human. Whatever we do, language is central to our lives and the use of language underpins the study of every other discipline. We discover our identity as individuals and social beings when we acquire it during childhood. It serves

Figure 1.1　Tower of Babel

as a means of cognition and communication: it enables us to think for ourselves and to cooperate with other people in our community; it is a key to the understanding of so much of human behavior, both of ourselves and of our interaction with others. It provides for present needs and future plans, and at the same time carries with it the impression of things past. By language, we live, we communicate, and we get things done. By language, we read, we write, and we keep a harmonious relationship with the people around us. People with a good mastery of language and its skill are more likely to succeed in their life and career. What is language, then?

1.2 Language

1.2.1 Definition of language

Language has fascinated people for thousands of years, and linguists have studied every detail, from the number of languages spoken in New Guinea to why the English people say *razzle-dazzle* instead of *dazzle-razzle*. Every day we speak language, and hear language, but we never stop to ask what language is. Linguists have offered various definitions of language. Yet none succeeds in satisfying all. According to the important features of languages that most linguists agreed on, a generally acceptable definition is: **Language** is a system of arbitrary vocal symbols used for human communication.

Language is a **system**— elements in it are not arranged and combined randomly, but according to some rules and principles. For example, we can say "I can speak English", but we cannot say "I English can speak". Man is born free, and everywhere he is in chains. So it is in using language. Language is **arbitrary**— there is no intrinsic connection between the word (e.g. *pen*) and the thing (e.g. with what we write). Language is **vocal**— the primary medium for all language is sound. Language is used for human communication— it is **human-specific**, which differs greatly from the systems of animal communication. Birds, bees, crabs, spiders, and most other creatures communicate in a certain way, but the information imparted is severely limited and stimulus-bound, confined to a small set of messages.

1.2.2 Features of language

If language is viewed only as a system of communication, then many species communicate. Then it seems that language is not the exclusive property of the human species. But, as a matter of fact, the human natural language is quite different from the system of animal communication. Although the human language has some features shared with other animals, at least five features are specific to early hominoids and modern humans: arbitrariness, cultural transmission, displacement, productivity, and duality.

(i) Arbitrariness

What's in a name? That which we call a rose.

By any other name would smell as sweet.

(Shakespeare, *Romeo and Juliet*, Act Ⅱ, Scene 2)

Human language is arbitrary. There is no logical or intrinsic connection between meanings and sounds, or between the things signified and the words used to signify them—between **signified** and **signifier**. This feature of language is usually called **arbitrariness**. In English, for example, bakers make bread. The French call it *pain*, the Russians *xleb*. In Chinese, the word is *mianbao*. Not only can a given thing be signified differently in different languages, but even in a single language several signs can represent the same entity or notion. We purchase a *dozen* or *twelve* books for the same price. We can write 12 or XII for the same concept, as well as TWELVE, twelve, or Twelve. Thus, to represent even a straightforward numerical concept, English permits several alternative signs. For more complex content, the variety of possible expressions in phrases and sentences seems limitless.

(ii) Cultural transmission

Language is also culturally transmitted rather than genetically transmitted. Human language is only acquired through a process of learning: a child who is completely cut off from the sound of language will acquire absolutely no facility in the use or understanding of a language. Moreover, a child will acquire only that language which forms part of the culture in which it is brought up. Although the language faculty rests upon our genetic endowment, we learn the specific words and grammatical structures of the language community in which we are raised. For example, a Chinese baby born and brought up in New York by an English family will speak English while an English child, brought up in Beijing by a Chinese aunt, will speak Chinese.

(iii) Displacement

Displacement is that feature of language which allows us to talk about things remote in time or space, or both, from the site of communication: about the past or the future, about places which are far away, even about hypothetical and non-existent state of affairs. With the sole exception of the bee dance, displacement appears to be unique to human beings.

(iv) Productivity

Another feature of language is **productivity** or **creativity** by which there is no limit to the number of different things we can say. Language users can produce and understand indefinite numbers of utterances they ever or never heard before. This feature appears to be unique to human language: all other creatures are restricted to choosing from a short fixed list of possible "utterances".

(v) Duality

Language has at least two levels of structure. First, minimal meaningless units are combined into larger, meaningful units. Specifically, meaningless sounds are combined into meaningful words. For example, the four meaningless English phonemes /p/, /t/, /k/ and /æ/ can be arranged into /æt/ at, /pæt/ pat, /kæt/ cat, /tæp/ tap, /tæk/ tack, /tæt/ tat, /æpt/ apt, /ækt/ act, /tækt/ tact or tacked, /kæp/ cap, /kæpt/ capped, /pækt/ pact or packed, and several other items. Second, these minimal meaningful units can be combined into longer, more complex expressions. Thus, words can be combined into phrases and sentences. This higher level of organization is the essential basis for productivity: even if the range of words are limited to a small, fixed repertoire (e. g. the 850 words of C. K. Ogden's *Basic English*), an enormous number of sentences can be made. This feature of language is crucial, since, if every speech sound had its own meaning, we would not be able to produce more different meanings than we can produce speech sounds. Animal systems of communication generally lack this feature, though bird songs and whale songs arguably contain an element of duality.

1.2.3 Functions of language

Language is a tool of communication and thought, which can be applied to perform some functions. Generally speaking, language has seven basic functions: phatic, directive, informative, interrogative, expressive, evocative, and performative.

Phatic function: language is used to establish an atmosphere or maintain social contact among the communicators. Greetings, farewells, and comments on the weather serve this function.

Directive function: language is used to get the hearer to do something. Most imperative sentences are of this function.

Informative function: language is used to tell something, to give information about facts, or to reason things out. Declarative sentences serve this function.

Interrogative function: language is used to obtain information from others. All questions expecting replies serve this function. However, rhetorical questions do not have interrogative function. For example, *O, wind, if winter comes, can spring be far behind?* This is a rhetorical question which does not expect a reply.

Expressive function: language is used to reveal the speaker's attitudes and feelings. Ejaculations serve this function.

Evocative function: language is used to create certain feelings in the hearers. Jokes, advertising, and propaganda serve this function.

Performative function: language is used to do things or to perform things. The judge's imprisonment sentence, the president's war or independence declaration, etc. serve this function.

1.3   Linguistics

1.3.1   Definition of linguistics

The field of linguistics is a growing and exciting area of study, with an important impact on such fields as philosophy, cognitive psychology, education, anthropology, sociology, language learning and teaching, computer science, neuroscience, and artificial intelligence, among others. That is why linguistics is called the pilot science of humanities and social sciences. If we have much knowledge of linguistics, it is much easier for us to understand other disciplines such as language learning and teaching, translation studies, and literature. At first glance this approach might seem to lie in the great academic tradition of knowing more and more about less and less until you know everything about nothing. But please don't put the book down just yet. Read it, and you will be interested in it. It will be a travel guide to lead you into the wonders of human language and the kingdom of linguistics.

What is linguistics, then? Fundamentally, the field is concerned with the nature of language and verbal communication. **Linguistics** may be defined as the scientific study of language. Perhaps this definition is hardly sufficient to give you the positive indication of the fundamental principles of the subject. But it will be enough to say that by the scientific study of language is meant its investigation by means of controlled and empirically verifiable observations and with reference to some general theory of language. Many linguists today assume that theirs is an empirical and deductive science, and that scientific progress in the domain of their research is possible.

1.3.2　The scope of linguistics

The purpose of linguistics is to provide models of language which reveal features that are not immediately apparent. Linguistics seeks to describe and explain this human faculty. It is concerned with three things: discovering precisely what it means to "know a language"; providing techniques for describing this knowledge; and explaining why our knowledge takes the form it does.

Linguistics is a relatively young science, but it covers a wide scope of topics and its boundaries are difficult to define. A diagram in the shape of a wheel gives a rough impression of the scope covered (Figure 1.2). The major branches of linguistics include phonetics, phonology, morphology, syntax, semantics, and pragmatics. They are fields of enquiry purely about language itself.

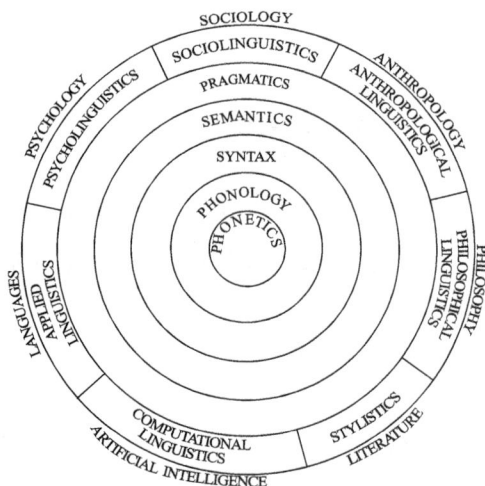

Figure 1.2　Scope of linguistics

Phonetics is the scientific study of speech sounds. It studies how speech sounds are articulated, transmitted, and received. It deals with the physical nature of speech sounds, and not with their relations to other speech sounds in particular languages. It is a pure science and examines speech sounds in general.

Phonology is the study of how speech sounds function in a language. It studies the ways speech sounds are organized. It can be seen as the functional phonetics of a particular language.

Morphology is the study of the formation of words. It is a branch of linguistics which breaks words into morphemes. It can be considered as the grammar of words as syntax is the grammar of sentences.

Syntax is the study of structure of sentences. It deals with the combination of words into phrases, clauses and sentences. It is the grammar of sentence construction.

Semantics is a branch of linguistics which is concerned with the study of meaning in all its formal aspects. Words have several types of meaning. A sentence needs to be well formed both syntactically and semantically. The sentence *Mary married the Mickey Mouse*, for example, is syntactically well formed but semantically ill formed, for we know that a lady cannot marry the Mickey Mouse. Semantics is concerned with such information.

Pragmatics can be defined as the study of language in use. It deals with how speakers use language in ways which cannot be predicted from linguistic knowledge alone, and how hearers arrive at the intended meaning of speakers. In a broad sense, pragmatics studies the principles observed by human beings when they communicate with one another. We can roughly say that pragmatics takes care of the meaning that is not covered by semantics. So people use the formula as its definition: **PRAGMATICS = MEANING - SEMANTICS.**

The branches of linguistics above are at the very center of its scope. However, language can be also studied in relation with something else. Here, for the sake of simplicity, we just list some of them:

Discourse analysis, or **text linguistics** is the study of the relationship between language and the contexts in which language is used. It deals with how sentences in spoken and written language form larger meaningful units such as paragraphs, conversations and interviews, and the various devices used by speakers and writers when they connect single sentences together into a cohesive and coherent whole.

Sociolinguistics is the study of language in relation to society: how social factors influence the structure and use of language. It studies such matters as the linguistic identity of social groups, social attitudes to language, standard and non-standard forms of language, the patterns and needs of national language use, the relations between language and ideology or language and power, linguistic aspects of social psychology, and so on. Another name for sociolinguistics is the **sociology of language**. Linguistic and social problems are closely related, so much so that linguistics itself has sometimes been regarded as a "social" science.

Psycholinguistics is the study of connections between language and mind: the mental structures and processes which are involved in the acquisition, comprehension and production of language. Perhaps the most well-developed part of psycholinguistics is concerned with language acquisition and development in children although there is a growing amount of work being done on second language acquisition and learning.

Stylistics is the study of style in language. Narrowly, it refers to the use of the concepts and techniques of linguistics in studying the language of literary texts like poetry and novels. Broadly, it refers to the study of the aesthetic use of language, in all circumstances, not just in literature.

Forensic linguistics is the examination of linguistic evidence for legal purposes. It refers to the use of linguistic techniques to investigate crimes in which language data forms part of the evidence, such as in the use of lexical or grammatical criteria to authenticate police statements. The field of **forensic phonetics** is often distinguished as a separate domain, which refers to the use of phonetics in criminal investigations, especially in trying to identifying the sex, age and geographical background of a person whose voice is recorded and hence in identifying the speaker.

Anthropological linguistics, also **linguistic anthropology**, is the discipline which combines the concepts and techniques of linguistics and anthropology in order to examine the relations between language and culture. Anthropological linguists typically look at such phenomena as kinship terms and methods of constructing personal names and place names.

Corpus linguistics is an approach to linguistic description based on the extensive accumulation of actually occurring language data and its analysis by computers.

Computational linguistics is an approach to linguistics which employs mathematical techniques, often with the help of a computer. It includes the analysis of language data, the research on machine-aided translation, electronic production of artificial speech and the automatic recognition of human speech. It has produced programs for collecting and evaluating large amounts of language data for making frequency word lists, for automatically indexing, and for producing concordances (word lists with contexts).

Applied linguistics is primarily concerned with the application of linguistic theories, methods and findings to the elucidation of language problems which have arisen in other areas of experience. The most well-developed branch of applied linguistics is the learning and teaching of foreign languages and sometimes the term is used as if this were the only field involved.

1.4   A brief history of linguistics

Nothing is more helpful to the student making his first acquaintance with the science of linguistics than some knowledge of the history of the subject. Many of the ideas about language which the linguist will question will seem less obviously self-evident if one knows nothing of their historical origin. Linguistics can be compared to a pathway which is being cut through the dark and mysterious forest of language. Different parts of the forest have been explored at different times.

1.4.1   Historical linguistics

Before the 19th century, language in the western world was of interest mainly to philosophers. It is significant that the Greek philosophers Plato and Aristotle made major contributions to the study of language. For example, Plato is said to have been the first person to distinguish between nouns and verbs.

1786 is the year that many people regard as the birthdate of linguistics. On the 27th of September, 1786, an Englishman, Sir William Jones, read a paper to the Royal Asiatic Society in Calcutta pointing out that Sanskrit, Greek, Latin, Celtic and Germanic all had striking structural similarities. He concluded that these languages must come from one common source. Jones' discovery fired the imagination of scholars. For the next hundred years, all other linguistic work was eclipsed by the general preoccupation with writing **comparative grammars**, grammars which first compared the different linguistic forms found in the various members of the Indo-European language family, and second attempted to set up a hypothetical ancestor, Proto-Indo-European, from which all these languages were descended.

The 19th century concern with reconstructing Proto-Indo-European, and making hypotheses about the way it split into various modern languages, was encouraged by the general intellectual climate of the times. In 1859, Darwin published his famous *Origin of Species*, putting forward the theory of evolution. It seemed natural to attempt to chart the evolution of language alongside the evolution of species. This emphasis on language change eventually led to a major theoretical advance. In the last quarter of the century, a young group of scholars nicknamed the "Young Grammarians" claimed that language change is regular. It was an important step forward for linguists to realize that language changes were not just optional tendencies, but definite and clearly stateable "laws".

1.4.2 Descriptive linguistics

In the 20th century, the emphasis shifted from language change to language description. Instead of looking at how a selection of items changed in a number of different languages, linguists began to focus on describing single languages at one particular point in time.

If any one person can be held responsible for this change of emphasis, it was the Swiss scholar Ferdinand de Saussure (1857—1913), who is labeled "the father of modern linguistics". His book *Course in General Linguistics* (1915) exerted a major influence on the course of linguistics, particularly in Europe. De Saussure's crucial contribution was his explicit and reiterated statement that all language items are essentially interlinked. This was an aspect of language which had not been stressed before. It was de Saussure who first suggested that language was like a game of chess, a system in which each item is defined by its relationship to all the others. His insistence that language is a carefully built structure of interwoven elements initiated the era of **structural linguistics**. All linguistics since de Saussure is structural, as "structural" in this broad sense only means the recognition that language is a patterned system composed of interdependent elements, rather than a collection of unconnected individual items.

In America, linguistics began as an offshoot of anthropology. Around the beginning of the 20th century, anthropologists were eager to record the culture of the fast-dying American-Indian tribes, and the American-Indian languages were one aspect of this. This state of affairs changed with the publication in 1933 of Leonard Bloomfield's comprehensive work entitled simply *Language*, which attempted to lay down rigorous procedures for the description of any language. Bloomfield considered that linguistics should deal objectively and systematically with observable data. So he is more interested in the way items were arranged than in meaning. He concluded that the study of meaning was "the weak point in language study, and will remain so until human knowledge advances very far beyond its present state". Bloomfield had far more influence than the European linguists working during this period, and the so-called "Bloomfieldian era" lasted for more than twenty years. The Bloomfieldians laid down a valuable background of linguistic methodology for future generations. But by around 1950, linguistics had lost touch with other disciplines and become an abstruse subject of little interest to anyone outside it. It was ready for a revolution.

1. 4. 3   Generative linguistics

In 1957, linguistics took a new turning. Noam Chomsky, then aged twenty-nine, a teacher at the Massachusetts Institute of Technology, published a book called *Syntactic Structures*, which started a revolution in linguistics. Chomsky is, arguably, the most influential linguist of the 20th century, whose reputation has spread furthest outside linguistics. He has transformed linguistics from a relatively obscure discipline of interest mainly to PhD students and future missionaries into a major social science of direct relevance to psychologists, sociologists, anthropologists, philosophers and others.

Chomsky has shifted attention away from detailed description of actual utterances, and started asking questions about the nature of the system which produces the output. According to him, a grammar should be more than a description of old utterances. It should also take into account possible future utterances. A grammar which consists of a set of statements or rules that specify which sequences of a language are possible, and which impossible, is a **generative grammar**. In Chomsky's words, a grammar will be "a device which generates all the grammatical sequences of a language and none of the ungrammatical ones". Such a grammar is perfectly explicit, in that nothing is left to the imagination.

1. 4. 4   Cognitive linguistics

The movement, known as **cognitive linguistics**, is one of the most rapidly expanding schools in modern linguistics and cognitive science. Cognitive linguistics is not a single theory but a paradigm within linguistics, subsuming a number of distinct theories and research programs. It began to emerge in the 1970s and flourish in the 1980s. By the end of that decade it had amassed a relatively large international community of adherents, an International Cognitive Linguistics Association (the ICLA) had been established, a journal *Cognitive Linguistics* founded and a series of biennial conferences established. From the outset, cognitive linguistics sought to create a scientific approach to the study of language, incorporating the tools of philosophy, psychology, neuroscience and computer science. While cognitive linguistic approaches to language were initially based on philosophical thinking about the mind, more recent work emphasizes the importance of convergent evidence from a broad empirical and methodological base. In the first decade of the 21st century, cognitive linguistics represents one of the most exciting and innovative interdisciplinary approaches on offer for the study of the complex relationship between language and mind.

Cognitive linguistics is an approach to the analysis of natural language that focuses on language as an instrument for organizing, processing, and conveying information. The analysis of the conceptual and experiential basis of linguistic categories is of primary importance within cognitive linguistics: it primarily considers language as a system of categories. Therefore, the main topics that cognitive linguistics is interested in are categories and categorization, conceptual metaphor and metonymy, image schemas, iconicity, subjectivity, and grammaticalization.

1.5　Summary

This chapter is a very general introduction to language and linguistics. We have explained language, its features and functions. Linguistics is the scientific study of language. Language is the central object of study in linguistics, but one which can be approached from several points of view. So linguistics has various branches such as phonetics, syntax, semantics, pragmatics, and some other fields such as sociolinguistics, stylistics, psycholinguistics and applied linguistics. Linguistics is a pilot science, which is relatively young but has a wonderful history ranging from historical linguistics to cognitive linguistics. Language is deep in the human heart and humankind is deep in the heart of language. If we know linguistics, can we be far behind in learning language?

Self-study Activities

1. Define the following terms briefly.
   (1) language　(2) linguistics　(3) arbitrariness　(4) duality
   (5) phonetics　(6) phonology　(7) syntax　(8) semantics
   (9) pragmatics　(10) sociolinguistics　(11) psycholinguistics
   (12) stylistics　(13) discourse analysis　(14) corpus linguistics
2. If language is partially defined as communication, can we call the noises that dogs make language? Why or why not?
3. Suggest at least four features of language which are rare or absent in animal communication.
4. Why is de Saussure an important figure in linguistics?
5. Why were the 19th century linguists so interested in historical linguistics?
6. Suppose you taught a dog to *heel*, *sit up*, *roll over*, *play dead*, *stay*, *jump*, and *bark* on command, using the italicized words as cues. Would you be teaching it language? Why or why not?

Sources and Suggestions for Further Reading

Aitchison, J. 1992. *Linguistics*. London: Hodder & Stoughton.
Akmajian, A. et al. 2008. *Linguistics: An Introduction to Language and Communication* (5th

ed.) . Beijing: Foreign Language Teaching and Research Press.

de Saussure, F. 2001. *Course in General Linguistics.* Beijing: Foreign Language Teaching and Research Press.

Finch, G. 1998. *How to Study Linguistics.* New York: Palgrave.

Finegan, E. 1999. *Language: Its Structure and Use* (3rd ed.). New York: Harcourt Brace College Publishers.

Fromkin, V. et al. 2004. *An Introduction to Language* (7th ed.). Beijing: Peking University Press.

Liu, R. Q. and Wen, X. 2006. *Linguistics: A New Coursebook.* Beijing: Foreign Language Teaching and Research Press.

Meyer, C. F. 2009. *Introducing English Linguistics.* Cambridge: Cambridge University Press.

Sapir, E. 2002. *Language: An Introduction to the Study of Speech.* Beijing: Foreign Language Teaching and Research Press.

Yule, G. 2000. *The Study of Language.* Beijing: Foreign Language Teaching and Research Press.

Chapter 2　Phonetics and Phonology

2. 1　Introduction

Read aloud this sentence, "The cat stopped chasing the mouse at the sight of the dog. " If you read it slowly enough, you can tell that this sound sequence is composed of a series of individual sound segments. If you want to analyze the pronunciation of the sentence in more detail, two groups of questions are to be answered.

One includes such questions as follows: What sound segments are exactly involved here? How can these sounds be identified, or described? How is each of them produced? And how can these sounds be classified?

The other group would in part include the following questions: How come the sound of the letter *t* in *cat* is different from that of the *ed* in *stopped*? What is the difference then? Is that difference of the same significance as the difference between the sound of *t* as in *cat* and the sound of *d* as in *dog*? Is there any rule governing the combination of the speech sounds? And which sounds or words in the sentence should be articulated with more strength?

The study of language that aims to answer the first group of questions is referred to as **phonetics**, while the study concerned with the second group is known as **phonology**.

2. 2　Phonetics

2. 2. 1　Definition and classification

Phonetics is the branch of linguistics which studies the characteristics of human sound-making, especially those sounds used in speech, and provides methods for their description, classification and transcription.

According to which aspect of speech sounds is the subject of investigation, three sub-branches of phonetics are generally recognized:

i) **articulatory phonetics**: the study of the way in which speech sounds are made or articulated by the vocal organs;

ii) **acoustic phonetics**: the study of the physical properties of speech sounds, as transmitted between mouth and ear, which often involves analyzing sound waves;

iii) **auditory phonetics**: the study of the perception of speech sounds, as mediated by the ear, the auditory nerve and the brain.

For the purpose of an introductory textbook, we will be mainly concerned with the findings of articulatory phonetics, and English phonetics in particular.

2.2.2 The organs of speech and their functions

In order to produce sound, a physical system must include a source of energy, a vibrating body and a resonance chamber. Speech sounds are produced by a stream of air which comes up from the lungs and passes through the vocal cords into the oral and nasal cavities (see Figure 2.1).

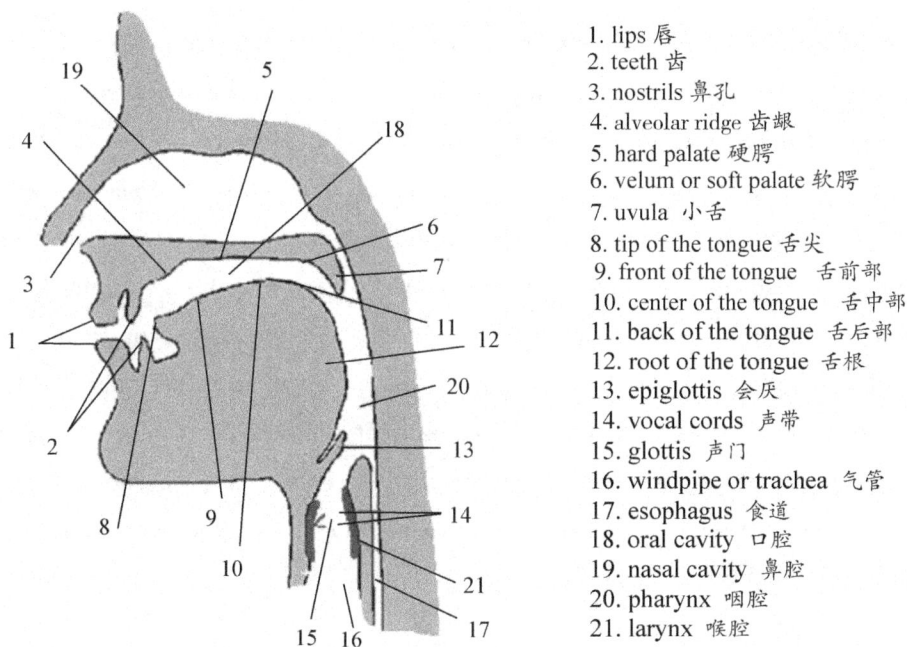

1. lips 唇
2. teeth 齿
3. nostrils 鼻孔
4. alveolar ridge 齿龈
5. hard palate 硬腭
6. velum or soft palate 软腭
7. uvula 小舌
8. tip of the tongue 舌尖
9. front of the tongue 舌前部
10. center of the tongue 舌中部
11. back of the tongue 舌后部
12. root of the tongue 舌根
13. epiglottis 会厌
14. vocal cords 声带
15. glottis 声门
16. windpipe or trachea 气管
17. esophagus 食道
18. oral cavity 口腔
19. nasal cavity 鼻腔
20. pharynx 咽腔
21. larynx 喉腔

Figure 2.1 Organs of Speech

Except esophagus, all of the organs shown in Figure 2. 1 form the vocal apparatus. Obviously, each of the vocal organs may get involved in other functions, including breathing and eating. In fact, on those occasions when we are eating and talking at the same time, many of the organs are performing three different functions simultaneously.

The functioning of the system of vocal organs can be summarized like this. The lungs, by expanding and contracting to bring air in and let it out, supply the basic force which is needed in sound-making. The primary vibration needed for speech is produced in the larynx by the vocal cords. The three interconnected areas above the larynx (popularly referred to as the "Adam's apple"), i. e., the pharynx, the nasal cavity and the oral cavity, serve as **resonance chambers** which are called the **vocal tract**. The air stream expelled from the lungs travels up the windpipe, passes through the vocal cords inside the larynx and enters the three resonance chambers. In this process, it is manipulated with our lips, tongues and other vocal organs in various ways so as to produce sounds of different quality. In general, variations in the force with which air is expelled from the lungs result in differences of intensity or loudness in speech sounds. Variations in the frequency of vibration of the vocal cords are responsible for variations in pitch. Variations in the shape of the vocal tract are related to different speech sounds.

Arguably, the tongue is the most important organ in speech production. The production of most individual speech sounds will involve the tongue, and especially, it is the small movements of the tongue that result in the differences between all **vowels**, sounds that are produced without any restriction in the mouth, such as the second sound in *cat*. The prominent function of the tongue is in part reflected by the facts that the word "language" comes from the Latin *lingua* meaning "tongue", and that such common idioms as *a smooth/sharp tongue* or *hold your tongue* equate the tongue with speaking. The tongue is so important in the production of speech sounds that, for ease of reference, it has been divided into four main areas: the tip, the front, the center, and the back. When the tongue is at rest, the front lies opposite the alveolar ridge, with the center opposite the hard palate and the back opposite the velum.

The vocal cords, like the strings of a guitar, are also worth particular mentioning. The opening between the cords is called the **glottis**. When the cords are somewhat loose and the air stream passes without causing them to vibrate, a **voiceless** or **unvoiced sound** is produced. On the contrary, when the cords are somewhat tense, the pressure of the outgoing air causes them to vibrate with a **voiced sound** being produced. The cords can be stretched to different degrees of tension, so that they vibrate at different frequencies, producing different pitches in the sounds articulated. Here is a good test you can apply to tell if a speech sound is voiced or voiceless. Take for example the ending sound of the word *buzz* and that of the word *bus*. Produce the two sounds in order, as you put your thumb and your index finger on each side your throat. You can feel vibration as you say the former sound, but not the latter.

Now, it might have become clear that the differences between individual speech sounds can be analyzed in terms of what vocal organs are involved and how the air stream is modified. As mentioned earlier, vowels are produced with the outgoing air meeting no restriction in the vocal tract. Try to say the second sound in each of the following words.

(1) p*e*t, b*a*ck, f*a*ce, p*u*t, b*u*s, f*i*rm, h*i*de

They are all vowels. By contrast, some other sounds are produced with the air stream being obstructed or restricted in various forms; these sounds are called **consonants**. Try to say the initial sound of each word in (1) and you can tell that they are all consonants, since the restriction occurs either at the vocal cords or at other vocal organs, such as the lips, teeth, tongue, etc. In short, a consonant is a speech sound produced by partial or complete closure of part of the vocal tract, thus obstructing the air flow and creating audible friction.

2.2.3　Classification of English speech sounds

It should have become clear by now that, as we pointed out earlier, speech sounds can be classified into two general categories: **consonants** and **vowels**, according to whether they are produced by restricting the air flow in some way, either partially or totally. Besides, according to whether the vocal cords vibrate or not when they are produced, speech sounds can be categorized as **voiceless** sounds and **voiced** ones. All vowels are voiced, but not all consonants are. Both consonants and vowels can further be classified into various subcategories.

i) English consonants

Consonants are sounds made by a closure or narrowing in the vocal tract with the air stream either completely or partially obstructed. As a result, they are most conveniently described in terms of where the obstruction is formed and what kind of obstruction is involved, or technically speaking, in terms of **place** and **manner of articulation**.

Say the following two pairs of words slowly: *pat/bat*, *fan/van*. In producing the initial sounds in *pat/bat*, /p/ and /b/, the air stream is blocked by bringing the two lips together, while in producing /f/ and /v/, the air stream is obstructed by pressing the bottom lip against the upper teeth. Consonants can be named according to the speech organs involved in the obstruction. Thus, /p/ and /b/ are called **labial sounds** or **labials**, /f/ and /v/ **labiodental sounds** or **labiodentals**.

The following list serves as a summary of the classification of English consonants in terms of their **places of articulation**.

Bilabial (lips coming together): /p/ /b/ /m/ (/w/) *, as in *per*, *bet*, *met*, *wet*

Labiodental (upper teeth touching lower lip): /f/ /v/, as in *fan*, *van*

Dental (tip or blade of tongue touching upper teeth): /θ/ /ð/, as in *thank*, *than*

Alveolar (tip or front of tongue touching alveolar ridge): /t/ /d/ /s/ /z/ /n/ /l/ /r/, as in *tie*, *die*, *sip*, *zip*, *not*, *lot*, *rot*

Postalveolar (tongue touching back of alveolar ridge): /ʃ/ /ʒ/, as in *fish*, *measure*

Palatal (front of tongue touching hard palate): /tʃ/ /dʒ/ /j/, as in *cheap*, *jeep*, *yes*

Velar (back of tongue touching velum): /k/ /g/ /ŋ/ /w/, as in *cold*, *gold*, *sing*, *wing*

Glottal (vocal folds coming close enough, with no other restriction): /h/, as in *hot*

*Note: when /w/ is articulated, the lips narrow and the back of the tongue touches the soft palate; It is thus taken bilabial or velar.

You may have noticed that although some sounds may have the same place of articulation and share the same voicing, there is still something which makes them different. Take the initial sounds of *sip* and *tip* for example. Here, /s/ and /t/ are both alveolar sounds and thus have the same place of articulation, and they are also both voiceless. However, they are clearly different from each other, with *sip* and *tip* standing as two distinct words.

/s/ and /t/ differ in the **manner of articulation**.

Saying /t/ involves stopping the flow of air in your mouth, and then releasing it suddenly. The result is something like a mini-explosion, and sounds produced this way are thus called **stops**, or **plosives**. Saying /s/, however, involves just some constriction of the airflow in the oral cavity. The speech organs involved do not completely block the flow of air; instead, they are brought close so as to create a narrow opening through which the air flows, with some turbulence or friction caused by the air between them. Not surprisingly, sounds produced like this are named **fricatives**. In fact, with such fricatives as /s/ and /z/, one can even hear a hissing sound as the sound is produced.

Below are the main classifications of English consonants according to manner of articulation.

Plosives (air stream completely obstructed and released suddenly): /p/ /b/ /t/ /d/ /k/ /g/

Fricatives (air stream almost completely obstructed and released with friction): /f/ /v/ /θ/ /ð/ /s/ /z/ /ʃ/ /ʒ/ /h/

Affricates * (air stream completely obstructed and released with friction): /tʃ/ /dʒ/

Nasals (air stream completely stopped somewhere in the mouth and allowed to flow through the nasal cavity): /m/ /n/ /ŋ/

Approximants (speech organs involved approaching each other, but producing no significant obstruction and thus resulting in no audible friction): /l/ /r/ /w/ /j/

* Note: /tr/ /dr/ /ts/ and /dz/ also occur in English but are usually regarded not as affricates, but as consonants (see 2.3.3).

Different from the other consonants, approximants are further divided into various subcategories by phoneticians to emphasize relevant distinctive features among them. For instance, /l/ is called **lateral approximant**, with the name approximant used in particular for the rest three, which may also be called **central approximant**. That is because, /l/, different from the others, is articulated with the sides of the tongue curled in and air escaping over the sides. In addition, /l/ and /r/ are somewhere else named **liquid**, since in their articulation the tongue is raised, partly impeding the flow of air, but the tongue is shaped in such a way that air flows along it, creating particular patterns of vibration. Because of the impedance, liquids are classed as consonants. Very often, /w/ and /j/ are referred to as **glides,** for a more or less gradual glide from one quality to another is an essential part of them. If you make the initial sound of *wet* and *yet* very long, you will be able to tell that they are closely similar to /uː/ and /iː/ respectively, but are very short.

Thus far, we have distinguished three ways of describing consonants: voicing, place of articulation, and manner of articulation. The following table is a summary:

Table 2. 1 English Consonants

	Bilabial	Labiodental	Dental	Alveolar	Postalveolar	Palatal	Velar	Glottal
Plosive	p b			t d			k g	
Fricative		f v	θ ð	s z	ʃ ʒ			h
Affricate						tʃ dʒ		
Nasal	m			n			ŋ	
Approximant	(w)			r		j	w	
Lateral Approximant				l				

In each column, the symbol put to the right represents a voiced consonant.

ii) English vowels

Try saying the sounds in the middle of the following three words: *seat*, *sat*, *side*. They, called vowels, are all produced with no obstruction to the air stream as it passes from the larynx to the lips, and thus are different from consonants. In other words, vowels are articulated without a complete closure in the mouth or a degree of narrowing which would produce audible friction; the air escapes evenly over the centre of the tongue. The differences between vowels largely depend on small movements we make with our tongues, and as a consequence, they are the most mobile of all speech sounds, and the most frequent indicators of differences in pronunciation and accent. Vowels differ from one another in several kinds of features, the most important of which is **quality**, determined by the shape of the resonance chamber, which in turn depends mainly on the position of the tongue. Vowel quality mainly has to do with two dimensions, **tongue height** and **tongue advancement**, with the additional feature of lip shape.

Tongue height concerns the height of the tongue in producing a sound: if the tongue is near the roof of the mouth the sound is described as **high**, and if it is near the bottom it is **low**. Following a general convention, we recognize five degrees of height and label them High, High-mid, Mid, Low-mid, and Low. Try saying in sequence the vowel in *feet* (/iː/), the vowel in *fed* (/e/) and then that in *farm* (/ɑː/). You can feel your tongue keeps dropping to a lower position. A point should be made clear here. It happens that the different degrees of tongue height are roughly equivalent to the degree of openness of the mouth in sound-making. For instance, in saying /iː/, when the tongue is near the roof of the mouth, the mouth is almost close; by contrast, in saying /ɑː/, the mouth is widely open with the tongue near the bottom of it. Thus, we recognize five degrees of openness and label them Close, Close-mid, Mid, Open-mid, and Open.

Tongue advancement concerns which part of the tongue is raised nearest to the palate in sound-making. If it is the front of the tongue that is raised nearest to the palate, the vowel produced is classed as a front vowel. Likewise, if it is the central part or back of the tongue, the vowel will correspondingly be classed as a central or back one. The idea is quite clear, but it is a tricky thing for you to tell exactly which part of the tongue is raised highest in producing a certain vowel. However, if you say in sequence the vowel /iː/ in *he*, the vowel /ɜː/ in *her* and the vowel /uː/ in *boot*, it is possible to sense small movements backwards, with /ɜː/ somewhere in between. It is important to realize that notions such as height, frontness and backness are just "labels" that are used by linguists as a convenient way to describe and compare vowels; they are by no means absolute descriptions of the position of the body of the tongue.

Still, the quality of a vowel, to a lesser extent, depends on the shape of the lips—whether they are rounded or spread (also referred to as unrounded) . Say in sequence the vowels in the following words and see what happens to your lips: /ɑː/ in *arm*, /ɔː/ in *saw*, /uː/ in *room*. You should feel them gradually rounding; with /uː/ they are completely rounded. If you say the vowel in *feet* (/iː/) , the vowel in *fed* (/e/) , however, you will notice that the lips are spread rather than rounded. All vowels are described in terms of this shape: they are either spread or rounded. Of course, some are more spread than others and there are degrees of rounding, but despite these individual variations, they are conventionally put into one of the two categories: round vowels and spread ones.

Vowels can also differ in length. It is sure that any vowel can be stretched out or clipped short; in this sense length depends on the importance of a word in an utterance and on the habits of the speaker. However, in describing vowels in a language, phoneticians are more concerned with determining whether some vowels are typically shorter than others,

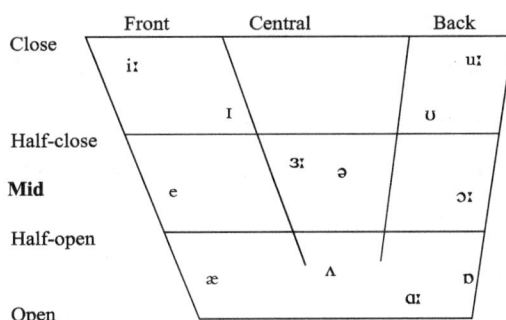

Figure 2. 2 Monophthongs in RP
(**adapted from Finch 1998: 81**)

especially whether two vowels similar in quality differ in length. The vowels in *feet* and *fit*, for example, are somewhat similar in quality but the former is typically longer than the latter. What closely goes with length is the feature of tenseness. Muscles in the lips and, more importantly, in the tongue can be tightened or relaxed in producing a sound. You can feel the muscles in the root of the tongue by putting your fingers where chin and neck come together and thus compare the tension in different vowel articulations. Generally, long vowels are tense, while short vowels are lax. Compare *feet* and *fit*, for example. Figure 2.2 illustrates the simple vowels in British "Received Pronunciation" (**RP**) in terms of their quality.

Another important feature that distinguishes vowels from one another is complexity. Compare the vowel in *cup* (/ʌ/) with that in *out* (/aʊ/). This is the familiar distinction between a simple or pure vowel, or **monophthong**, and a compound vowel, or **diphthong**. For a monophthong, such as /ʌ/, the tongue and lips remain relatively stable throughout the articulation. A diphthong, such as /aʊ/, however, is made with tongue (and lips) moving, involving the movement of the tongue from one vowel position to another.

The eight diphthongs in RP are as follows:

/eɪ/ /aɪ/ /ɔɪ/ /əʊ/ /aʊ/ /ɪə/ /eə/ /ʊə/
face *five* *noise* *boat* *out* *fear* *care* *gourmand*

2.3 Phonology

It is clear that in order to study speech sounds, we have to divide a stream of speech into small pieces that we call segments. The smallest perceptible discrete segment of sound in a stream of speech is a **phone**. For instance, the word *hat* has three phones: two consonants beginning and ending the word and a single vowel between the two consonants. We have shown that phones can be distinguished from each other in terms of how they are produced. In phonetic study, focus is put on what the differences between phones are, with the issue left aside whether particular differences make sense or not. Phonetics is concerned with the characteristics of the speech sounds that the human vocal apparatus can produce in all languages. Phonology, however, is concerned with only those sounds that are used distinctively in any specific language, aiming to demonstrate the patterns of distinctive sound found in a language and to make as general statements as possible about the nature of sound systems in the languages of the world.

2. 3. 1　Phoneme and allophone

Now it is the right time for us to deal with the question: Why are the two phones, /t/ and /d/, taken as distinctive, while the two phones, the aspirated and unaspirated /p/, are not taken as distinctive sounds? The answer is that /t/ and /d/ create meaningful differences in words while the aspirated and the unaspirated /p/ do not. That is, if we replace /t/ with /d/ in the same place of a word, we can change the meaning of a word; nonetheless, the same does not hold true for the aspirated and the unaspirated /p/. For example, if we substitute /t/ for /d/ in the word *dip* we get a different word: *tip*; however, if we substitute the aspirated /p/ in the word *spring* for the unaspirated, we do not get a different word, and a change in the meaning of a word does not occur. So there is a sense in which although the aspirated /p/ and the unaspirated /p/ are *different* sounds they are also the *same* sound.

To capture that sense, we need a new term or concept, **phoneme**. A phoneme is the smallest segment of sound which can distinguish two words. In other words, a phoneme is a phone of distinctive value. The fact that *tip* and *dip* are different words provides evidence that the phones /t/ and /d/ in English are phonemes. By contrast, the aspirated and the unaspirated /p/ are not phonemes in their own right, for they are not of distinctive value. Rather, they are just predictable variations in pronunciation of a same phoneme /p/, i. e. the voiceless bilabial stop. It is observed that the phoneme /p/ is aspirated initially in a syllable and unaspirated elsewhere. In phonology, the variants of a same phoneme are called the **allophones** of the phoneme. Now, we can say that the two phones, the aspirated and the unaspirated /p/, are the allophones of the phoneme /p/. In other words, we can say that the phoneme /p/ is realized in English by two phones: the aspirated and the unaspirated /p/.

2. 3. 2　Minimal pair

One way to determine whether a speech sound is distinctive is to examine minimal pairs. Two words that differ in meaning only by a single phoneme in the same position in a word are referred to as a **minimal pair**, e. g. *pin* vs. *bin*, *cot* vs. *cut*. Linguists or native speakers making these judgments are said to be carrying out a minimal pair test. A group of words which differ from each other only by a single phoneme in the same position, e. g. *pat*, *bat*, *cat*, *hat*, and *fat* (the list can go longer if necessary), is sometimes called a **minimal set**.

Using minimal pair tests, or making minimal sets, it is possible to begin building up an inventory of phonemes within a language. In fact, this is one of the principal ways in which linguists set about mapping the phonemes of different languages.

2. 3. 3　Suprasegmental features

The study of speech sounds can involve either individual segments, namely phones or phonemes, or suprasegmentals, i. e. units larger than individual segments, such as syllables, words, phrases, and clauses. **Suprasegmental features** are the features of sound that describe these units, especially **stress**, and **intonation**, to both of which the notion of **syllable** is of great importance.

i) Syllable

In a certain sense, speaking is like singing: The sounds we produce are notes, and rhythm, tempo, and pitch are all important in speech production. The syllable is the smallest rhythmic unit in English. Most people have an intuitive sense of what a syllable is; for instance, even a non-linguist could tell the word *happiness* contains three syllables. Thus, a syllable is "one pulse of speech", which usually contains one loud or prominent part (almost always a vowel sound), and may optionally have consonant sounds preceding or following the vowel.

In phonological terms, a syllable consists of three parts: an **onset**, a **nucleus** or **center**, and a **coda**. For example, in a simple word such as *hat*, the nucleus is the vowel /æ/, the onset /h/, and the coda /t/. More often than not, both the onset and the coda, or either of them can be absent in a syllable, as shown in *ear*, *at* and *me*. Typically, the nucleus is a vowel, and consonants always do not stand alone as the center of a syllable, apart from some special cases, such as /n/ and /l/. It is possible for the nasal consonant /n/ or the lateral /l/ to form a syllable with other consonants in words such as *button* /b ʌtn/ and *little* /lɪtl/. In such cases, /n/ and /l/ are called **syllabic consonants**.

If a syllable has a coda, it is often called a **closed syllable**, for it is "closed" by a consonant; otherwise, it will be called an **open syllable**. In addition, if a word contains a single syllable, it is called a monosyllable or a monosyllabic word; words containing more than one syllable are called polysyllables or polysyllabic words.

ii) Consonant clusters

In English and some other languages, we can find several consonants (C for short) appear in a sequence, with no vowel (V for short) between them. For instance, the word *spring* begins with three consonants, and *sixths* ends with four. Sequences of two or more consonants as such within the same syllable are called **consonant clusters**. Of course, there will be restrictions on the type of combination which can occur in particular languages. In English, the maximum consonant cluster in the initial position of a syllable contains 3 consonants, while that in the final position contains 4 consonants. So, we can have CCCVCCCC as a possible English syllable or word, for example, *strengths*.

iii) Stress

Speech is a sequence of syllables, some of which may receive more emphasis or strength and thus be more prominent than the others. In the study of speech sounds, the term, **stress**, is used to refer to the degree of force used in producing a syllable, and the usual distinction is between stressed and unstressed syllables, the former being more prominent than the latter. Most discussions of word stress in English only cover the **primary stress** and the **secondary stress**. For example, the word *international* is marked as ˌ*in. ter*ˈ*na. tion. al* /ˌɪntəˈnæʃənəl/. In most cases, a shift in stress pattern can lead to a shift in the way a word functions. For instance, such words as the following function as nouns with the stress on the first syllable, but will function as verbs when the stress is put on the second syllable:

Noun	Verb	Noun	Verb
ˈaccent	acˈcent	ˈcontract	conˈtract
ˈexport	exˈport	ˈimport	imˈport
ˈobject	obˈject	ˈsubject	subˈject

Besides, some adjectives are also distinguished from verbs only by a difference in stress assignment:

Adjective	Verb
ˈabsent	abˈsent
ˈperfect	perˈfect
ˈpresent	preˈsent

In addition to word stress, sentence stress is also important. On the sentence level, stress is mainly employed as a means of distinguishing degrees of emphasis or contrast. Take for example *Tom left for Shanghai* ˈ*yesterday*. Here, with the stress falling on *yesterday*, the whole sentence emphasizes that it is yesterday rather than any other day that Tom left for Shanghai. The term **contrastive stress** is often used for this function.

iv) Intonation and tone

Intonation refers to the way the voice goes up and down in pitch when we are speaking. The different ways the voice fluctuates are known as **intonation patterns**, which can be seen as a sequence of pitch levels, or "tones". There are five types of intonation generally identified in phonology: rising, falling, fall-rise, rise-fall, and level intonation, which are conventionally marked as ↗, ↘, ∨ʼ, ∧ʼ, and →.

The most important function of intonation is to help determine meaning, serving as a signal of grammatical structure, where it performs a role similar to punctuation in writing. Here are some generalizations about the connections between intonation patterns and particular types of grammatical structures:

- Information questions with *who*, *what*, *how*, etc. : Falling (if being asked for the first time), e. g. *What's your name?*
- Yes-no questions: Rising, e. g. *Have you got a pen?*
- Statements: Falling, e. g. *It's over there.*
- Imperatives: Falling, e. g. *Put it on the table.*
- Question tags expecting confirmation: rising and falling, e. g. *You're French, aren't you?*
- Question tags showing less certainty: Rising, e. g. *You're French, aren't you?*
- Lists of items: Rising, rising and finally falling, e. g. *You need a pen, a pencil and some paper.*

Remember, these are just generalizations rather than rules. More often than not, a statement, said in the rising intonation, will be turned into a yes-no question, while an information question may as well go in a fall-rise intonation. Compare the following two sentences where the intonation pattern is marked with an arrow (taken from Kelly 2000: 88):

What time does your train leave?

What time does your train leave?

Here the words are the same, but the difference in intonation pattern makes a contrast between the two sentences. The former one is a question asking for new information, while the latter is one asking for confirmation of something the speaker thinks he has already been told.

When used in the analysis of intonation, the term **tone** refers to the main movement of pitch over a sequence of words. However, that use of the term should not be confused with the tone carried by a single syllable or word, called **lexical tone**. In many languages, the tone carried by a word is an essential feature of the meaning of that word, e.g. in Mandarin Chinese the word *ma* means "mother" if pronounced in a level tone, but "scold" if said in a falling tone. Such languages, where word meanings or grammatical categories (such as tense) are dependent on pitch level, are known as **tone languages**. Many languages of South-East Asia and Africa are tone languages.

2.3.4 Variations of sounds

More often than not, we find that people do not pronounce every sound clearly in their speaking. For example, sometimes, they leave out some sounds or run them together, or even change them, but can still be understood. Such features are usually more evident in rapid, everyday speech than in slow, careful speech. Here we will look at some of the principal variations of sounds in connected speech.

i) Liaison

Liaison involves the insertion of a sound in connected speech. Say the following phrases and try to tell what is happening at the word boundaries: *see it, do it.*

You may have noticed that when a word ends in /iː/, or a diphthong ending in /ɪ/, there is a tendency to introduce a /j/ to ease the transition to the following vowel (e.g. /siːjit/). Likewise, when a word ends in /uː/, or a diphthong finishing with /ʊ/, a /w/ is often introduced to ease the transition to the following vowel (e.g. /duːwit/).

The other sound which is often inserted at word boundaries is /r/. Words like *father, here, far* have an "r" in their spelling, but may not in their pronunciation. However, when they form part of a phrase in which the succeeding word begins with a vowel, /r/ appears or reappears, for example: *father and son* /faːðər ən sʌn/, *her English* /hɜːr ɪŋglɪʃ/.

ii) Assimilation

Assimilation is a process in which phonemes are modified to be similar with their neighboring sounds. It usually occurs across word boundaries, but within words too. This happens because when we are preparing to articulate a phoneme, we are already thinking of the one which will follow it. Try saying the phrase *that book* and observe what happens at the word boundaries when you say it rapidly.

The phoneme /t/ is an alveolar sound, which on its own is produced with the tongue blade forming a temporary closure against the alveolar ridge. However, in saying *that book*, we will notice that the tongue does not actually get there at the end of the word *that*. Rather than having our tongue make the unnecessarily long journey all the way to the alveolar ridge, we employ an economy of effort, and get our lips ready for the next sound /b/. The modified sound /t/ retains its original voice quality and assimilates to a /p/, both being unvoiced. Consequently, *that book* is pronounced as /ðæp bʊk/. However, that does not mean that here we give the /p/ its full plosive manner of articulation, but that our lips are in the position to make a /p/. The best description is that in preparing our articulators for the next sound, the preceding sound acquires some qualities of it. In the phrase *that book*, labial assimilation occurs. The following are some rules for assimilation:

● The phonemes /t/, /d/ and /n/ often become bilabial before bilabials /p/, /b/ and /m/ (e. g. *good boy* /gʊb bɔɪ/, *ten men* /tem men/).

● The phonemes /t/, /d/ and /n/ often become velar before velars /k/, /g/ (e. g. *that cat* /ðæk kæt/, *good concerts* /gʊb kənsɜːts/, *his own car* /hɪz əʊŋkɑː/).

● /s/ can assimilate to /ʃ/ before /ʃ/ (e. g. *this shiny skirt* /ðɪʃ ʃaɪnɪ skɜːt/)

.

The above cases are referred to as **anticipatory assimilation**, where one sound changes to another because of the following sound. There are also cases where two sounds combine to form a different one, called **coalescent assimilation**:

● /t/ and /j/ coalesce to form /tʃ/ (e. g. *last year* /lɑːstʃɪə/).
● /d/ and /j/ coalesce to form /dʒ/ (e. g. *would you* /wʊdʒə/).

iii) Elision

There are many cases where sounds which are produced in words pronounced on their own, or in slow, careful speech, are not found in rapid, casual speech. This is known as **elision**, which is often explained in terms of the Principle of Least Effort: other things being equal, we try to avoid doing more work than is necessary. Elision is most commonly found in the simplification of consonant clusters. The loss of /t/ and /d/ in combination with other consonants serves as a good example, as in:

act badly /ˌæk'bædlɪ/

good books /'ɡʊbʊks/

Likewise, *acts* /ækts/ and *sixth* /sɪksθ/ can be simplified to /æks/ and /sɪks/ in rapid speech. In addition, before consonants /v/ can disappear in *of*, as in *a waste of time.*

The elision of vowels can also be found in rapid speech. A typical example is the disappearing of /ə/ in some unstressed syllables. For instance, *police* and *perhaps* can be produced as /pliːs/ and /phæps/ if said rapidly.

2.4　Summary

In this chapter we have shown how a linguistic description of speech sounds could be arrived at. With the two concepts, phone and phoneme, we can better understand the important distinction between phonetics and phonology. Phonetics is concerned with the acoustic properties of language; it examines phones, without any direct reference to their capacity to act as bearers of meaning. Its primary concern is with sounds as substance. Phonology, on the other hand, relates speech sounds to their linguistic function within the "meaning" structure of the language. As such, it is concerned with phonemes, or sounds as concepts. Having examined the major suprasegmental features and some of the changes in the pronunciation of words in connected speech, we are now enabled to look more closely at intonation patterns and how they affect the meaning of sentences in concrete contexts. This will lead us to the fields of pragmatics (Chapter 6), discourse analysis (Chapter 7) and stylistics (Chapter 9). Also, we can now explore the nature and diversity of accents and how and why changes occur in pronunciation. This will take us in the direction of sociolinguistics (Chapter 8). If you like, jump ahead and look at the relevant sections there; otherwise, we are moving to the next linguistic level, morphology.

Self-study Activities

1. Give the correct technical terms for the sounds made in the following places of articulation:

    (1) the bottom lip and top teeth coming together

    (2) the tongue touching the upper teeth ridge

(3) the tongue touching hard palate

(4) the tip or blade of tongue touching upper teeth

(5) the back of tongue touching soft palate

2. Give the correct technical terms for the sounds made in the following manner of articulation:

(1) complete closure of the oral cavity with the air going out through the nose

(2) complete closure followed by a sudden release of air stream

(3) complete closure followed by a slow release with friction

(4) partial closure where the air stream is allowed to flow out with no audible friction

(5) partial closure where the air stream is released with audible friction

3. Pick out the inappropriate member of each set and justify your choice.

(1) /ʊ/, /ʌ/, /w/, /ɜː/, /eɪ/

(2) /t/, /b/, /f/, /θ/, /ʃ/

(3) /l/, /m/, /n/, /ŋ/

4. Explain the relationships among *phone*, *phoneme*, and *allophone* with examples.

Sources and Suggestions for Further Reading

Aitchison, J. 1992. *Teach Yourself Linguistics* (4th ed.). London: Hodder & Stoughton.

Akmajian, A., et al. 2001. *Linguistics: An Introduction to Language and Communication* (5th ed.). Cambridge, Massachusetts: The MIT Press.

Ashby, M., & Maidment, J. 2005. *Introducing Phonetic Science.* Cambridge: Cambridge University Press.

Crystal, D. 2008. *A Dictionary of Linguistics and Phonetics* (6th ed.). Oxford: Blackwell Publishing Ltd.

Finch, Geoffrey. 1998. *How to Study Linguistics.* New York: Palgrave Macmillan.

Geigerich, H. 1992. *English Phonology: An Introduction.* Cambridge: Cambridge University Press.

Hewlett, N., & Beck, J. M. 2006. *An Introduction to the Science of Phonetics.* Oxford and New York: Routledge.

Jones, Daniel. 2006. *Cambridge English Pronouncing Dictionary* (17th ed.). Cambridge: Cambridge University Press.

Kelly, G. 2000. *How to Teach Pronunciation.* Harlow: Pearson Education Limited.

Kreidler, C. W. 2004. *The Pronunciation of English: A Course Book* (2nd ed.).

Oxford: Blackwell Publishing Ltd.

Meyer, C. F. 2009. *Introducing English Linguistics*. Cambridge: Cambridge University Press.

Todd, L. 1995. *An Introduction to Linguistics*. Harlow, Essex: Longman Group Ltd.

Trask, R. L. and Stockwell, P. 2007. *Language and Linguistics: The Key Concepts* (2nd ed.). New York: Routledge.

Chapter 3　Morphology

3.1　Introduction

Words like *come*, *go*, *book*, *love*, and *it* make up an important part of the vocabulary of English. But they are far outnumbered by words which look rather different:

classroom, *goldfish*, *happiness*, *unwise*, *nationalistic*, *worked*, *tables*

These words are composed of parts. And we can easily see the parts if we imagine them as having hyphens:

class-room, *gold-fish*, *happi-ness*, *un-wise*, *nation-al-ist-ic*, *work-ed*, *table-s*

This chapter is about words—their constituent parts, their internal organization, and their relationships. **Morphology**, as a branch of linguistics, is thus the study of the internal structure, forms and classes of words.

3.2　Morpheme

Many English words are morphologically complex. They can be broken down into smaller units that are meaningful. *Tables*, for instance, where *table* refers to one piece of furniture, while the *-s* serves the grammatical function of indicating plurality.

The term **morpheme** is used to refer to the smallest, indivisible units of semantic content or grammatical function from which words are made up. By definition, a morpheme cannot be decomposed into smaller units which are either meaningful by themselves or mark a grammatical function like singular or plural number in the noun.

3.2.1　Free morpheme

Some morphemes, which are capable of standing independently, are called **free morphemes**. For example,

(1) man, book, tea, sweet, cook, bet, very, pain

Single words like those in (1) are the minimal free morphemes capable of occurring in isolation. Such an element is also called a **root**. A root is the irreducible core of a word, with absolutely nothing else attached to it. It is the part that must always be present, possibly with some modifications.

When roots are used with bound morphemes, the basic word-form involved is technically known as the **stem**. For example,

(2) Word	Noun stem	Plural suffix
works	*work*	*work*　-s
workers	*worker*	*worker*　-s
workshops	*workshop*	*workshop*　-s

In the word-form *works*, the plural inflectional suffix -s is attached to the simple stem *work*, which is a bare root, that is, the irreducible core of the word. In *workers*, the same inflectional -s suffix comes after a slightly more complex stem consisting of the root *work* plus the suffix -er, which is used to form agentive nouns from verbs (with the meaning "someone who does the action designated by the verb", e. g. *singer*, *fighter*, *dancer*). Here *work* is the root, but *worker* is the stem to which -s is attached. Finally, in *workshops*, when *work* and *shop* are both roots, *workshop* is the stem to which -s is attached.

The free morphemes in (1) are also examples of **lexical morphemes**. They are nouns, adjectives, verbs, prepositions or adverbs. Such morphemes carry most of the semantic content of utterances—loosely defined to cover notions like referring to individuals (e. g. the nouns *Mike*, *mother*), attributing properties (e. g. the adjectives *kind*, *wise*), describing actions, process or states (e. g. the verbs *work*, *write*, *rest*) etc., expressing relations (e. g. the prepositions *in*, *on*, *under*) and describing circumstances like manner (e. g. *kindly*, *fiercely*, *quickly*).

Another class of free morphemes is **functional morphemes**. They differ from lexical morphemes in that the lexical morphemes carry most of the semantic content, while the functional morphemes mainly signal grammatical information or logical relations in a sentence. Typical functional morphemes include the following:

(3) Articles:　　　　　*the, a (an)*

　　Demonstratives:　*this, that, these, those*

　　Conjunctions:　　*if, but, and, yet, or, however*

　　Pronouns:　　　　*I, you, we, them; my, your, his, hers; who, which*

3.2.2 Bound morpheme

Some morphemes cannot normally stand alone, but function only as parts of words. For example,

(4) walk, walks, walked, walking, walker

Words in (4) can all be analyzed into the morphemes *walk*, *-s*, *-ed*, *-ing* and *-er* respectively. Obviously, only *walk* can occur on its own as a word, while *-s*, *-ed*, *-ing* and *-er* cannot be further divided into meaningful units and each occurs in many other words, such as *makes*, *looked*, *coughing* and *cooker*. Thus, they are not free and each must be attached to some other units. Morphemes that must be attached as word parts are said to be **bound**. Bound morphemes are actually **affixes**. All affixes in English are bound.

There are three basic types of affixes:

(i) Prefixes

A **prefix** is an affix attached before a root or a stem, like *re-*, *un-* and *in-* in (5):

(5) re-make, un-kind, in-decent, re-read, un-tidy, in-accurate

(ii) Suffixes

A **suffix** is an affix attached after a root or a stem, like *-ly*, *-er*, *-ist*, *-s*, *-ing* and *-ed* in (6):

(6) kind-ly, wait-er, social-ist, book-s, walk-ing, play-er, jump-ed

(iii) Infixes

An **infix** is an affix inserted inside the root itself. Infixes are common in some languages, though they are rare in English. Consider the following examples:

(7) a. Kalamazoo (place name) — Kalama-goddamn-zoo

     b. kangaroo — kanga-bloody-roo

Other examples can be found in the Native American language Nuuchahnulth, where the infix "*-t-*" is used to indicate the plural, as in (8):

(8) t'an'a (child)   t'atn'a (children)

    lim'aqsti (mind)   litm'aqsti (minds)

3.2.3 Derivational versus inflectional morphemes

Bound morphemes can be further classified into two categories: **derivational**

morphemes and **inflectional morphemes**. Derivational and inflectional morphemes form words in different ways.

Derivational morphemes form new words in two ways. One is changing the meaning of the stem to which they are attached. For example, *wise* vs. *un-wise* (both are adjectives but with opposite meanings) and *obey* vs. *dis-obey* (both are verbs but with opposite meanings). The other is changing the word-class that the stem belongs to. For example, the addition of *-ly* to the noun *friend* and the adjective *kind* produce the adjective *friendly* and the adverb *kindly*.

Unlike derivational morphemes, inflectional morphemes do not change the meaning or word-class of a word. Inflectional morphemes are only able to modify the form of a word so that it can fit into a particular syntactic slot. Thus, *book* and *books* are both nouns referring to the same kind of entity. The *-s* ending merely carries information about the number of those entities. The grammar dictates that a form marked as plural (normally by suffixing *-s*) must be used when more than one entity is referred to. The table below is a sample of frequently used inflectional suffixes in English:

Table 3.1   English inflectional suffixes

Suffix	Stem	Function	Examples
-s	N	plural	book-s
-s	V	3rd person, singular, present	sleep-s
-'s/-s'	N	possessive	worker-'s/worker-s'
-ed	V	past tense	walk-ed
-en	V	past participle	brok-en
-ing	V	progressive (incomplete action)	walk-ing
-er	Adj	comparative degree	tall-er
-est	Adj	superlative degree	tall-est

3.3   Morph and allomorph

A **morph** is a physical form representing some morpheme in a language. That is to say, morphs are the phonological (spoken) or orthographic (written) forms which realize morphemes, and they are minimal carriers of meaning.

Most morphemes are realized by single morphs, like *student*, *explain*, *great*, *handle*, etc. These morphemes can stand by themselves as words, and can be used freely in a sentence, but that is not always the case. Sometimes different morphs may represent the same morpheme. For instance, the past tense of regular verbs in English spelled as *-ed* is realized in speech by ［-id］, ［-d］ or ［-t］. The phonological properties of the last segment of the verb to which it is attached determine the choice, as shown in the following:

（9）It is realized as:

a. ［-id］ if the verb ends in ［-d］ or ［-t］

| *mend, mended* | ［*mend*］ ~ ［*mendid*］ |
| *paint, painted* | ［*peint*］ ~ ［*peintid*］ |

b. /d/ after a verb ending in any voiced sound except /d/

| *clean, cleaned* | ［*kli: n*］ ~ ［*kli: nd*］ |
| *weigh, weighed* | ［*wei*］ ~ ［*weid*］ |

c. /t/ after a verb ending in any voiceless consonant other than /t/

| *park, parked* | ［*pa: k*］ ~ ［*pa: kt*］ |
| *miss, missed* | ［*mis*］ ~ ［*mist*］ |

If different morphs represent the same morpheme, they are grouped together and they are called **allomorphs** of that morpheme. We can say that: (i) ［*-id*］, ［*-d*］ and ［*-t*］ are English morphs; and (ii) we can group all these three morphs together as allomorphs of the past tense morpheme.

Other examples are the allomorphs of the morpheme of plurality ［-s］, which is realized orthographically and phonologically as follows:

	orthographic form	phonological form
meaning	meaning*s*	［-z］
map	map*s*	［-s］
watch	watch*es*	［-iz］
mouse	m*i*ce	［-ai-］
foot	f*ee*t	［-i］
deer	*deer*	［∅］（zero change）

3.4 Word formation

As an English learner, do you know what the word in (10) is?

（10）pneumonoultramicroscopicsilicovolcanoconiosis

It is a word that contains 45 letters and is recognized as the longest word in English by the American National Puzzlers' League in 1935. It means "a special form of silicosis caused by ultra-microscopic particles of siliceous volcanic dust". Probably we are fascinated by words like this and wonder how they are created, or some of us must be irrationally scared of them, especially when we are learning English as a foreign language.

Fortunately, no matter how long or strange a word is, it is made up using just a few basic processes of word formation. That is the beauty of word creation. Once we have learned the word-building methods and word elements, we would never have a "*hippopotomonstrosesquipedaliophobia*" (a fear of long words).

3.4.1 Major ways of word formation

3.4.1.1 Affixation or derivation

Affixation or **derivation** is the process of creating separate but morphologically related words, which is done by adding derivational affixes to other words or morphemes. Typically, it involves one or more changes in form. It can involve prefixing, as in *unwise*, *impossible*, and suffixing, as in *wisdom*, *possibility*. A derivational word consists of at least a free morpheme and a bound morpheme (a derivational morpheme or affix).

As indicated in 3.2.2, affixes are classified into prefixes, suffixes and infixes. Here, only prefixes and suffixes will be taken into consideration.

A **prefix** is a derivational morpheme preceding the root-morpheme and modifying its meaning. For example (11),

a. negative prefixes: un- (*ungrateful*); non- (*non-sense*); in- (*incorrect*); dis- (*disloyal*); a- (*amoral*);

b. reversative prefixes: un- (*untie*); de- (*decentralize*); dis- (*disconnect*);

c. pejorative prefixes: mis- (*mispronounce*); mal- (*maltreat*); pseudo- (*pseudo-scientific*);

d. prefixes of time and order: fore- (*foretell*); pre- (*pre-war*); post- (*post-war*), ex- (*ex-president*);

e. prefix of repetition: re- (*rebuild*, *rewrite*);

f. locative prefixes: super- (*superstructure*), sub- (*subway*), inter- (*inter-*

continental）, trans- (*transatlantic*) .

A **suffix** is a derivational morpheme following the root, as in (12):

a. **noun suffixes**: -ing (*building*, *wasting*); -age (*breakage*, *bondage*); -ance/-ence (*assistance*, *reference*); -dom (*freedom*, *kingdom*); -er (*teacher*, *reader*); -ess (*actress*, *hostess*);

b. **adjective suffixes**: -able/-ible/-uble (*favourable*, *incredible*, *soluble*); -al (*formal*, *official*); -ic (*dynamic*); -ant/-ent (*repentant*, *dependent*);

c. **verb suffixes**: -ate (*activate*); -er (*glimmer*); -fy/-ify (*terrify*, *specify*); -ize (*minimize*); -ish (*establish*);

d. **adverb suffixes**: -ly (*quickly*, *coldly*); -ward/-wards (*backward*, *northwards*); -wise (*likewise*) .

3.4.1.2 Compounding or composition

The italicized words in (13) are created by combining *room* with some other words, rather than with a bound morpheme.

(13) a. Our *classroom* is at end of the corridor.

b. Joey and Chandler are *roommates*.

c. Is this your *bedroom*?

Such words are called **compounds**. They contain two or more words, or more accurately, two or more roots. This way of building new words is called **compounding** or **composition**.

In most cases, compounds are spelled as single words, as in *classroom* and *roommate*. Sometimes the parts are connected by a hyphen, as in *kind-hearted* and *lean-faced*, and sometimes they are spelled as two separate words, as in *green house* and *black bird*. It should be noted that the stress pattern of the compound word is usually different from that of the phrase composed of the same words in the same order. For example, "'green house" (stress on the first word) is a compound, while "*green 'house*" (stress on the second word) is a phrase.

There are a number of ways of approaching the study and classification of compound words, the most accessible of which is to classify them according to the word class of the compound and then sub-classify them according to the word class of its constituents. The following is based on the discussion in Bauer (1983) .

(14)

(i) Compound nouns

    a. Noun + noun: *bath towel*; *boyfriend*; *death blow*; *helicopter parent*; *ice queen*

    b. Verb + noun: *pickpocket*; *breakfast*

    c. Noun + verb: *nosebleed*; *sunshine*

    d. Verb + verb: *make-believe*

    e. Adjective + noun: *deep structure*; *fast food*

    f. Particle + noun: *in-crowd*; *downtown*

    g. Adverb + noun: *now generation*

    h. Verb + particle: *cop-out*; *dropout*

    i. Phrase compounds: *son-in-law*

(ii) Compound verbs

    a. Noun + verb: *sky-dive*; *water-cool*

    b. Adjective + verb: *fine-tune*; *quick-charge*

    c. Particle + verb: *overbook*; *outact*

    d. Adjective + noun: *brown-bag*

(iii) Compound adjectives

    a. Noun + adjective: *card-carrying*; *childproof*

    b. Verb + adjective: *fail safe*

    c. Adjective + adjective: *open-ended*

    d. Adverb + adjective: *cross-modal*

    e. Particle + adjective: *over-qualified*

    f. Verb + noun: *roll-neck*

    g. Adjective + noun: *red-brick*; *blue-collar*

    h. Particle + noun: *in-depth*

    i. Verb + verb: *go-go*; *make-believe*

    j. Adjective/Adverb + verb: *high-rise*

    k. Verb + particle: *see-through*; *tow-away*

An alternative approach is to classify compounds in terms of the semantic relationship between the compound and its head. The head of a compound is the constituent modified by the compound's other constituents. In English, heads of compounds are typically the rightmost constituent (excluding any derivational and inflectional suffixes). For example, *in traffic-cop* the head is *cop*, which is modified by *traffic*; in *line-backer* the head is *backer*, which is modified by *line*. There are at least three different semantic relations between the head and modifier(s) of compounds.

First, the compound represents a subtype of whatever the head represents. For instance, a *traffic-cop* is a kind of cop; a *teapot* is a kind of pot; a *fog-lamp* is a kind of lamp; a *blue-jay* is a kind of jay. That is, the head names the type, and the compound names the subtype. These are called **endocentric compounds**.

Second, the compound names a subtype, but the type is not represented by either the head or the modifier in the compound. For example, *pickpocket* and *redhead* represent types of people by denoting their distinguishing characteristics. A *pickpocket* is a person who steals money from other's pockets, and a *redhead* is a person who has red hair. These compounds are called **exocentric compounds**.

Third, there are compounds in which both elements are heads, and each contributes equally to the meaning of the whole, for example, *bitter-sweet*. Compounds like these can be paraphrased as both X and Y, e. g. "bitter and sweet". Other examples include *teacher-researcher* and *producer-director*, and such compounds are called **coordinative compounds**.

3. 4. 1. 3 Conversion

Conversion (also known as **zero derivation**) can be defined as the derivation of a new word without any overt marking. It is the formation of new words by changing their word class without altering their morphological structures. Consider the following examples:

(15) a. the *water*   to *water*
        the *bottle*   to *bottle*
        the *hammer*   to *hammer*
        the *file*   to *file*
    b. to *record*   a *record*
        to *dump*   a *dump*
        to guess   a *guess*
        to *spy*   a *spy*
    c. *soundproof*   to *soundproof*
        better   to *better*

empty	to *empty*
open	to *open*
d. *rich*	the *rich*
poor	the *poor*
well-fed	the *well-fed*
deaf	the *deaf*

From above, we can see that different types of conversion can be distinguished, in particular (a) noun to verb, (b) verb to noun, (c) adjective to verb, and (d) adjective to noun. Other types can also be found, though they are marginal (e. g. the use of prepositions as verbs, as in *to down the can*).

3. 4. 2   Minor ways of word formation

3. 4. 2. 1   Clipping

Clippings appear as a rather mixed bag of forms abbreviated from larger words, which share a common function with words they are from. Clippings originate as terms of a special group like schools, army, police, the medical profession, etc. For example, *exam* (ination), *math* (ematics), and *lab* (oratory) originated in school slang; *spec* (ulation) and *tick* (et) in stock-exchange slang; and *vet* (eran) and *cap* (tain) in army slang. Clipping mainly consists of the following types:

(i) Back clipping

Back clipping is the most common type of clippings, in which the beginning part is retained. Examples are: *ad* (advertisement), *cable* (cablegram), *doc* (doctor), *exam* (examination), *gas* (gasoline), *gym* (gymnastics or gymnasium), *memo* (memorandum), *mutt* (muttonhead), *pub* (public house), and *pop* (popular music).

(ii) Front clipping

Front-clipping retains the final part. For example: *chute* (parachute), *coon* (raccoon), *gator* (alligator), *phone* (telephone), *pike* (turnpike), and *varsity* (university).

(iii) Middle clipping

In **middle clippings**, the middle part of the word is retained. Examples are: *flu* (influenza), *jams* or *jammies* (pajamas/pyjamas), and *tec* (detective).

(iv) Complex clipping

Clipped forms are also used in compounds. One part of the original compound remains intact, while other parts are clipped. Examples are: *cablegram* (*cable* tele*gram*), *op art* (*op*tical *art*), and *org-man* (*org*anization *man*).

3.4.2.2 Acronym

Acronyms are words formed by taking the initial letters from the words in a compound or phrase, which are pronounced as words, such as OPEC (Organization of Petroleum Exporting Countries), AIDS (acquired immune deficiency syndrome), and laser (light amplification by stimulated emission of radiation). Some other examples are:

APEC	Asia Pacific Economic Cooperation
CARE	Cooperative for Assistance and Relief Everywhere
CALL	computer assisted language learning
CALT	computer assisted language teaching
NATO	North Atlantic Treaty Organization
PIN	personal identification number
radar	radio detecting and ranging
SARS	Severe Acute Respiratory Syndrome
TEFL	teaching English as a foreign language
TESL	teaching English as a second language
TOEFL	Test of English as a Foreign Language
VAT	value added tax
WAR	women against rape

When an acronym becomes fully accepted as a word, it often comes to be spelled with lower-case letters, like other ordinary words.

3.4.2.3 Initialism

Initialisms are words formed from the initial letters of words and pronounced as letters, such as USA (the United States of America), VIP (very important person), and CD (compact disk). Other examples are:

ATM	automatic teller machine
CPU	central processing unit
CIA	the Central Intelligence Agency
DVD	digital video disc
EEC	European Economic Community
FBI	Federal Bureau of Investigation
GDP	gross domestic product
GNP	gross national product
GPS	Global Positioning System
GRE	Graduate Record Examination
ID	identification card
IIRC	if I remember correctly
IOC	International Olympic Committee
IQ	intelligent quotient
MBA	Master of Business Administration

3.4.2.4   Back-formation

Back-formation is considered as a reversal process of suffixation, through which a new word is formed by removing an imagined suffix from an already existing form. Back-formation is characterized by the fact that it involves the shortening of a longer word by the subtraction of a morpheme, as shown in the following:

burgle (from *burglar*), *laze* (from *lazy*), *proofread* (from *proofreading*), and *scavenge* (from *scavenger*)

Back-formation is different from clipping. Back-formation may change the word class or the word's meaning, whereas clipping creates shortened words from longer words, but does not change the word class or meaning of the word. Other examples are:

adsorb from *adsorption*, *air-condition* from *air-conditioning*, *biograph* from *biography*, *couth* from *uncouth*, *cross-refer* from *cross-reference*, *diagnose* from *diagnosis*, *edit* from *editor*, *euthanase* from *euthanasia*, *gamble* from *gambler*, *kidnap* from *kidnapper*, *proliferate* from *proliferation*, *resurrect* from *resurrection*, *self-destruct* from *self-destruction*, *spoonfeed* from spoonfeeding, *televise* from *television*, and *vacuum-clean* from *vacuum cleaner*.

3. 4. 2. 5 Blending

Blending involves taking two or more words, removing parts of each, and joining the residues together to create a new word whose form and meaning are taken from the source words. For example, *smog* derives from *smoke* and *fog*, *motel* derives from *motor* and *hotel*, *eracism* derives from *erase* and *racism*, and *webinar* derives from *web* and *seminar*. Other examples are:

boat + hotel	boatel
boom + hoist	boost
breakfast + lunch	brunch
breath + analyzer	breathalyzer
channel + tunnel	chunnel
compressor + expander	compander
goat + sheep	geep
guess + estimate	guesstimate
modulator + demodulator	modem
science + fiction	sci-fi

3. 4. 2. 6 Imitative words

Imitative words, also called **onomatopoeia**, are combinations of speech-sounds, which aims at imitating sounds produced in nature (wind, sea, thunder, etc.), by things (machines or tools, etc.), by people (singing, laughter, patter of feet, etc.), and by animals (barking of a dog, cooing of a dove, chirping of a cricket, etc.). There are two varieties of imitative words: direct and indirect.

Direct imitative words are contained in words that imitate natural sounds. For example, *ding-dong*, *buzz*, *cuckoo*, *tintinnabulation*, *mew*, *Ping-Pong*, *roar*.

These words have different degrees of imitative quality. Some of them immediately bring to mind whatever it is that produces the sound. Others require the exercise of a certain amount of imagination to decipher it. Imitative words can be used in a transferred meaning. For instance, *ding-dong*, which represents the sound of bells ringing continuously, may mean: (a) noisy, or (b) strenuously contested, as in a *ding-dong struggle* and *a ding-dong go at something*.

Indirect imitative words are combinations of sounds, the aim of which is to make the sound of the utterance an echo of its sense. It is sometimes called "**echo-writing**". For example, "*and the silken, sad, uncertain, rustling of each purple curtain*", where the repetition of the sound "*s*" actually produces the sound of the rustling of the curtain.

Indirect imitative words demand some mention of what makes the sound, as "rustling of curtains" in the line above. The same can be said of the sound "*w*" if it aims at reproducing let us say the sound of wind. The word "*wind*" must be mentioned as follows:

Whenever the moon and stars are set,

Whenever the wind is high,

All night long in the dark and wet,

A man goes riding by.

3.4.2.7   Reduplication

Reduplication is a process whereby an affix is realized by phonological material borrowed from the root, for example, *pooh-pooh*, *goody-goody*, *wishy-washy*, *sing-song*, *ruly-poly*, and *harum-scarum*.

English uses some kinds of reduplication, mostly for informal expressive vocabulary. There are three types:

(i) **Rhyming reduplication**: *claptrap*, *hokey-pokey*, *honey-bunny*, *razzle-dazzle*, *slim jim*, *super-duper*, *teenie-weenie*, *wingding*, etc.

Occasionally this morphological tendency to reduplicate is strengthened by a semantic component. In the word *walkie-talkie*, for instance, not only do the combined parts rhyme but also the linking of their independent meanings captures the word's connotation.

(ii) **Exact reduplications** (baby-talk-like): *bye-bye*, *choo-choo*, *night-night*, *no-no*, *pee-pee*, *poo-poo*, etc.

Exact reduplication can be used with contrastive focus (generally where the first noun is stressed) to indicate a literal, as opposed to figurative, example of a noun, as in "Is that carrot cheesecake or carrot *CAKE-cake*?". Consider the following example:

Student: I'm all done.

Professor: *ALL-DONE-all-done?*

(iii) **Ablaut reduplications**: *chit-chat*, *criss-cross*, *ding-dong*, *jibber-jabber*, *kitty-cat*, *knick-knack*, *pitter-patter*, *splish-splash*, *zig-zag*, *honky-tonk*, etc. In the ablaut reduplications, the first vowel is always a high vowel and the reduplicated ablaut variant of the vowel is a low vowel. There is also a tendency for the first vowel to be front and the second vowel to be back.

3.5 Summary

This chapter is about words. More specifically, it deals with the internal structure of complex words, i. e. words that are composed of more than one meaningful element. This area of study is traditionally referred to as morphology, which is sub-classified as Lexical Morphology and Inflectional Morphology. The purpose of this chapter is to enable the readers to engage in their own amalysis of English words. After reading this chapter, the readers should be familiar with the key concepts of morphological analysis and major ways of word-formation in English. Thus, the discussion will be of great value to anyone who is learning English as a first or second language.

Self-study Activities

1. Define the following terms briefly.

    (1) morphology   (2) bound morpheme   (3) free morpheme

    (4) prefix   (5) suffix   (6) infix

    (7) morph   (8) allomorph   (9) inflection

    (10) derivation   (11) compounding   (12) conversion

    (13) back-formation   (14) acronym   (15) initialism

2. The following sentences contain both derivational and inflectional affixes. Underline all of the derivational affixes and circle the inflectional affixes.

    (1) The farmer's cows escaped.

    (2) It was raining.

    (3) Those socks are inexpensive.

    (4) Jill needs the newer copy.

    (5) Fido has a broken leg.

    (6) The strongest rower won.

    (7) The pit bull has bitten the cyclist.

    (8) She quickly closed the book.

    (9) The dramatization went well.

(10) The dispute was eventually resolved after protracted negotiations.

3. Give the full forms and meanings of the following initialisms and acronyms.

   (1) NATO   (2) WWW   (3) SOS
   (4) TOEFL   (5) UN   (6) GMT
   (7) NSC   (8) AM   (9) VIP
   (10) IBM   (11) UNESCO   (12) asap
   (13) dink   (14) FAQ   (15) VAT
   (16) laser   (17) radar

4. Explain the formation of the following blends.

   (1) brunch   (2) motel   (3) talkathon
   (4) mingy   (5) comsat   (6) stagflation
   (7) hi-fi   (8) heliport   (9) smog
   (10) chunnel   (11) guesstimate (12) breathalyser   (13) chortle

5. The following sentences contain verbs created from nouns in accordance with the process described in this chapter. Describe the meaning of each of these new verbs.

   (1) We punk-rocked the night away.

   (2) She dog-teamed her way across the arctic.

   (3) We MG'd to Perth.

   (4) We Concorded to London.

   (5) He Maradonna'd the ball into the net.

   (6) I microwaved the parsnips.

   (7) She Robinson Crusoed in the Galapagos.

   (8) We'll have to Ajax the sink.

   (9) He Windolened the windows.

   (10) You should Clairol your hair.

6. In English dozens of suffixes can change a word into its corresponding noun form. Give at least ten examples of noun suffixes. Adding noun suffixes may result in a shift of stress such as 'real to re 'ality and 'situate to situ 'ation. Can this phonetic feature be widely applied to all noun suffixes? Find some examples to support your ideas.

Sources and Suggestions for Further Reading

Bauer, L. 1983. *English Word Formation*. Cambridge: Cambridge University Press.

Katamba, F. and Stonham, J. 2006. *Morphology*. New York: Palgrave Macmillan.

Liu, R. Q. and Wen, X. 2006. *Linguistics: A New Coursebook*. Beijing: Foreign

Language Teaching and Research Press.

Matthews, P. H. 1991. *Morphology.* Cambridge: Cambridge University Press.

Napolie, J. D. 2003. *Language Matters: A Guide to Everyday Questions about Language.* Oxford: Oxford University Press.

Plag, I. 2003. *Word-formation in English.* Cambridge: Cambridge University Press.

Poole, S. C. 2000. *An Introduction to Linguistics.* Beijing: Foreign Language Teaching and Research Press.

Yule, G. 2000. *The Study of Language.* Beijing: Foreign Language Teaching and Research Press.

Chapter 4   Syntax

4.1   Introduction

Obviously, any speaker of English language could produce and understand the following sentences:

(1) a. He met a girl.

    b. He met a blonde girl.

    c. He met a blonde girl wearing blue jeans.

    d. He met a blonde girl wearing blue jeans and a red hat.

Sentences in (1) vary in length and meaning, but they share the same pattern SVO: a personal pronoun + a predicate in past form + a nominal phrase. Different elements in the sentences are combined by rules or patterns. **Syntax** is the study of these rules and patterns. It is about the infinite uses of finite means: finite in that in most languages the number of basic words is relatively limited and more importantly syntax rules and patterns are finite; infinite because there is no longest sentence and syntax rules can be applied to their own output in a repeated way to create unlimited number of structures. Such infiniteness is labeled "recursion" or "recursiveness". The typical examples are as follows:

(2) a. Mary likes Bill.

    b. John thinks that Mary likes Bill.

    c. Bill thinks that John thinks that Mary likes Bill.

    d. Mary thinks that Bill thinks that John thinks that Mary likes Bill.

    ...

(3) Children's rhyme:

    This is the farmer sowing the corn, that kept the cock that crowed in the morn, that waked the priest all shaven and shorn, that married the man all tattered and torn, that kissed the maiden all forlorn, that milked the cow with the crumpled horn, that tossed the dog, that worried the cat, that killed the rat, that ate the malt, that lay in the house that Jack built. (Cited from Fromkin, et al. 2007: 133)

Recursion makes it possible to produce and understand an infinite number of sentences and the unbounded length of sentences. It reflects the creativity of language. This chapter will show how the rules or patterns are employed to make larger units such as phrases, clauses and sentences.

4.2 The domain of syntax

The major task within the domain of syntax is to construct structures, including identifying structure building blocks, representing different structures and judging their grammaticality.

4.2.1 Grammatical categories

Formally a sentence is the grouping of meaningful phrases which are formed out of words. Each word or phrase belongs to a specific class and serves a specific function within the sentence containing it. Word class or part of speech is also termed "category", including **lexical categories**, **functional categories** and **phrasal categories**.

1) **Lexical categories**

A **lexical category** has obvious descriptive content, for instance, N denoting entities, V actions, Adj attributes, Adv manner, Prep location, etc.

Noun (N)	furniture, happiness, room, water
Verb (V)	arrive, destroy, die, give
Adjective (Adj)	alive, brute, friendly, isolated
Adverb (Adv)	again, happily, never, very
Preposition (Prep)	across, at, with, within

Each lexical category has a corresponding phrasal category. A phrase is an extension of the head word.

2) **Phrasal categories**

a. Noun phrase (NP)   *enemies* of the human race, *people* who lived long ago
b. Verb phrase (VP)   *eat* the cake, *realize* that the earth is flat

c. Adjective phrase (AdjP)　all the more *fascinating*, *afraid* of upsetting him

d. Adverb phrase (AdvP)　more *easily*, very *clearly*

e. Prepositional phrase (PP)　*in* the Near East, *on* the table

It should be noted that a bare word in a sentence is also assigned the status of phrase, for example, "Gardens are beautiful", where the bare plural noun *Gardens* and the adjective *beautiful* are NP and AdjP respectively.

3) **Functional categories**

a. Determiner (Det)　*the*, *a*, and demonstratives such as *this*, *that*, *these*, *those*

b. Auxiliary (Aux)　*have*, *be*, *do*, and modals such as *can*, *may*, *must*, *will*

Det and Aux are functional because they carry grammatical information within a sentence, for instance, Det is about whether an entity is definite or not.

Every phrase or sentence in a language is the combination of different categories. For example,

(4) Culture opens the sense of beauty.

Groupings recognized in (4) are NP_1 (*culture*), and VP (*opens the sense of beauty*). The VP is grouped further by smaller elements V (opens) and NP_2 (the sense of beauty). The clearest way to represent the hierarchical structures is using phrase structure rules or bracket-labeling, as illustrated in the next.

4.2.2 **Phrase structure rules**

NP_2 in (4) can be described as strings of words of different categories like the following:

$NP_2 \rightarrow$ Det - N - Prep - N (the - sense - of - beauty)

However, such flat ordering gives us nothing about the internal structure of the constituent. Examples (1) — (4) indicate that language is hierarchical in nature, that is, language is not a string of words but structured out of larger constituents. We can build a constituent structure in the guide of phrase structure rules (PS rules for short).

In traditional understanding, a sentence is a statement containing a subject and a predicate. This can be formalized as: **S →NP VP**, meaning "S can be rewritten as NP plus VP". Such formulation can also be explicitly represented in the form of tree diagram:

S
NP   VP

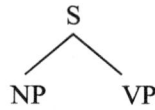

In the same spirit, all phrasal categories in English can be rewritten as PS rules like this:

NP → (Det) (Adj) N (PP)

VP → V (NP/AdjP/AdvP/CP) (PP)

AdjP → (Degree modifier) Adj (PP)

AdvP → (Degree modifier) Adv (PP)

PP → (modifier) P NP

CP → C S (C = complementizer, such as *that*, *if*, *whether*)

The following examples clarify the rules above.

(5) a. The children played on the ground.

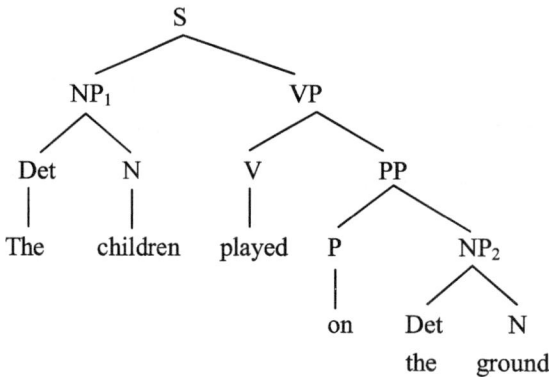

```
                    S
           NP₁              VP
        Det    N         V        PP
        The  children  played   P       NP₂
                                on   Det      N
                                     the    ground
```

b. The troops expect that the war will end very quickly.

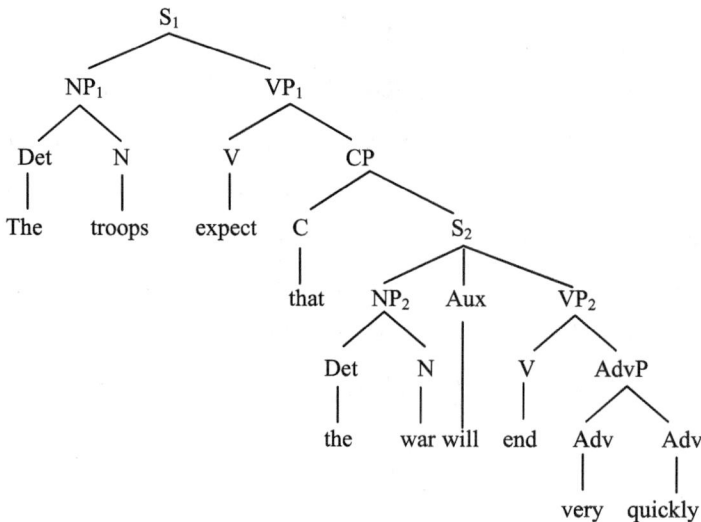

```
                      S₁
         NP₁                    VP₁
      Det    N              V          CP
      The  troops        expect     C         S₂
                                   that   NP₂   Aux      VP₂
                                       Det   N    will  V     AdvP
                                       the  war       end  Adv    Adv
                                                          very  quickly
```

c. (He is) afraid of snakes.

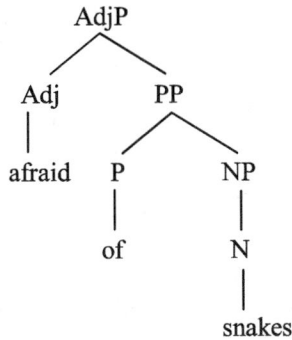

```
            AdjP
          /      \
        Adj       PP
         |       /   \
       afraid   P    NP
                |     |
                of    N
                      |
                    snakes
```

PS rules, especially represented in the tree form, reflect the linear order of grammatical elements (from left to right) and the hierarchical nature of structures. Language can be regarded as a recursive procedure that takes primitive elements (like words) and applies rules repeatedly to expand structures. For instance, the rule "S→NP VP" occurs twice in (5b), S_1 being the main clause and S_2 subordinate to S_1. Besides subordination, coordination is also one sort of recursion, jointing two coordinating constituents using coordinating conjunctions such as *and*, *or*, or *but* in English. For example,

(6) a. War and peace

   b. Stay home or go shopping

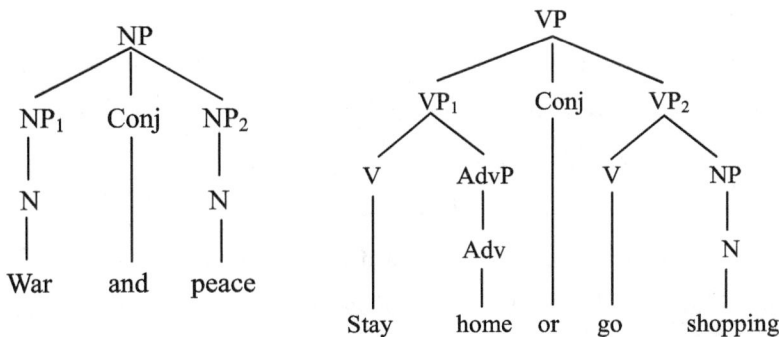

```
            NP                                    VP
         /  |  \                          /        |        \
      NP₁  Conj  NP₂                    VP₁       Conj       VP₂
       |    |    |                      /  \                /  \
       N    |    N                     V   AdvP            V    NP
       |    |    |                     |    |              |    |
      War  and peace                   |   Adv             |    N
                                     Stay  home    or     go  shopping
```

4.2.3   Senses of syntax rules

The rules of syntax reflect the speaker's knowledge of his or her language. Language users could take word-like elements and apply these rules to generate structures. On the other way, they can use syntax rules to check or interpret whether a structure conforms to rules or whether a structure is grammatical. In this sense, syntax rules have two senses:

generating and interpreting, both of which converge on the distinction of the well-formed or grammatical sentences from ill-formed or ungrammatical ones. For example,

(7) a. There is no such thing as a free lunch.

b. *It is no such thing as a free lunch. (The misuse of expletive)

(8) a. He that dies pays all debts.

b. *He dies debts pays all that. (Improper word order)

(9) a. I think that you are right.

b. *I think that you to be right. (The misuse of infinite clause)

Syntax rules can also help us to identify or constrain grammatical elements.

(10) a. A policeman gave me a ticket for speeding.

b. A policeman gave a ticket for speeding to me.

c. * A policeman gave me. (*give* should be followed by direct and indirect objects)

d. * A policeman gave a ticket for speeding. (*give* NP should be followed by a PP.)

(11) a. Put those bags on the table.

b. * Put those bags. (*put* must be followed by adv/prep denoting a place or a position)

c. * Put on the table. (*put* is a transitive verb)

(12) a. The woman died.

b. * The woman died the man. (*die* is an intransitive verb)

The rules of syntax also specify grammatical relations of a sentence, such as subject, (direct, indirect) object.

(13) Nothing can come of nothing.

The two "nothing" in (13) take the same grammatical category (NP) but function differently. The first is the subject and the second the object of the preposition.

(14) a. They are expecting you to contact them. (*you* is the object of the verb *expect*)

b. They are expecting themselves to contact you. (*you* is the object of the verb *contact*)

(15) a. Your dog chased my cat. (*your dog* is the subject, *my cat* is the object)

b. My cat chased your dog. (*my cat* is the subject, *your dog* is the object)

Different word orders in (14) and (15) lead to the change of meanings. Thus, syntax rules are also crucial to understanding the meaning of a sentence, though the meaning issues are of semantics in nature. Moreover, one can remove semantic ambiguities by resorting to grammatical rules since these ambiguities are a result of different structures. For example,

(16) More interesting books

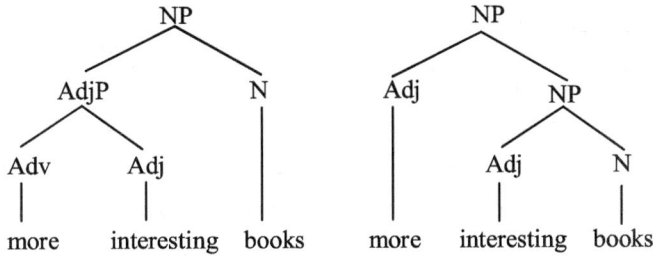

(17) Spot the man with a telescope

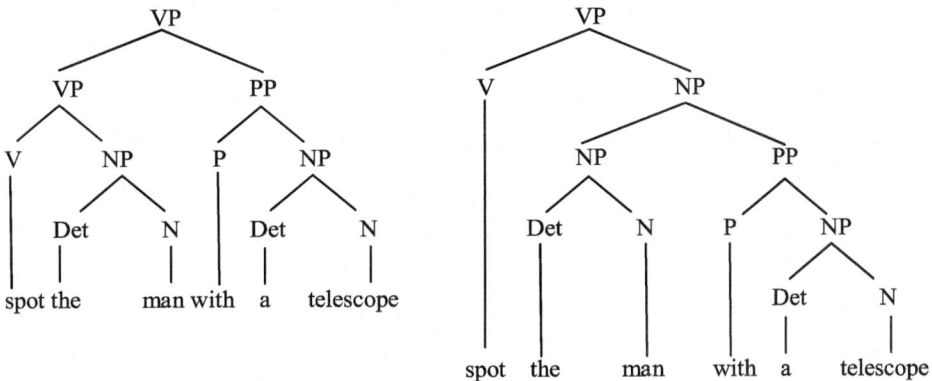

Besides the free diagram, bracker-labeling is another explicit way to represent and disambiguate structures. For example:

(18) More interesting books →

    a. [[more interesting] books]

    b. [more [interesting books]]

(19) Spot the man with a telescope →

    a. [[spot the man] [with a telescope]]

    b. [spot [[the man] [with a telescope]]]

It seems that there is a close interaction between sentence structures and meanings. Indeed, both issues can come into the domain of syntax. What's more, other branches of linguistics such as morphology and discourse analysis are also closely related to syntax. In this sense, syntax is not a completely independent discipline, but relating to morphology, semantics, discourse analysis, and other linguistic fields.

Within contemporary linguistics there are two camps: **formalism** and

functionalism. The formalism-functionalism distinction has evolved into different approaches to language with alternating theories and hypotheses. Linguistic formalism generally agrees with Chomsky's position and functionalism holds the commonsense view that language is used for communication. The following two sections will introduce the two major lines of research of syntax.

4.3 Generative grammar

Since the 1950s, generative grammar, led by Noam Chomsky, has dominated the linguistic world. The central task of generative grammar is to try to solve the "Plato's problem", i. e. how it is that children are able to acquire their language in a rapid and relatively uniform way but with the impoverished input data. Here the concept of "language", defined as **I-language** (internalized language) instead of **E-language** (externalized language), is the knowledge of language or knowledge of rules which govern the formation of structures. It is genetically determined and internal to the human mind/brain. The ultimate goal of generative grammar is to devise a theory of **Universal Grammar** (**UG** for short) about the nature of the grammar of human languages.

Linguistic theory should be adequately descriptive as well as explanatory. However, a fully accurate description of language properties may lead to the complexity of grammar, but a uniform and efficient explanation requires the grammar to be simple and invariant. Thus there is serious tension between the two. The effort to balance the tension drives linguists to develop generative grammar. The developing theory has undergone successive stages: the **Standard Theory**, the **Extended Standard Theory**, the **Revised Extended Standard Theory**, **Government and Binding Theory** and the latest **Minimalist Program**. Each stage is an improvement of the previous one, driven by the desire to achieve the explanatory adequacy. We briefly introduce some notions about the latest development in this section.

4.3.1 Principles and parameters

Children acquire their native languages rapidly and uniformly. Chomsky maintains that language acquisition is determined by a genetically endowed innate Language Faculty (or language acquisition program). Language acquisition processes in the following way: the experience of particular language such as parents' language serves as the trigger or input; then language faculty, like a factory, analyzes the input and devises a grammar, which leads to the output—the grammar of the language being acquired. The process can be schematized as:

UG is assumed to be a set of universal principles (or principles of UG). For instance,

(20) a. He expects much.

　　 b. Does he expect much?

　　 c. He can expect little.

　　 d. Can he expect little?

(21) a. He who expects much can expect little.

　　 b. ∗ Does he who expect much can expect little?

　　 c. Can he who expects much expect little?

From (20a-b) and (20c-d) we can conclude that in English yes-no question is formed by raising the first auxiliary to the position preceding the subject. However, (21b) is ungrammatical in that the operation of raising the first auxiliary violates the Structure Dependence Principle:

All syntactical operations are structure-dependent.

In (21) NP (*he who expects much*) is an intact structure and the first auxiliary raised is the modal verb *can*. Grammatical operations like moving an auxiliary can only apply to complete structures. Thus (21c) is grammatical, following one of the UG principles: Structure Dependence Principle.

However, not all grammatical structures are determined by principles. Some are subject to language variation. For example, English wh-question requires the movement of wh-elements to the initial position, while wh-elements in Chinese are kept in original site. e. g.

(22) a. What are you doing?

　　 b. ni zai-　　　　　　gan shenme?

　　　　you Progressive Marker do what

　　　　What are you doing?

This variation is known as the wh-parameter: English is a wh-movement language and Chinese wh-in-situ (ation). Parameter is thought to be like "on/off" switch. Switching on or off denotes different languages. In sum, a theory of UG incorporates a set of UG principles and a set of open parameters. UG principles do not have to be learned. Language acquisition is reduced to the process of setting parameters on the basis of language experience. The overall approach is called the **Principles and Parameters Theory (PPT)**.

4.3.2 Structure-building

All phrasal categories in Section 4.2 are expansions of the heads. A phrase XP is formed by projecting the head X, as is diagramed:

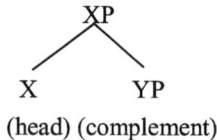

```
        XP
       /  \
      X    YP
   (head) (complement)
```

We can also say that X and YP are merged to form a new category XP, X being the head, YP the complement of the head. Merger is a primitive syntactic operation that takes two elements to construct a new one. For instance,

(23) take the cake

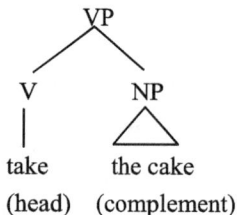

```
         VP
        /  \
       V    NP
       |    /\
      take the cake
    (head) (complement)
```

What about NP *the cake*? The noun *cake* is the head and the article *the* is to specify the definiteness of the noun. So we call it **Specifier**.

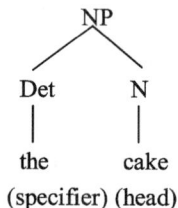

```
           NP
          /  \
        Det    N
         |     |
        the   cake
    (specifier) (head)
```

(24) a. take the birthday cake

b. take the birthday cake from the store

In (24a) *birthday* is the modifier of N *cake*, located in an intermediate position, i. e., between NP and its Head. In (24b) PP *from the store* as a modifier of the VP *take the birthday cake* is a part of the whole VP, so it is located in an intermediate position. Such intermediate position is signed as X-bar (X'), which is a projection of the Head. Such way of structure building is known as **X-bar theory (X'-theory)**.

(24a)

```
        VP
       /  \
      V    NP
          /  \
        Det   N'
             /  \
          AdjP   N
            |
           Adj

take  the birthday  cake
```

(24b)

```
              VP
              |
              V'
             /  \
           V'    PP
          /  \    |
        V    NP   △
            /  \
         Det    N'
               /  \
            AdjP    N
              |
             Adj

take  the birthday  cake from the store
```

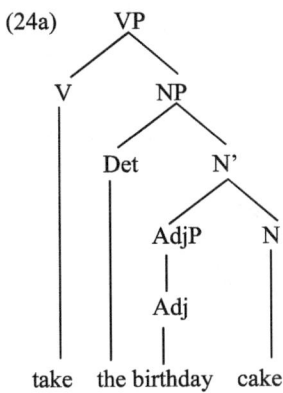

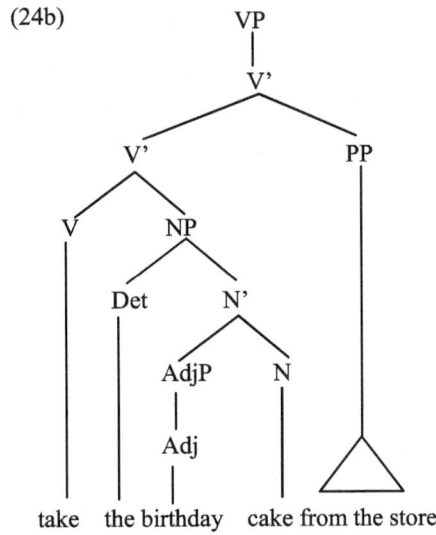

The general schema of X' theory is:

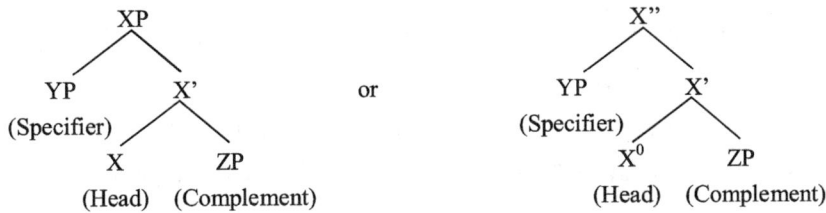

```
       XP
      /  \
    YP    X'
(Specifier) / \
          X    ZP
       (Head) (Complement)
```

or

```
        X"
       /  \
     YP     X'
(Specifier) / \
          X⁰   ZP
       (Head) (Complement)
```

The head X is the zero projection X^0, X' is the intermediate projection, and XP, also labeled X", is the maximal projection.

X-bar theory has important implications for the nature of language. First, X-bar theory provides a unified account for phrasal categories. Second, language is endocentric. Endocentricity is an inherent property of all structures in natural languages, that is, every head projects a phrase and all phrases have heads. Thirdly, all structures, formed by Merger, have two branches (binary-branching), reflecting the simplicity of language design. Finally, a local grammatical relation has been established including Specifier-Head relation, Head-Complement relation, all immediately contained within the projection of Head.

Other phrasal categories are in the same as VP and NP. For example,

(25) a. all the more fascinating

　　 b. very afraid of snakes

　　 c. quite independently of the pressure

　　 d. right on the table

(25a) AdjP
        /\
    Spec   Adj
     △ |
all the more fascinating

(25b) AdjP
        /\
    Spec   Adj'
     | /\
            Adj   PP
             | △
very   afraid of snakes

(25c) AdvP
        /\
    Spec   Adv'
     | /\
            Adv   PP
             | △
Quite independently of the pressure

(25d) PP
        /\
    Spec   P'
     | /\
            P   NP
            | △
right   on   the table

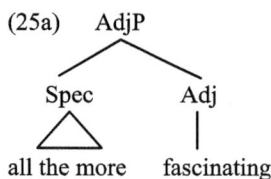

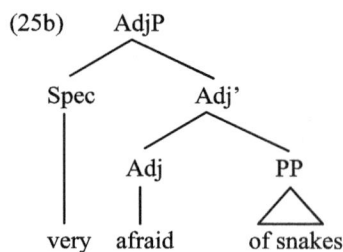

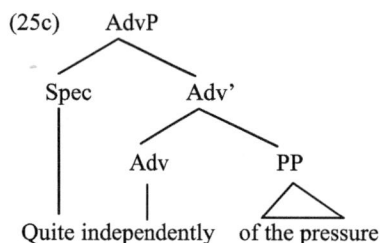

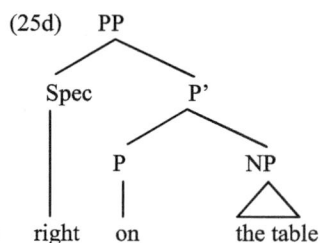

In order to devise a unified structural model, clauses, on a par with phrases, are also viewed as projections of heads.

Complement clauses are headed by complementizers (C for short) such as *that*, *for*, and *if/whether*, representing different clause types: *that* marks declarative clauses, *for* marks infinitive clauses, and *if/whether* marks questions.

Finite and non-finite clauses are headed by Inflection (INFL or I for short) . INFL in finite clauses, including modal verbs and tense affixes, has the features of [+ Tense] and [+ Agreement]; while INFL in non-finite clauses, generally in the form of infinitive marker *to*, does not have [+ Tense] and [+ Agreement] features. For example,

(26) a. God helps those who help themselves.

b. He managed to help her out of the trouble.

In (26a) the first predicate *helps* indicates present tense and the agreement with the subject *God*, and the second predicate *help* denotes the present tense and the agreement with plural subject *who* (referring to *those*) . Thus the two *help* are in finite forms. However, in (26b) the infinitive *to help* involves no agreement with subject and no tense information. More examples are given in (27):

(27) a. No one has found a solution to this problem.

b. They expected us to pay the rent.

c. I wonder whether she was coming.

d. (It is difficult) for foreigners to study Mandarin Chinese.

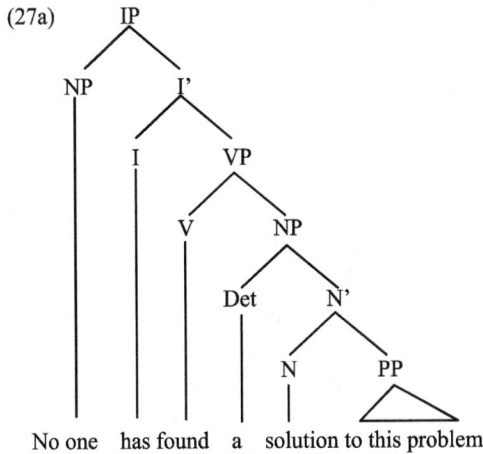

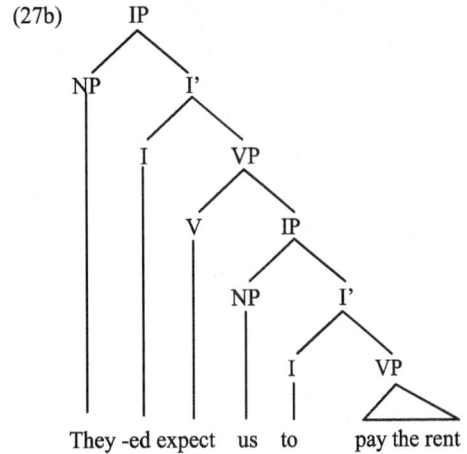

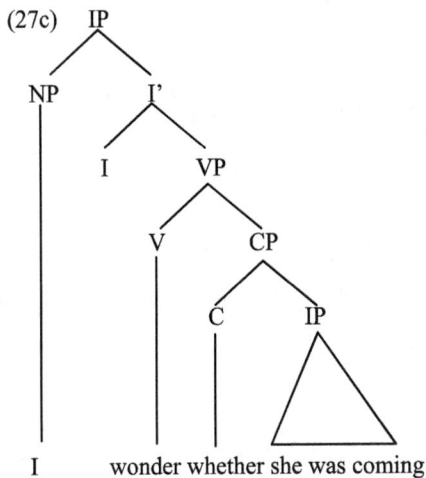

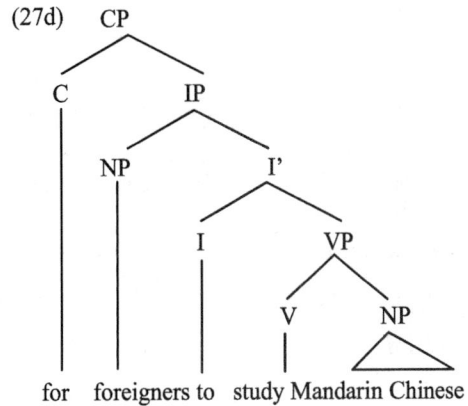

(27a)

```
              IP
            /    \
          NP      I'
                /    \
              I       VP
                    /    \
                  V       NP
                        /    \
                     Det      N'
                            /    \
                          N       PP
                                  /\
                                 /  \
No one   has found   a   solution to this problem
```

(27b)

```
              IP
            /    \
          NP      I'
                /    \
              I       VP
                    /    \
                  V       IP
                        /    \
                      NP      I'
                            /    \
                          I       VP
                                  /\
                                 /  \
They -ed expect   us   to        pay the rent
```

(27c)

```
              IP
            /    \
          NP      I'
                /    \
              I       VP
                    /    \
                  V       CP
                        /    \
                      C       IP
                              /\
                             /  \
I        wonder whether she was coming
```

(27d)

```
              CP
            /    \
          C       IP
                /    \
              NP      I'
                    /    \
                  I       VP
                        /    \
                      V       NP
                              /\
                             /  \
for   foreigners to   study Mandarin Chinese
```

All the cases discussed above are relatively simple structures. Complex constructions such as double object structures are beyond the present introduction.

4.3.3   Movement

In addition to recursion, language has another property: displacement, that is, we pronounce a constituent in one position but interpret it somewhere else. For example,

(28) What are you doing?

We know that *what* functions as the object of the verb *doing* as in *we are doing our work*, but it is pronounced at the initial position of the sentence. Why? Such observation can be accounted for by the theory of movement, which is a central component of generative grammar. Based on the nature of moved elements and the landing site, movement is classified as **Head movement**, **NP movement** and **Wh-movement**.

1) Head movement

(29) a. He is causing trouble.

    b. Is he causing trouble?

(30) a. The end justifies the means.

    b. Does the end justify the means?

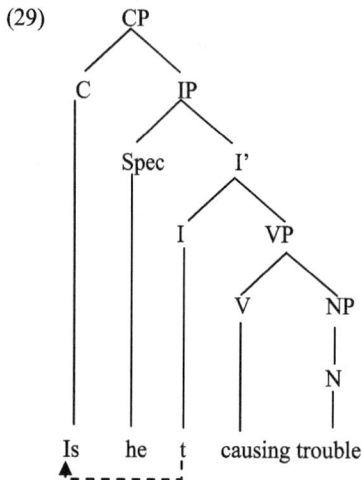

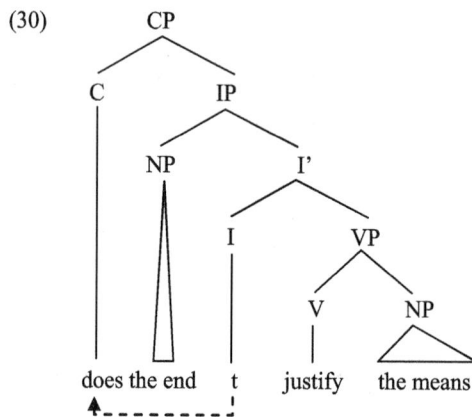

The moved elements and the landing sites in (29) and (30) are heads, I and C. Such kind of movement is called Head movement. In (29) the auxiliary *is* moves from I to C position leaving a trace(t) in the original position. In (30) the present tense third person marker *-es* in *justifies* moves from I to C. Since *-es* is a suffix which has to be attached to a stem, so the auxiliary *do* inserts in C position. Such operation is known as Do-support.

C is the clause-type marker, indicating statement or question. The driving force of head movement is the head C. It is assumed that in questions, the head C has a strong [+ Question] feature, which triggers the movement of I to C. While in statement, no [+ Question] feature is presented, thus no head movement is involved.

2) NP movement

(31) a. The man murdered her.

    b. She was murdered.

In (31a) the subject *the man* is the **agent** and the complement (the object) *her* is the **patient**. The passive subject in (31b) originates as the complement of VP and moves to the subject position [Spec, IP] . The moved elements are NPs, so it is named as NP movement.

(31)

What leads to NP movement in passivisation? The participial *murdered* has lost its power to assign accusative case to its complement *her*. So the patient has to move to a position to obtain a case. The empty subject/specifier position has the power to assign nominative case so it provides the chance for the movement of the patient. Thus NP movement in passivisation is case-driven, that is, to move to a position in order to obtain a (nominative) case.

3) **Wh-movement**

(32) a. What are you doing? b. Where does he live?

Wh-element *what* in (32a) is the complement of the verb *doing*, and *where* in (32b) is the adverbial of *live*, adjoining to V'. Both move from their original position to the sentence initial [Specifier, CP]; at the same time the auxiliaries move from the head of IP to the head of CP. C has the [+ Question] feature, and *what* and *where* also have [+ Question] feature, thus the Specifier and the head are in agreement with each other. So there are two types of movement involved: head movement and wh-movement. Each type of movement leaves behind a trace in the original position.

It should be clear that this section gives a very tiny introduction to some notions of generative theory. Since generative grammar is in the process of developing, many technical devices are changing. In the 1990s, Chomsky sketches **Minimalist Program (MP)**. As the title suggests, it is not yet a theory but a program defining that any linguistic theory of UG should be minimal or economical. The best way to keep pace with UG theory is to read the original.

4.4 Functional grammar

What is the primary function of language? Probably the most common answer would be that language is used for communication. The function of language could be focused on either from pragmatic perspective concentrating on the meaning and the conditions on the appropriate uses of language (see Chapter 6), or from discourse perspective concerned with the construction of texts or discourses using grammatical and lexical devices. There is a great diversity of views under the name of Functional Grammar such as Dik's Functional Grammar, Van Valin's Role and Reference Grammar, and Halliday's Systemic Functional Grammar. For a brief review of the different approaches, see Van Valin (2001). This section will introduce the basic ideas of Halliday's Systemic Functional Grammar.

4.4.1 Halliday's view of language

Halliday's systemic functional grammar insists that everything in grammar can be explained by reference to how language is used. Language is a social rather than an individual phenomenon. Language is a system of making meanings. All languages are organized around three modes of meaning (also called three meta-functions): the ideational, interpersonal and textual meaning, which are realized by different lexical-grammatical systems.

Ideational meaning is concerned with understanding the environment or construing experience, that is to say, we could use language to interpret and represent the world for one another and for ourselves. It is actualized by transitivity, voice (active, passive or middle voice) and polarity (positive or negative), transitivity being the major system. e. g.

    (33) a. We all love to talk about ourselves. (Active voice)

        b. Agreement is made more precious by disagreement. (Passive voice)

        c. Tickets for the concert just aren't selling well. (Middle voice)

        d. <u>Change your life today; Don't gamble on the future</u>, act now without delay.

           (Positive)   (Negative)

        e. Things do not change, we do. (Negative + Positive)

Interpersonal meaning is related to interacting with one another to construct and maintain social relations. It is construed by mood, modality (probability, usuality, obligation and inclination) and key (tone system), mood being the leading system.

    (34) a. It is likely / I think that Mary knows the situation.   (Probability)

        b. The truth, as always, is more complicated.   (Usuality)

        c. Women usually live longer than men.   (Usuality)

        d. Drivers are required by law to wear a seat belt.   (Obligation)

        e. Passengers are allowed one item of hand luggage each.   (Obligation)

        f. The government is keen for peace talks to start again.   (Inclination)

        g. How much are they willing to pay?   (Inclination)

        h. What are you doing?   (Falling tone)

        i. Is smoking permitted?   (Rising tone)

Combined with the two meanings above is the third one, textual meaning, i. e. , the creation of text, organizing information to convey the ideational and interpersonal meanings. Textual meaning is unfolded by thematic structure, information structure and cohesion (see chapter 7), thematic structure being the core system.

In this section only the three leading systems of each meta-function are discussed: transitivity, mood, and thematic structure.

4. 4. 2   Transitivity

Transitivity specifies different types of process and the participants involved. Halliday & Matthiessen (2004/2009) identify six processes, each consisting of a process, the participants involved in the process, and circumstances associated with the process.

1) **Material Process**: process of doing

(35) a. <u>Fred</u>   <u>cut</u>   <u>the lawn</u>   <u>once a week</u>.
      Actor   Material   Goal   Circumstance

   b. <u>The company</u>   <u>is giving</u>   <u>a new teapot</u>   <u>to my aunt</u>.
      Actor   Material   Goal   Recipient

2) **Mental Process**: process of sensing such as feeling, thinking, knowing, seeing and perceiving

(36) a. <u>She</u>   <u>realized</u> <u>her mistakes</u>.
      Sensor Mental Phenomenon

   b. <u>Tim</u>   <u>knows</u>.
      Sensor Mental

3) **Relational Process**: process of being, that is, a relation is being set up between two separate entities

(37) a. <u>Sarah</u>   <u>is</u>   <u>the wise one</u>.
      Identified Relational Identifier

   b. <u>This teapot</u>   <u>is</u>   <u>beautiful</u>.
      Carrier   Relational Attribute

4) **Behavioral Process**: process of physiological and psychological behavior, such as breathing, dreaming, smiling and coughing

(38) a. <u>She</u>   <u>is crying</u>.
      Behaver Behavioral

   b. <u>He</u>   <u>is always grumbling</u>.
      Behaver Behavioral

5) **Verbal Process**: process of saying

(39) a. <u>John</u>   <u>said</u>   <u>'I'm hungry'</u>.
      Sayer Verbal Quoted

   b. <u>John</u>   <u>said</u>   <u>he was hungry</u>.
      Sayer Verbal Reported

6) **Existential Process**: representing that something exists or happens

(40) a. There <u>was</u>   <u>a storm</u>.
      Existential Existent event

b. <u>On the wall</u>　there <u>hangs</u>　　<u>a picture.</u>
　　Circumstance　　Existential Existent entity

There are no obvious markers such as affixes and particles to differentiate the process types. Their distinctions depend on the predicates, participants, and other elements like adverbials.

4. 4. 3　Mood

Mood is often signaled by predicates in clauses, namely declarative, expressing a fact or action; imperative, expressing a command; and interrogative, expressing a question. The network of the Mood System:

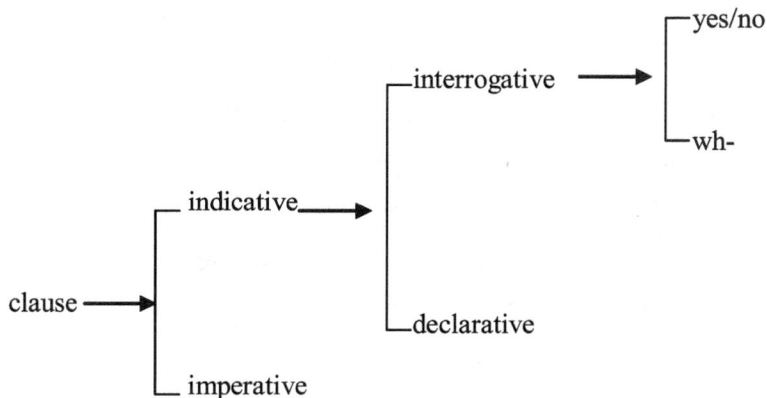

```
                                                      ┌ yes/no
                                   ┌ interrogative ──→ │
                                   │                   └ wh-
                  ┌ indicative ──→ │
                  │                └ declarative
clause ──→ │
                  └ imperative
```

Halliday and Matthiessen (2009: 44)

For example,

(41) a. They rode horses. (Declarative)

　　　b. Did they ride horses? (Yes-no question)

　　　c. Who rode horses? (Wh-question)

　　　d. Ride horses! (Imperative)

Semantically, Mood denotes the interactive event involving speaker and audience. For example, in asking a question, the speaker plays a particular speech role of seeking information and requiring the listener to provide information for her. The most fundamental speech roles are giving and demanding, relating to the exchange of goods and services or exchange of information. For example,

	Clause	Speech role	Exchange	Function
(42) a.	Would you like this teapot?	Giving	Goods & services	Offer
b.	He is giving her the teapot.	Giving	Information	Statement

    c. Give me that teapot!   Demanding   Goods & services   Command

    d. What is he giving her?   Demanding   Information   Question

4.4.4　Thematic structure

Thematic structures tell us the way to organize message and relate a clause to its context. A message consists of a **Theme** followed by a **Rheme**. Theme is the starting point of the message and Rheme is the remainder of the message to develop Theme. In English, a theme can be realized by a nominal group, an adverbial group or a prepositional phrase. The following examples are taken from Halliday & Matthiessen (2004/2009):

（43）

Theme	**Rheme**
a. The duke	has given my aunt that teapot
b. My aunt	has been given that teapot by the duke
c. That teapot	the duke has given to my aunt
d. Once upon a time	there were three bears
e. Very carefully	she put him back on his feet again
f. For want of a nail	the shoe was lost
g. Who	killed cock robin
h. Is anybody	at home?
i. In your house	who does the cooking?
j. Answer	all five questions!
k. If winter comes	can spring be far behind?
l. It was his teacher	who persuaded him to continue

Thematic structure is speaker-oriented in that it is the speaker who chooses the theme as his starting point of the message. In contrast, information structure is listener-oriented since whether information is new or given is determined by the listener's access to it. An information unit is made up of the New and the Given. The new is new to the listener, while the given is known to the speaker. The preferred flow of information in a clause is from given to new, with the New having prominence and carrying information focus. For example,

（44）　a. The boy stood on <u>the burning deck</u>.

       b. Some old people are oppressed by <u>the fear of death</u>.

However, it is possible to place the New before the Given for stylistic consideration. For example,

(45) a. <u>A rectangular conference table and four chairs, of a type provided for senior public servants</u>, stood between the tall windows.

b. Listening and reading requires many skills in common. <u>Finding the main idea in a paragraph</u> is just one of these skills.

4.5 Summary

This chapter has briefly introduced a set of notions and operations that are relevant to the Chomsky's generative grammar and Halliday's functional grammar. However, many other aspects concerning the two approaches are beyond the present analysis. We end this chapter with the wording: It is always the best to read the original.

Self-study Activities

1. Define the following terms and give examples if necessary.

Syntax	Recursion
PS rules	Movement
I-language	Universal Grammar
Meta-functions	Transitivity

2. Paraphrase each of the following sentences in two or more ways to show that you understand the ambiguity involved.

(1) Nutritious food and drink.

(2) Student film club.

(3) Visiting professors can be boring.

(4) Dick finally decided on the boat.

(5) They said she would go yesterday.

3. Draw a tree diagram for each of the following sentences according to the X-bar format.

(1) To help you is my honor.

(2) We would like you to stay.

(3) We know that he enjoys syntax.

(4) He wants to try to help others.

(5) That Julie admired Romeo surprised us.

4. Which type(s) of movement is (are) involved in the following structures? Draw tree diagrams to show the landing sites and traces of the moved elements.

(1) Which foreign language can you speak?

(2) Did Rosie look wonderful?

(3) He forgot where she lived.

(4) Was anyone arrested?

(5) I don't know which exams he has failed.

5. Identify the theme and rheme, given and new information in the following sentences.

(1) What kids need is love and support.

(2) Under the hill lived an old man.

(3) When lead is added to petrol, it improves the car's performance.

(4) What tremendously easy questions you ask.

(5) (-Who broke the window?)

-My brother broke the window.

6. Is syntax a completely independent discipline? If necessary, give examples to illustrate your point.

Sources and Suggestions for Further Reading

Akmajian, A. et al. 2001/2009. *Linguistics: An Introduction to Language and Communication* (5th ed.). Cambridge, Mass.: The MIT Press/Beijing: Foreign Language Teaching and Research Press.

Chomsky, N. 1957. *Syntactic Structures*. The Hague: Mouton.

Chomsky, N. 1965. *Aspects of the Theory of Syntax*. Cambridge, Mass.: The MIT Press.

Larson, R. K. 2010. *Grammar as Science*. Cambridge, Mass.: The MIT Press.

Radford, A. et al. 2009. *Linguistics: An Introduction* (2nd ed.). Cambridge: Cambridge University Press.

Thompson, G. 2000. *Introducing Functional Grammar*. Beijing: Foreign Language Teaching and Research Press.

Yule, G. 2000. *The Study of Language*. Beijing: Foreign Language Teaching and Research Press.

Chapter 5　Semantics

5.1　Introduction

Semantics is more interesting than you can imagine. Probably you don't believe that. Never mind. Just enjoy the following wordplay and see how you would feel:

(1) ——Why is the river rich?

　　——Because it has two banks.

(2) ——What makes a road broad?

　　——The letter B.

(3) ——What flower does everybody have?

　　——Tulips.

You see, these conversations sound funny. Why are they funny? It is meanings of some words that make the conversations funny in their contexts. This implies that words don't have meanings in isolation. Meanings come from the way words are connected to other words. Consider the following examples:

(4) She bought a red and a yellow dress.

　　She bought a red and yellow dress.

(5) This tool is no more useful than that one.

　　This tool is not more useful than that one.

(6) He hurled the bone to the dog.

　　He hurled the bone at the dog.

There are only slight differences in examples (4) — (6), but the meanings of these sentences are quite different. How words are connected with one another is important in deciding the meaning you would like to convey.

Semantics is the systematic study of meaning communicated through language. In reading history, we may discover that scholars seem always to have been singularly fascinated with the subject of meaning. Xun Zi, a Chinese philosopher, said more than 2,000 years ago that even names have no fixed meaning. "It is only by agreement that we apply a name. Once agreed, it becomes customary, and the standard is thus fixed... A name has no fixed actuality; it is a product of such agreement". We may thus infer from Xun Zi's observation that the only useful definition is the one that all can accept. The word "semantics" itself denotes a range of ideas, from the popular to the highly technical. In linguistics, semantics is the subfield that is devoted to understanding meanings inherent at the levels of words, phrases, sentences, and larger units of discourse (also referred to as text). The present chapter will focus on these areas.

5.2   Word meaning

One important point made by the linguist Ferdinand de Saussure is that the meaning of linguistic expressions derives from two sources: the language they are part of and the world they describe. The relationship by which language hooks onto the world is usually called **reference**. Roughly, a term's reference is the object it refers to and its **sense** is the way in which it refers to that object. For instance, the reference of the American president is Barack Obama, but the sense of the expression may be the "highest executive officer".

5.3   Semantic relations between words

Semantic relations between words can be put into the following eight types: **homonymy, polysemy, synonymy, antonymy, hyponymy, meronymy, member-collection**, and **portion-mass**.

5.3.1   Homonymy

A **homonym** is one of a group of words that share the same spelling and the same pronunciation but have different meanings. The state of being a homonym is called **homonymy**. Examples of pairs of homonyms are *stalk* (part of a plant) and *stalk* (follow/harass a person), and *left* (opposite of right) and *left* (past tense of *leave*).

Homographs are usually defined as words that share the same spelling, regardless of how they are pronounced. If they are pronounced the same then they are also homophones (and homonyms) . For example, *bark* (the sound of a dog) and *bark* (the skin of a tree) . If they are pronounced differently then they are also heteronyms. For example, *bow* (the front of a ship) and *bow* (a type of knot) .

Homophones are usually defined as words that share the same pronunciation, regardless of how they are spelled. If they are spelled the same then they are also homographs (and homonyms); if they are spelled differently then they are also heterographs. Homographic examples include *rose* (flower) and *rose* (past tense of rise) . Heterographic examples include *to*, *too*, *two*, and *there*, *their*, *they're*, etc.

5.3.2 Polysemy

Polysemy is the capacity for a sign (e.g. a word, phrase, etc.) or signs to have multiple meanings. A polyseme is a word or phrase with multiple, related meanings. Most items of the vocabulary are polysemous. Let's, again, take the word "bank" for example. If we look it up in any dictionary, we will find that it has at least the following three meanings:

(a) a financial institution;

(b) the building where a financial institution offers services;

(c) a synonym for "rely upon" (e.g. "*I'm your friend, you can bank on me*") .

The third meaning of "bank" is different from, but related to, as it derives from the theme of security, the first meaning. Polysemy, as many linguists suggested, should be distinguished from homonymy, though the boundary between the two is not always clearly drawn. An important, but not absolute, criterion is that polysemous items are assigned distinct senses in an entry, while homonyms are treated in different entries. Thus, in dictionaries, we can find that words like *face*, *foot*, *over*, *get* and *run* are examples of polysemy, whereas *lap*, *hooker*, *sole* and *mail* are examples of homonymy.

5.3.3 Synonymy

Synonyms are different words with identical or very similar meanings. Words that are synonyms are said to be synonymous, and the state of being a synonym is called **synonymy**.

Synonyms can be any part of speech (e.g. nouns, verbs, adjectives, adverbs), as long as both members of the pair are the same part of speech. See the following examples:

Noun: *student* and *pupil*

Verb: *buy* and *purchase*

Adjective: *sick* and *ill*

Adverb: *quickly* and *speedily*

Synonyms can be divided into the following types:

(i) Dialectal synonyms

These words belong to different dialects and then become synonyms for speakers familiar with both dialects, like British English *autumn* and American English *fall*.

(ii) Stylistic synonyms

These words belong to different styles of language, colloquial, formal, etc. that belong to different situations. For example, *male parent* and *father* are more formal than *old man* and *daddy*.

(iii) Collocational synonyms

These words differ in their collocation. That is, they go together with different words, for example: *accuse ... of*, *charge ...with*, *rebuke ...for*, but they express the same meaning.

(iv) Synonyms that differ in their emotive or evaluative meaning

These words may portray positive or negative attitudes of the speaker. For example, *stingy* and *mean* are more critical than *frugal* and *economical*.

(v) Semantically different synonyms

These words differ slightly in what they mean. For example, *allege* and *proclaim* are very close in meaning to the word *announce*. While *allege* implies that somebody states something as a fact without proof, *proclaim* indicates that somebody makes something known officially or publicly.

5.3.4 Antonymy

The term **antonymy** has also been commonly used as a term that is synonymous with opposite. Antonyms are words with opposite or nearly opposite meanings. There is a very classical example of antonyms in Charles Dickens' *A Tale of Two Cities*:

(7) It was the *best* of times, it was the *worst* of times, it was the age of *wisdom*, it was the age of *foolishness*, it was the epoch of *belief*, it was the epoch of *incredulity*, it was the season of *light*, it was the season of *darkness*, it was the spring of *hope*, it was

the winter of *despair*. We had *everything* before us, we had *nothing* before us.

Generally speaking, there are three subtypes of antonyms:

(i) Complementary antonyms

Complementary antonyms are pairs that express absolute opposites, like *mortal* and *immortal*, *male* and *female*. The denial of one means the assertion of the other or vice versa. For example: If Peter is not *married*, he is *single*; if Peter is not *single*, he is *married*.

(ii) Gradable antonyms

Gradable antonyms lie at opposite ends of a continuous spectrum of meanings; examples are *hot* and *cold*, *slow* and *fast*, and *fat* and *skinny*.

(iii) Relational antonyms

Relational antonyms are pairs in which one describes a relationship between two objects and the other describes the same relationship when the two objects are reversed, such as *parent* and *child*, *teacher* and *student*, or *buy* and *sell*.

5.3.5　Hyponymy

Hyponymy is the lexical relation described in English by the phrase *kind/type/sort of*. A chain of hyponyms define a hierarchy of elements. For example, *sports car* is a hyponym of *car* since a sports car is a kind of car, and car, in turn, is a hyponym of *vehicle* since a car is a kind of vehicle.

A **hyponym** is a word or phrase whose semantic field is included within that of another word, its hypernym or superordinate. In simpler terms, a hyponym shares a type-of relationship with its hypernym. Hyponyms of the same hypernym or superordinate are co-hyponyms. For example, *scarlet*, *vermilion*, *carmine*, and *crimson* are all hyponyms of *red* (their hypernym /superordinate), which is, in turn, a hyponym of *color*.

5.3.6　Meronymy

Meronymy is a term used to describe a part-whole relationship between lexical items. Meronymy reflects the semantic relation that holds between a part and the whole. A **meronym** denotes a constituent part of, or a member of something. That is, X is a meronym of Y if Xs are parts of Y (s), or X is a meronym of Y if Xs are members of Y (s).

For example, *finger* is a meronym of *hand* because a finger is part of a hand. Similarly, *wheel* is a meronym of *automobile*.

5.3.7 Member-collection

Member-collection refers to the relationship between a member and the collective to which the member belongs. Examples include: *student* and *class*, *tree* and *forest*, *bird* and *flock*, *book* and *library*.

5.3.8 Portion-mass

Portion-mass refers to the relationship between a portion and the mass from which the portion is taken. Examples include: *slice* and *bread*, *centimeter* and *meter*, *grain* and *wheat*, *strand* and *hair*.

5.4 Sentence meaning

The meaning of a sentence is not simply the sum total of the meanings of the constituent words used in it. Sentence meaning depends on the meanings of the constituent words and the sentence structure. That is, grammatical meaning and semantic meaning are two indispensable factors in sentence meaning.

Firstly, grammatical meaning of a sentence provides the grammatical classification of words. For example, *rise* is not just a verb, but an intransitive verb.

Secondly, semantic meaning of a sentence offers the semantic information which includes two sub-types. One type of information is of a more general nature which is shown by semantic markers, such as (human), (adult), (female). The other one is word-specific which is shown by distinguishers. For example, the word *prince* has the following distinguishers:

a. [male member of a royal family who is not the king, esp. (in Britain) a son or grandson of the sovereign]

b. [hereditary royal ruler, esp. of a small state]

c. [(figurative) excellent or outstanding man in a particular field]

The projection rules are responsible for combining the meanings of words together. The rules are called **selectional restrictions** which constrain the way words are combined. Therefore, some sentences are formed grammatically, but they are not semantically meaningful. The classical example "Green ideas sleep furiously" violates the selectional restrictions, thus is semantically meaningless in common contexts.

5. 5 Semantic relations between sentences

As there are certain semantic relations between words, so are there certain semantic relations between sentences, and they are analyzed in terms of truth-conditions. **Truth-conditional semantics** attempts to define the meaning of a given proposition by explaining when the sentence is true. So, for example, the proposition "snow is white" is true if and only if snow is white.

5. 5. 1 Presupposition

In ordinary language, to presuppose something means to assume it. In the following example, sentence (a) is said to presuppose sentence (b):

(8) a. I don't regret leaving Beijing.

b. I left Beijing.

The following is the analysis of the relation of presupposition in terms of truth-condition.

If *a* is true, *b* must be true.

If *a* is false, *b* is still true.

If *b* is true, *a* could be either true or false.

5. 5. 2 Entailment

There are fixed truth relations between sentences regardless of the empirical truth of the sentences. In the following example *a* is said to entail *b*:

(9) a. She has been to Japan.

b. She has been to Asia.

The following is the analysis of the relation of entailment in terms of truth-condition.

If *a* is true, *b* is necessarily true.

If *a* is false, *b* may be true or false.

5.5.3 Implicature

Implicature refers to what is suggested in an utterance, even though not expressed nor strictly implied by the utterance. For instance, a speaker responds to the question "How did you like the guest speaker?" with the following utterance: "Well, I'm sure he was speaking English." Then the utterance must have an additional nonliteral meaning, such as: "The content of the speaker's speech was confusing."

5.5.4 Synonymy

When the two sentences express the same meaning, then they are synonymous. For example, sentence (*a*) is synonymous with sentence (*b*) in the following:

(10) a. The politician assassinated the president.

b. The president was assassinated by the politician.

5.5.5 Contradiction

A **contradiction** sentence consists of a logical incompatibility between two or more sentences. It occurs when the propositions yield two conclusions which form the logical, usually opposite inversions of each other. For example, the sentence "Now is not now." is a contradiction.

5.5.6 Inconsistency

Inconsistency sentences contain a contradiction which consists of a logical incompatibility between two or more sentences. For example, (*a*) is inconsistent with (*b*) in the following:

(11) a. He is murderer.

b. He's never killed anyone.

In terms of truth condition, if (*a*) is true, (*b*) is false, and if (*a*) is false, (*b*) is true.

5.5.7 Semantic anomaly

The elements of semantic anomaly are semantically incompatible with each other, although possibly grammatically sound. For example, the sentence "Dark green leaves rustle furiously" is semantically anomalous, but it is obviously absurd.

5.6　Mechanisms of semantic change

Semantic change, also known as semantic shift or semantic progression, describes the evolution of word usage — usually to the point that the modern meaning is radically different from the original usage. Semantic change is a change in one of the meanings of a word. Every word has a variety of senses and connotations which can be added, removed, or altered over time, often to the extent that cognates across space and time have very different meanings.

A number of classification schemes have been suggested for semantic change. Metaphor and Metonymy are the major sub-types of semantic change.

5.6.1　Metaphor

Metaphor is the concept of understanding one thing in terms of another. A metaphor is a figure of speech that constructs an analogy between two things or ideas; the analogy is conveyed by the use of a metaphorical word in place of some other word. For example: "Her eyes were glistening jewels". There are three common types in metaphor:

(ⅰ) A dead metaphor is one in which the sense of a transferred image is absent. Examples: "*to grasp a concept*" and "*to gather what you've understood*" use physical action as a metaphor for understanding.

(ⅱ) An extended metaphor, establishes a principal subject (comparison) and subsidiary subjects (comparisons). The *All the world is a stage, / And all the men and women merely players. / They have their exits and their entrances; /And one man in his time plays many parts* quotation is a good example. The world is described as a stage, and then men and women are subsidiary subjects further described in the same context.

(ⅲ) Mixed metaphors are different metaphors occurring in the same utterance. They are used to express the same concept. And they leap from one iden-tification to a second identification inconsistent with the first. For example:

a. *At this point our argument doesn't have much content.*

b. *In what we've done so far, we have provided the core of our argument.*

c. *If we keep going the way we're going, we'll fit all the facts in.*

5.6.2　Metonymy

Metonymy is a figure of speech used in rhetoric in which a thing or concept is not called by its own name, but by the name of something intimately associated with that thing or concept. For instance, "*Washington*", as the capital of the United States, can be used as a metonym for the United States government. "*Hollywood*", as a section of Los Angeles, can be used as a metonym for the American film and television industry.

5.7　Summary

The study of linguistic meaning is called semantics. It typically focuses on the relation between signifiers, such as words, phrases, signs and symbols, and what they stand for. The meaning of words may be in part the objects referred to by the word, or its reference, but often there is more to a word than the object it denotes, and that part of meaning is called sense. And words are related in various ways.

Sentence meaning includes knowing the truth-conditons of declarative sentences. And semantic relations between sentences include presupposition, entailment, implicature, synonymy, contradiction, inconsistency and semantic anomaly.

Semantic change describes the evolution of word usage. Metaphor and metonymy are the major sub-types of semantic change.

Self-study Activities

1. Consider the following paired sentences below. Decide whether sentences (a) entail sentences (b).

   (1) a. Margarita passed her driving test. b. Margarita didn't fail her driving test.

   (2) a. Cassidy inherited a farm. 　　b. Cassidy owned a farm.

   (3) a. Arnold poisoned his wife. 　　b. Arnold killed his wife.

   (4) a. We brought this champagne. 　b. This champagne was brought by us.

2. Decide whether sentences (a) below entail or presuppose sentences (b) in the following.

(1) a. Dave is angry because Jim crashed the car.　b. Jim crashed the car.

(2) a. Zaire is bigger than Alaska.　b. Alaska is smaller than Zaire.

(3) a. The minister blames her secretary for leaking the memo to the press.

b. The memo was leaked to the press.

(4) a. Everyone passed the examination.　b. No one failed the examination.

(5) a. Mr Singleton has resumed his habit for drinking stout.

b. Mr Singleton had a habit of drinking stout.

3. Explain the semantic ambiguity of the following sentences by providing two or more sentences that paraphrase the multiple meanings.

a. She can't bear children.

b. I saw him walking by the bank.

4. Circle any deictic expression in the following sentences.

a. I saw her standing there.

b. The name of this book rock band is "The Beatles".

c. The Declaration of Independence was signed last year.

d. These are the times that try men's souls.

5. Each of the following single statements has at least one implicature in the situation described. What is it?

a. Statement: The restaurants are open until midnight.

Situation: It's 10 o'clock and you haven't eaten dinner.

b. Statement: Mr. Smith dresses neatly, is well-groomed, and is on time to class.

Situation: The summary statement in a letter of recommendation to graduate school.

Sources and Suggestions for Further Reading

Fromkin, V. , Rodman, R. , and Hyams, N. 2007. *An Introduction to Language* (8 th ed.). Beijing: Peking University Press.

Lyons, J. 2000. *Linguistic Semantics: An Introduction.* Beijing: Foreign Language Teaching and Research Press.

Poole, S. 2000. *An Introduction to Linguistics.* Beijing: Foreign Language Teaching and Research Press.

Robins, R. H. 2000. *General Linguistics* (4 th ed.) . Beijing: Foreign Language Teaching and Research Press.

Saeed, J. I. 2009. *Semantics* (3 rd ed.). Oxford: Wiley-Blackwell.

Chapter 6　Pragmatics

6.1　Introduction

There is an old joke that goes like this: "When a diplomat says 'yes', he means 'perhaps'; when he says 'perhaps', he means 'no'; and when he says 'no', he is no diplomat. When a lady says 'no', she means 'perhaps'; when she says 'perhaps', she means 'yes'; and when she says 'yes', She is no lady". Is it funny? Maybe most people will answer *yes*, but please do not take it seriously, since such a saying can offend some ladies, especially, feminists. This joke certainly implies that both diplomats and ladies may provide no fixed meanings for *yes*, *no* and *perhaps* in communication. Therefore, this snippet is more of a pragmatic phenomenon than a joke, in respect that it suggests that, what is said (coded information) and what is meant (its use) do not seem to coincide in all cases, and this is what pragmatics is about. So what is pragmatics? **Pragmatics** is a subfield of linguistics which studies the ways in which context contributes to meaning. See the following example:

(1) I'm working on my course paper.

All that can be claimed with certainty is that the speaker of (1) at the time of speaking is right in the process of finishing her course paper. This is a typical English declarative sentence, simply stating a fact, argument or an idea without requiring either an answer or action from the hearer. What if we put the sentence in different contexts as in (2) and (3):

(2) Who's at the door?

　　—I'm working on my course paper.

(3) What are you doing?

　　—I'm working on my course paper.

As shown in (2) and (3), the same line of words is used to answer different questions. In other words, it can be used to fulfill different functions in different contexts. It is clear that in (3) the sentence is simply providing information concerning what the speaker is engaged in when the conversation takes place. However, the same sentence used in (2) is arguably explaining why she cannot go to find out who is at the door. Clearly, the same line of words conveys different meanings or functions in different contexts. Take a look at another example:

(4) as luck would have it

It is almost universally understood that (4) is ambiguous, meaning *by chance*. Still not very informative! This is until we put this snippet of language in a specific context as in (5):

(5) We run out of petrol on the way home, but as luck would have it, we are very near a garage.

With this additional context, the meaning of (4) becomes more translucent: the speaker of (5) is talking about her good fortune. Nevertheless, that is still not the end of the story: what does *way home* specifically mean? And who does *we* refer to? Irrespective of the answers, which are the ingredients of a full comprehension of (5), these are questions for pragmatics which deals with analyzing language in context.

If semantics is the study of meaning isolated from context, pragmatics is concerned with how that meaning is used and negotiated between speakers and hearers. In other words, pragmatics focuses on how language is used in actual communication. Accordingly, the study of pragmatics concerns issues such as when it is used, how it is used, who is involved in the communication, for what purpose it is used, and how the use of language is interpreted by language users. This chapter provides an introduction to pragmatics and covers topics like **deixis, presupposition, speech acts, conversational implicatures,** and **conversation analysis**.

6. 2   Deixis

Reconsider example (5) above. How shall we interpret the use of *we* in the example? Or who are *we*? This seems to be a simple question, but the answer cannot be revealed via semantic inquiries, because the interpretation of *we* in (5) needs to take the context into consideration prior to any attempt to work out the complete specification of the proposition expressed by the sentence. Look at the following conversation between two colleagues:

(6) Mary and John are discussing the new marketing plan in Mary's office. During

their discussion, Mary receives a phone call and her presence is expected at their boss's office.

Mary: I will be back in 30 minutes.

John: OK.

In this face-to-face conversation, Mary's words pose no challenge to John, as the latter unambiguously understands that *I* refers to Mary herself, *be back* means *Mary will return to her office*, and *in* 30 *minutes* refers to the time point 30 minutes after the time point at which the conversation is taking place. To put it another way, the interpretation of these expressions depends heavily on the context. Words like *we* in (5), *I* and *in* 30 *minutes* in (6) whose interpretation requires context are called **deictic words** or **deictic expressions**.

Deixis denotes the act of using such deictic expressions. It is one of the basic things we do with utterance: pointing through language. Deictic expressions can be used to refer to people through person deixis (e. g. *I*, *we*, *they*) or location through spatial deixis (e. g. *there*, *here*, *above*, *behind*, *left*, *right*) or time through time deixis (e. g. *in* 30 *minutes*, *then*, *yesterday*, *now*). A small boy, gazing at the toffee apple on the table, points and says:

(7) Mom, I want that.

Or, a boss who is directing one of his employees to move the files in the office says:

(8) Put it there.

The mother in (7) and the employee in (8) can immediately pick up the meanings of *that*, i. e. the toffee apple and *there*, i. e. a particular place the boss is looking at or pointing at with his hand.

The following example involves all the three types of deixis:

(9) *I'll meet you downstairs tomorrow.*

This sentence doesn't make any sense unless we know who the speaker and hearer (s) are and where the building is and when the conversation is taking place.

In the English language, a basic distinction of deictic expressions can be made between **proximal terms** and **distal terms**. Proximal terms are usually construed in relation to the speaker's location or "close to the speaker". Consequently, *here* can be understood as referring to some place that takes the speaker's location as the center. Distal terms are used to denote the meaning of "away from the speaker". So *there* is interpreted as referring to some place that is away from the location of the speaker. Note that, the spatial or temporal distance as discussed above can be not only physical but also mental.

6.3 Presupposition

In the discussion of semantic relations between sentences in Chapter 5, we have encountered the term **entailment**, as shown in the following examples:

(10) a. Mary managed to stop the car.

b. Mary stopped the car.

(10a) entails (10b), in other words, the truth of (10b) requires that of (10a) in any circumstances. However, this is not the whole picture about the relationship between sentences. Consider the following examples:

(11) a. Mary stopped beating her husband.

b. Mary used to beat her husband.

What is the relationship between sentences (11a) and (11b)? This is definitely not entailment, because the truth of (11b) does not require that of (11a) . These two sentences in (11) serve as good examples of **presupposition**. Other examples are:

(12) a. John is no longer the caption-writer-in-chief.

b. John was once the caption-writer-in-chief.

(13) a. Mary managed to stopped the car.

b. Mary tried to stopped the car.

In both groups, the sentences (a) presuppose the sentences (b) . Traditionally, presupposition is treated as a relationship between two propositions. If we use p as the proposition contained in (11a) and q as the proposition in (11b), then using " >> " for "to presuppose", we can represent (11) in the following way:

(11') a. Mary stopped beating her husband.   (= p)

b. Mary used to beat her husband.   (= q)

c. p >> q

The relationship as exemplified in (11) serves as a good case of semantic presupposition or logic presupposition, which can be best characterized as follows:

(14) Sentence A semantically presupposes Sentence B iff:

a. *in all situations where* A *is true*, B *is true*

b. in all situations where A *is false,* B *is true*

According to this definition, if we negate a sentence, its original presupposition still exists:

(15) a. Mary did not stop beating her husband.

> > b. Mary used to beat her husband earlier.

(16) a. Mary did not manage to stop the car.

> > b. Mary tried to stop the car.

This property of presupposition is described as constancy under negation. In other words, presupposition remains Constant under negation.

However, few cases of such semantic presupposition as defined and exploited above exist in real language usage. This can be best illustrated in the following example:

(17) Mary did not manage to stop the car; in fact, she never ever tried.

It is interesting to note that (17) which is logical no longer presupposes (16b). This is due to the fact the (16b) is explicitly denied by the linguistic context. Besides, presuppositions can also be cancelled by situational context, as shown below:

(18) Every one knows that Mary failed to get a doctoral course and would say:

At least Mary won't have to regret that she did a PhD.

The presupposition *Mary did a PhD* triggered by *regret* would be easily cancelled by such common assumption. This property of presupposition is termed defeasibility, which gives rise to a looser understanding of presupposition, sometimes called pragmatic presupposition. This is due to the fact that presuppositions are liable to evaporate in certain contexts, either immediate **linguistic context** or the **situational context**. **Pragmatic presupposition** can be defined in the following way:

(19) An utterance A pragmatically presupposes a proposition B iff A is appropriate only if B is **mutually known** by participants. (Levinson 1983: 205)

This definition, then, is to emphasize the **appropriateness** and **mutual knowledge** of the use of sentences. Consider example (20):

(20) John fed the horse.

The utterance of (20) would be inappropriate if John had more than one horse. In this case, we may suggest that the use of *the horse* is associated with the pragmatic presupposition that both the speaker and the hearer are familiar with only one particular horse in the circumstance or when this utterance is uttered the speaker and the hearer are talking about a specific horse. Examples of pragmatic presupposition are prevalent in language use, and it is important for us to keep the notions of appropriateness and context in our mind, because they are crucial to our understanding of the next topic: speech acts.

6.4   Speech acts

6.4.1   Doing things with words

How would you perform the action of congratulating someone? Yes, you may say:

(21) Congratulations!

By this utterance, you performed the action. In the same line, the utterance in (22) can be used to perform the action of calling someone's attention to the television set.

(22) Look at the television.

It is true that we have other options. In the case of (21), we may simply use the thumbs up sign and in (22) it can be done by pointing to the television. However, words are the most common and efficient way to express the meaning. And actions performed (or *done*) through utterances are called **speech acts**.

In daily language usage, we not only produce utterances with grammatical patterns and structures but also use them to perform certain actions, such as congratulating, suggesting, commanding, and promising. This idea was first sparked by Austin's work. Austin (1975) further pointed out that in analyzing a speech act, we need to make a distinction among **locutionary act, illocutionary act** and **perlocutionary act**. Locutionary act refers to the utterance of a sentence with ostensible sense and reference. In (22) the speaker uttered the words *Look at the television* which can be semantically paraphrased as "focus your attention on the program being broadcast in the television". With the uttering of (22), the speaker performed the act of requesting the addressee to look at the television. This is an illocutionary act, which is the real, intended meaning in the making of an utterance, such as commanding, offering, and promising. A perlocutionary act can be understood as the actual effect brought about on the addressee by means of the utterance. However, the primary interest will be illocutionary acts in speech act study.

6.4.2 Indirect speech acts

Consider the following utterance:

(23) Peter, can you open the window?

The utterance of (23) would be commonly understood as the speaker making a request. But why does it take the form of an interrogative sentence? Actually, everyday conversation is abundant in such indirect illocutionary acts, whose meanings are different from the content intended to be communicated, as illustrated in (23). In such cases, form and function do not match and we call them **indirect speech acts**. Thus, a declarative sentence used to make a statement is a **direct speech act**, but a declarative sentence can be an indirect speech act when used to make a request, ask for information, etc. More examples are given in (24) — (26).

(24) Couldn't you turn down the voice? (Interrogative used to make a command)

(25) (At the ticket office of a railway station)

Traveler: I'd like a ticket to Chicago. (Declarative used to make a request)

(26) It's cold in here. (Declarative used to make a request)

So in cases of indirect speech act, often what someone says is not actually what she means, for the illocutionary force is indirect. Accordingly, we must ask how it is that we seem to be able to figure out the intended or implicit meaning of an illocutionary act. The next section may provide a solution to this problem.

6.5 Conversational implicatures

6.5.1 Saying one thing while meaning the other

Considering the following examples of language in use:

(27) (At a jeweler's)

Wife: Honey! What a beautiful ring! I can' wait to wear it. Can I have it?

Husband: Oh, Darling, the restaurant is right across the street. Hurry up!

(28) (A critical review of the performance of a singer)

The singer produced a series of sounds corresponding closely to the score of an aria from Rigoletto.

(29) Student: Tehran's in Turkey, isn't it, Professor?

Teacher: And the Pope is a Buddhist, I suppose.

(30) Boys are boys.

All these utterances in (27) — (30) would seem a little odd if taken literally. The husband in (27) does not answer his wife's request. Instead, his utterance lacks relevance to that of his wife. In (28), why does the writer bother to use so many words in the report instead of the simple one: *Miss Singer sang an aria from Rigoletto*? In (29), we might doubt what kind of relationship there might be between Tehran's being in Turkey and the Pope's being a Buddhist. Furthermore, it seems clear that the teacher deliberately makes a wrong statement in his utterance. Why? As for (30), the speaker is at first blush expressing something utterly uninformative. True, these examples seem odd taken at face value, but they are commonly used in our daily communication. What's more, we can easily figure out the inference of these utterances with a little logic work:

(27') Husband: Honey, I don't think that ring is what we need.

(28') Miss Singer's performance can hardly be called singing.

(29') Teacher: No.

(30') Boys are always naughty.

All these inferences are cases of conversational implicature, which are implicitly conveyed and often different from what is said by the speaker.

6.5.2　The Cooperative Principle

After analyzing these conversational implicatures, we need to ask another question: how do these implicatures come into being? Or how is this possible? Paul Grice's **Cooperative Principle (CP)** may within certain limits shed light on these issues.

Grice (1975) was interested in how it is that we can say something while meaning something else, as illustrated in (27) — (30). According to him, reasonable interlocutors are expected to be cooperative and helpful to each other in communication and utterances should be properly understood in the given context. This is what Grice called the Cooperative Principle. The CP is reflected in communication by interlocutors' observation of the four maxims underlying the efficient cooperative use of language:

(31) **Maxim of Quality**: try to make your contribution one that is true.

Maxim of Quantity: make your contribution as informative as is required for the current purposes of the exchange.

Maxim of Relevance: make your contributions relevant.

Maxim of Manner: be perspicuous.

The purpose of the CP is not to ask people to observe it in communication. The significance resides in that interlocutors can flout the four maxims in order to imply something different from what is said. The CP can help us work out this implied meaning or the conversational implicature in Grice's term. In (28), the writer relies for its effect on the verbosity of his utterance, thus violating or flouting the maxim of manner, which gives rise to understatement. In (29), the teacher's response violates the maxim of relation, and this deliberate flouting invites the addressee to conclude that Tehran is not in Turkey. It is necessary for us to understand that flouting a maxim is still observing the CP at the level of conversational implicatures.

6.6 Conversation analysis

Till now, our discussion in this chapter has been mainly concerned with single utterances or short stretches of speech, most of which are constructed to exemplify specific topics or various pragmatic meanings such as presupposition, illocutionary force and conversational implicature. There is still another area in the study of pragmatics that has not been touched in our discussion and that principally deals with a large group of utterances which are closely and logically organized – conversation. When we listen to a group of people discussing a certain topic, we may wonder how they negotiate the "floor-taking" right so efficiently as well as how well-organized the discussion is among these participants. The study of these phenomena is called **conversation analysis (CA)**.

CA is different from **discourse analysis (DA)**. DA tends to adopt a deductive methodology and employs the theoretical principles and concepts typical of linguistics. In contrast, CA, interested in the sequential organization of talks, tends to adopt an inductive methodology, that is, researchers avoid any premature theory construction and search for recurring patterns of naturally occurring conversations. In the following part, we will offer a brief introduction to some key concepts in conversation analysis.

Conversation organization is always characterized by turn-taking. Participants in conversation do not take their turns randomly. Instead, the prototypical turn-taking follows the sequence order: one participant talks, stops; then another takes the floor, talks and stops. The end of each participant's utterance may constitute a **transition**

relevance place (TRP) where speaker change can occur. The commonest example of TRPs is the noticeable silence which might signal that the current interlocutor has finished his or her talk.

Talk tends to occur in the form of responsive, paired utterances, such as question-answer, greeting-greeting, offer-acceptance, apology-minimization. Such pairs are called **adjacency pairs**, as shown below.

(32) How do you do?

—How do you do?

(33) What time is it?

—It's four o'clock.

(34) Would you like some beer?

—Yes, Thank you very much.

Of course, in daily conversation, talks may consist of more complex sequential organizations, as in (35).

(35) A: Are you ready for the interview now?   (Q1)

B: Has the manager arrived?   (Q2)

A: Yes.   (A2)

B: OK. I think I'm ready now.   (A1)

One problem that arises with the notion of adjacency pair is the concept of **preference organization**, which designates that not all the potential responses to a first part of an adjacency pair are of equal status, and there is at least one preferred response (36) and one dispreferred (37).

(36) Could you put on the light for me?

—Yes.

(37) After the dinner let's go to the show, shall we?

—Well, I'd like to, but I have to work on my course paper tonight.

Basically, preferred responses are unmarked while dispreferred ones are marked in terms of structural complexity, that is to say, preferred responses occur in structurally simpler turns.

6. 7 Summary

In our understanding of language use, we often go beyond the literal meaning of the linguistic form and venture into the various contextual information involved so as to reach the intended meaning. The intended meaning based on context falls right into the scope of pragmatics. What this chapter has shown is that we cannot exclusively depend on the literal meaning and syntactic ordering (or grammar) in interpreting an utterance. We also need to consider issues concerning when, where, and how the utterance is issued as well as who is involved. In short, it is pragmatics that provides us with a better understanding of the language in use.

Self-study Activities

1. What are the differences between entailment and presupposition?
2. For the following example, explain in detail how Grice's CP and Maxims help account for the way the utterances are interpreted.

   A: *Can you tell me the time?*

   B: *Well, the milkman has just come.*

3. Decide whether each of the following statements is True or False.

   (1) The contextual view is often considered as the initial effort to study meaning in a pragmatic sense. (   )

   (2) All utterances take the form of sentences. (   )

   (3) A locutionary act is the act of conveying literal meaning by means of syntax, lexicon, and phonology. (   )

   (4) All the utterances that can be made to serve the same purpose share the same syntactic form. (   )

   (5) Gradually linguists found that it would be impossible to give an adequate description of meaning if the context of language use was left considered. (   )

4. Define the following terms.

   (1) context   (2) locutionary act   (3) illocutionary act

5. What implicatures might be generated by the following examples?

   (1) *It's cold in here.*

   (2) *The phone is ringing.*

   (3) *Some students went to the lab.*

Sources and Suggestions for Further Reading

Cutting, J. 2002. *Pragmatics and Discourse: A Resource Book for Students.* London: Routledge.

Grundy, P. 2000. *Doing Pragmatics.* London: Edward Armold.

Huang, Y. 2009. *Pragmatics.* Beijing: Foreign Language Teaching and Research Press.

Levinson, S. C. 1983. *Pragmatics.* Cambridge: Cambridge University Press.

Peccei, J. S. 1999. *Pragmatics.* London: Routledge.

Thomas, J. 1995. *Meaning in Interaction: An Introduction to Pragmatics.* London: Longman.

Chapter 7 Discourse Analysis

7.1 Discourse and discourse analysis

7.1.1 Discourse

Since its introduction to modern science the term **discourse** has taken various, sometimes very broad, meanings. However, this chapter only discusses discourse in the domain of linguistics.

There is no agreement among linguists as to the use of the term **discourse** in that some use it in reference to **text**, while others claim it denotes speech. Despite the differences, grammarians have become convinced of the usefulness of considering stretches longer than individual sentences in their analyses since the late 1960s. Consequently, the terms **text** and **discourse** are almost interchangeably used today. If we do not make distinctions between discourse and text, discourse can be defined as "language above the sentence or above the clause" (Stubbs, 1983: 1) . More specifically, it is a continuous stretch of language larger than a sentence, often constituting a coherent unit such as a sermon, argument, joke, or narrative. Understood from this perspective, novels, as well as short conversations or groans might be equally rightfully named discourses.

7.1.2 Discourse analysis

Discourse analysis, also known as discourse linguistics and discourse studies, or text analysis, is therefore an area of linguistics that primarily deals with the analysis of language "beyond the sentence", a study of how sentences in spoken and written language form larger meaningful units such as paragraphs, conversations, and interviews. This contrasts with types of analysis more typical of modern linguistics, which are chiefly concerned with the study of grammar: the study of smaller bits of language, such as sounds (phonetics and phonology), parts of words (morphology), meaning (semantics), and the organization of words in sentences (syntax). Discourse analysis studies larger chunks of language that are not explainable at the grammatical level as they flow. Similar to pragmatics, discourse analysis is concerned with language in use. But the distinction can be arguably made that pragmatics is more concerned with meaning, while discourse analysis is more concerned with the information structure.

It is generally assumed in discourse analysis that there are several criteria that have to be fulfilled to qualify either a written or a spoken text as a discourse. These include:

Cohesion—lexical and grammatical relationship between parts of a sentence essential for its interpretation;

Coherence—the order of statements relates one another in meaning;

Intentionality—the message has to be conveyed deliberately and consciously;

Acceptability—the communicative product needs to be satisfactory in that the audience approves it;

Informativeness—some new information should be included in the discourse;

Situationality—circumstances in which the remark is made are important;

Intertextuality—reference to the world outside the text or the interpreters' schemata.

It is worth noting that, however, not all of the criteria mentioned above are perceived as equally important in discourse analysis, therefore some of them are valid only in certain methods of research. Let's consider the following two passages:

(1) a. The price of different fish can vary enormously, so always check out the price per kilo before you buy. Buying the same variety of fish on a different day can also have a very different effect on your wallet. This is because fish catches vary a lot and weather conditions and availability can play havoc with stocks, so fishermen, and subsequently fish buyers, don't know what they're going to buy until the boats are in.

b. Fish is low in fat and it's a good source of protein. Fish can be cooked in many different ways. Baking is a good option if you want to include some other flavors with the fish. This is a simple technique that ensures the fish remains moist.

Passage (1a) is clearly a discourse or text. Probably there is no problem for you to understand it, even if you are not interested in the topic, and you are able to guess that it might be an extract from a cookbook or an encyclopedia. But passage (1b) is quite different—it is not a discourse. In fact, it was created by copying the first sentence from every fifth page in the book on cooking that passage (1a) comes from. You may find yourself wondering what the passage is about, and think that something is missing or mixed up. Each of the four sentences is a perfectly grammatical English sentence but together they do not form a discourse.

In discourse analysis one of the primary tasks is to explore the linguistic features which characterize discourses. Discourses have structure, just as single sentences have structure. The goal of discourse analysis is to examine how the reader or user of a discourse recognizes that the words/phrases/sentences in a discourse must be co-interpreted—that parts of a discourse are dependent on others. One of the most important features of discourse is that a discourse needs to be cohesive. Readers recognize this cohesion in their interpretations. In reading passages (1a, b) we recognize that (1a) is cohesive, whereas (1b) is not—it does not "hang together". Besides cohesion, there are some other topics of discourse analysis, including information structure, coherence, discourse markers, conversational analysis, etc. which will be discussed one by one in the following parts.

7.2 Information structure

When producing a discourse, it is important for the addressor, in order to transmit their message or information properly, to give it a structure that may support the appropriate understanding of the message on the part of the addressee. This is normally done by marking some words or word groups as more important than others and by "packaging" the message into units of different sizes. The addressee, on the other hand, will perceive words or word groups as being more or less important and will detect different types of boundaries that will enable him or her to interpret the utterance on the basis of a division into units to be identified as paragraphs, subparagraphs, sentences, clauses, phrases, and others. The message as produced by the addressor and interpreted by the addressee will thus have a structure that can be characterized in terms of important information and of boundaries between units of difference extension. This type of structure is commonly referred to as the **information structure** of a discourse.

In practice, information structure is the most common term for those aspects of a sentence's meaning that have to do with the way in which the addressee integrates the information into already existing information. Put more simply, information structure is the domain of language structure and language study that is concerned with notions such as **given** and **new information**, **topic**, **comment**, **presupposition**, **focus**, etc. In this section, we will consider how information is packaged within discourse, and particularly, what resources are available to speakers or writers for indicating the status of information to their hearers or readers.

7. 2. 1 Given and new information

Given versus **new information** is a distinction between information that is assumed or supplied by the speaker or writer and that is presented for the first time. Let's first consider the following exchange:

(2) Alice: Who did break the window?

Tom: Mary broke the window.

The noun phrase *Mary* in Tom's answer is the message or information that Alice wants to know; *the window* in the reply, in contrast, is the information shared by both Alice and Tom. In other words, *Mary* is new information to Alice because it is just being introduced into the discourse for the first time, but *the window* is given or old information to Alice because it can be presumed to be in the mind of Alice, who has just introduced it into the discourse in the previous turn. **Given information** is the information that is assumed by the speaker to be known to, assumed by, or inferable by the addressee at the time of the speaker's utterance, while **new information** is the information that is assumed by the speaker not to be known to or assumed by the addressee, or the information that is not previously established in the discourse.

The given and new information distinction reflects the different cognitive status of the information transmitted by the addressor, and the difference is usually marked in one way or another. For instance, given information is often coded in condensed form—the more natural reply to Alice's question in (2) will be "Mary broke it" or "Mary did".

It has often been observed that, in English, new information is characteristically introduced by indefinite expressions and subsequently referred to by definite expressions. The use of the two articles *a* and *the* is a case in point as in the following sentences:

(3) a. There goes *a* beggar, with a long beard.

b. There goes *the* beggar, with the long beard.

(3a) is identical with (3b) except for the use of article. *The article a* in (3a) respects our primary perception, and denotes individuals as unknown, while *the* in (3b) respects our secondary perception, and denotes individuals as known.

In (4), we will exemplify a range of syntactic forms that have been frequently identified in the literature as expressions referring to given information. The expression that claims to be "given" is italicized in each case.

(4) a. Yesterday I saw a little girl got bitten by a dog.

   I tried to catch *the dog*, but *it* ran away.

   b. Mary got some beer out of the car.

   The beer was warm.

   c. Mary got some picnic supplies out of the car.

   The beer was warm.

   d. Yesterday, Beth sold her Chevy.

   Today, Glen bought *the car*.

   e. I bought a painting last week.

   I really like *paintings*.

   f. Robert found an old car.

   The steering wheel had broken off.

   g. What happened to the jewels?

   They were stolen by a customer.

   h. I saw two young people there.

   He kissed *her*.

   i. Sag produces a cleaver and prepares to hack off his left hand.

   He never actually *does it*.

   j. Look out.

   It's falling.

   k. William works in Manchester.

   So do I.

In the examples in (4), we find that the syntactic forms that are regularly in association with "given" information include: (i) Lexical items which are mentioned for the second time as in (4a, b), particularly those in definite expressions; (ii) Lexical items which are presented as being within the semantic field of a previously mentioned lexical item as in 4 (c), 4 (d), 4 (e) and 4 (f), again particularly those in definite expressions; (iii) Pronominals used anaphorically following a full lexical form in the preceding sentence as in 4 (a, g, h); (iv) Pronominals used exophorically (to refer to the physical context of situation) where the **referent** is present, as in 4 (i, j); (v) Pro-verbals as in 4 (i, k).

The contrast between given and new information is important in characterizing the functions of some constructions in English and other languages, as will be shown in the next section.

7. 2. 2   Topic and comment

The use of the term **topic** is usually associated with descriptions of sentence structure. A distinction can be made between the topic and the comment in a sentence, in that the speaker announces a topic and then says something about it. In other words, there is something that has to be regarded as the already established matter of current concern about which new information is added. The added information is named **comment**, whereas the information that has already been established and thus can serve as an anchoring point for the new information is designated as *topic*. It is this "aboutness" relation that connects the two categories, in that the **topic** represents what the utterance is about whereas the comment is what is said about the topic. Let's have a look at the following example:

(5) I saw John yesterday. He was angry.

Here, the pronoun *He* in the second sentence refers to the topic (it is the topic expression), whereas *was angry* designates the comment that is about the topic. In English, topics are usually subjects and comments are usually predicates, as is shown in (5). However, this is not always the case, and other elements in the sentence can also take the role of topic as in (6).

(6) a. *This article*, Mr. Morgan has written when he was still young.

b. *This article* was written by Mr. Morgan when he was still young.

c. *As for this article*, it was written by Mr. Morgan when he was still young.

Regarding this article, it was written by him when he was still young.

d. Mr. Morgan wrote *this article* when he was still young.

As is shown in (6), topics can be expressed in various ways, for example, by special syntactic movement as in (6a), by diatheses like passivization as in (6b), by specialized syntactic constructions as in (6c), or by deaccentuation as in (6d), etc.

Although the topic-comment distinction often coincides with the opposition between given and new information, it is important not to confuse them. The given-new distinction depends on the point of view of the listener, whereas the topic-comment distinction relates to that of the speaker. The given element is the information that the speaker presents as already known to the listener, while the topic element is the one that the speaker decides to take as the starting point. So, given information is not always the topic. In the second sentence of the following sequence, the noun phrase *her little sister* is both new information and the topic.

(7) Mary ate the bread. As for *her little sister*, she drank the Coca-Cola.

Similarly, given information can serve as the comment, as the italicized element in the following sequence illustrates:

(8) Peter didn't believe anything the charlatan said. *As for Mary, she believed everything* he said.

7.2.3 Focus and presupposition

A third distinction can be made between **focus** and **presupposition**. Although the term **focus** means different things to different people, we will use it here to refer to that portion of an utterance that represents new information. A focus marks some discourse unit by setting it off against a background which corresponds to presupposition in such a way that the relation to a set of possible alternatives it asserted. A focused constituent is realized intonationally with some kind of prosodic prominence, generally unclear accent. Presupposed information is the complement of focus: it represents the information that the speaker assumes is already part of the common ground, i. e. either salient or inferable in context.

Because utterances are intended to be informative, the presupposition typically does not exhaust the information in the utterance; instead, the proposition being presupposed is "open" —that is, lacking certain information. Such a proposition is represented with a variable in place of one or more constituents. For example, the utterance in (9a) would give rise to the presupposed open proposition in (9b), in the sense that a person hearing (9a) would immediately be licensed to treat (9b) as part of the common ground:

(9) a. Pat brought those cookies to the BBQ.

   b. Pat brought X to the BBQ.

Although only a single word, or syllable, of the focus bears nuclear accent, the focus itself can be indefinitely large. Consider (10):

(10) Pat brought a bag of those yummy cookies from Treasure Island to the BBQ.

If in a context someone asked "What did Pat bring?", the focus in (10) would be *a bag of those yummy cookies from Treasure Island.*

It is also possible for a clause to have more than one focus, as in the exchange in (11):

(11) a. Who brought what to the BBQ?

　　 b. Pat brought cookies.

The presupposition in this case is X *brought* Y, and *Pat* and *cookies* are foci. Notice that *Pat* need not represent entirely new information in order to count as new in this context. Even if Pat is salient in the discourse, *Pat* here is new as an instantiation of the variable in the presupposition. In effect, to say that *Pat* represents new information in this way is to say that the proposition *Pat brought cookies* is (believed to be) absent from the hearer's mental store of propositions, despite the presence of the proposition X *brought* Y.

Not all utterances involve presuppositions. For example, (10) may felicitously be uttered in a context in which it is not presupposed that anyone brought anything. In such a context, the entire utterance may be considered the focus (often called "broad focus").

7.3　Cohesion and coherence

Discourse is more than a random set of utterances: it shows connectedness. A central objective of linguists working on the discourse level is to characterize this connectedness. An addresser usually attempts to help his or her addressee to perceive the coherence of the text by organizing the way in which the meanings are expressed. Therefore, some devices are essential for creating a "texture", i. e. the quality of being recognizably a discourse or text rather than a collection of unconnected words or clauses. These resources are generally grouped together under the label of "**cohesion**". In this section, we will firstly examine the major cohesive devices that people usually apply to achieve cohesion, and then discuss the coherent nature of discourse.

7.3.1 Cohesion

Cohesion occurs "when the interpretation of some element in the discourse is dependent on that of another" (Halliday & Hasan, 1976: 4). It is concerned with the grammatical and/or lexical relationships between different elements of a discourse. There are five ways by which cohesion is created: **reference**, **substitution**, **ellipsis**, **conjunction**, and **lexical organization**. We will illustrate all of these cohesive devices from the following example:

(12) Little Boy Blue, come blow your horn!

The sheep's in the meadow, the cow's in the corn.

Where is the boy that looks after the sheep?

He's under the haycock, fast asleep.

Will you go wake him? No, not I!

For if I do, he'll be sure to cry.

In (12), the use of *he*, *him*, and *he* to refer back to "the boy that looks after the sheep" is an instance of reference. The forms *no*, *not I* and *if I do* are examples of ellipsis and substitution; they have to be interpreted as *no I (will)*, *not (wake him)* and *if I (wake him)*. The word *for* expresses a conjunctive relationship between "I will not" and "if I do, he will cry", *sheep* in line three reiterates *sheep* in line two, *cow* relates to *sheep*, *corn* to *meadow*, and *wake* to *asleep*. These are all examples of lexical cohesion. In the following part, we will examine these cohesive devices one by one.

7.3.1.1 Reference

Reference is the set of grammatical resources, which allows the speaker to indicate whether something has appeared somewhere else in the text, (i. e. we have already been told about it), or it has not yet been presented in the text (i. e. it is new to us). A participant or circumstantial element introduced at one place in the text can be taken as the reference point for something that follows. In simplest case this means that the same thing comes in again. Consider:

(13) If *a wife* is beautiful, two eyes are not enough for *her* husband. (J. Ray)

In (13), *her* is a repetition of the element *a wife* that is previously introduced into the discourse. This referring back to what is already mentioned in the discourse is known as **anaphoric reference**.

If the interpretation of an element has to resort to the element that follows in the discourse as is shown in (14) where the understanding of *her* depends on the following word *Jane*, this is called **cataphoric reference**.

(14) When I met *her*, *Jane* looked happy.

No matter whether it is an anaphoric reference in (13) or a cataphoric reference in (14), if the interpretive source lies in the co-text, so that the referent can be retrieved from the text, this kind of reference is called **endophora**. Sometimes, the interpretive source can be only found in the situational context as is shown in (15), where *her* refers to the girl that is standing there when the speaker is speaking. In this case, this kind of reference is called **exophoric reference** or **exophora**.

(15) (Mary is standing there) I like her.

Reference may also serve as a basis for comparison. For example:

(16) Henry can't play today. We'll have to find someone else.

In this discourse, *Henry* and *someone else* form a comparison where *someone else* means "someone other than Henry".

7.3.1.2　Substitution

There are some special words in English which contribute to cohesion by substituting for words that have already been used. The process or result of replacing one word by another at a particular position in a structure is called **substitution**. The word that refers back to a previously occurring element of structure may be called a **substitute word**. In substitution, a linguistic form is put in the place of the wording to be repeated from elsewhere. Let's see the following example:

(17) It's large for five months, but not abnormally so.

In (17), *so* substitutes for *large for five months*, which has been previously introduced into the discourse.

In English, there are three types of substitution, that is, **nominal** (to replace a noun or noun phrase), **verbal** (to replace a verb phrase) and **clausal** (to replace a clause) **substitution**.

(i) **Nominal substitution**

(18) By all means marry: if you get a good wife, you will become happy; if you get a bad *one*, you will become a philospher. (one = wife)

(19) She chose the roast duck; I chose *the same*. (the same = the roast duck)

（ii）**Verbal substitution**

（20）Some people like a shower after they have played tennis. Peter *does* for example.

（21）Did Mary take that letter? She might *have* (done).

（iii）**Clausal substitution**

（22）A: He is smart.

B: I don't think *so*.

（23）God send me a friend that may tell me of my faults; if *not*, an enemy, and he will.

7. 3. 1. 3 Ellipsis

A common cohesive device in discourse is to leave out a word or phrase rather than to repeat it. This device is called **ellipsis**. An elliptical item is one which, as it were, leaves specific structural slots to be filled from elsewhere. This is exactly the same as presupposition by substitution, except that in substitution an explicit "counter" is used, e. g. *one* or *do*, as a place-marker for what is presupposed, where in ellipsis nothing is inserted into the slot, so that there is a "gap" in the text which refers back. This is why we say that ellipsis can be regarded as substitution by zero. Here are some examples:

（24）All the children had an ice-cream today. Eva chose strawberry ø. Arthur had orange ø and Willem too.

（25）If aggression should instantly be punished, why was not a man, not a gun sent to deal with the aggressors in the occupied territories of the Middle East, Cyprus and East Timor? Our middle-of-the-road warmonger waves this aside. International force was not used in the past, he agrees. It should have been ø.

（26）To learn a new language you've got two options: either you study grammar, vocabulary and phonetics for months and months or you can go back to the way you learnt things as a child. A child learns to speak almost "by chance". He imitates his parents without knowing why ø.

In the above examples, the place where words are left out is marked with the symbol ø. It isn't hard to say what words have been omitted: *ice-cream* in (24), *used in the past* in (25) and *he imitates his parents* in (26). Like substitution, we can distinguish nominal, verbal and clausal ellipsis.

(i) **Nominal ellipsis**

(27) If one word be worth one shekel, silence is worth two (shekels).

(28) The good life is one (life) inspired by love and guided by knowledge. (B. Russell)

(ii) **Verbal ellipsis**

(29) A man can be destroyed, but not defeated (= but can not be defeated). (E. Hemingway)

(30) Reading makes a full man; conference (makes) a ready man; and writing (makes) an exact man. (Francis Bacon)

(iii) **Clausal ellipsis**

(31) We can live without our friends, but not (= we cannot live) without our neighbors.

(32) A: Would you like to see a little of it?

B: Very much indeed. (= I would very much indeed like to see a little of it.)

7.3.1.4　Conjunction

The fourth type of cohesion is conjunction. Conjunctive elements are cohesive not in themselves but indirectly, by virtue of their specific meanings; they are not primarily devices for reading out into the preceding (or following) discourse, but they express certain meanings which presuppose the presence of other components in the discourse. Consider the following example:

(33) A wise man likes to learn, *while* a fool likes to teach others. (A. Chekhov)

The two parts of sentence (33) constitute a cohesive whole, and the cohesive relation is expressed by the word *while*. **Conjunction** refers to an item or a process whose primary function is to connect words or other constructions. According to Halliday (1994), conjunction falls into four categories: additive, adversative, causal, and temporal. Let's consider the following examples:

(34) For the whole day he climbed up the steep mountainside, almost without stopping.

a. *And* in all this time he met no one. (additive)

b. *Yet* he was hardly aware of being tired. (adversative)

c. *So* by night time the valley was far below him. (causal)

d. *Then*, as dusk fell, he sat down to rest. (temporal)

The words *and*, *yet*, *so* and *then* can be taken as typifying these four general conjunctive relations, which help us interpret the relation between clauses.

7.3.1.5 Lexical cohesion

Lexical cohesion comes about through the selection of lexical items that are related in some way to those that have gone before. In general, we can classify two relations that a selected lexical item is likely to bear in relation to those that have gone before in the discourse: **reiteration** and **collocation**.

Reiteration takes place not only through repetition of an identical lexical item but also through occurrence of a different lexical item that is systematically related to the first one, as a synonym or superordinate of it. For example:

(34a) An invasion of armies can *be resisted*; an invasion of ideas cannot *be resisted*. (repetition)

(35) He was just wondering which road to take when he was startled by a noise from behind him. It was *the noise* of trotting *horses*... He dismounted and led his horse as quickly as he could along the right-hand road. *The sound* of *the cavalry* grew rapidly nearer... (synonym)

(36) Peter met *a bear*. *The animal* was bulgy. (superordinate)

In addition to reiteration, there are other instances of lexical cohesion which depend on a particular association between the items in question – a tendency to co-occur. This "co-occurrence tendency" is known as **collocation**. For instance:

(36a) A little fat man of Bombay

Was smoking one very hot day.

But a bird called a snipe

Flew away with his pipe,

Which vexed the fat man of Bombay.

In (36), there is a strong collocational bond between *smoke* and *pipe*, which makes the occurrence of *pipe* in line 4 cohesive.

7.3.2 Coherence

In 7.3.1, we have briefly examined some of the resources for creating "texture",

i. e. the quality of being recognizably a text rather than a collection of unconnected words or clauses. These are generally grouped together under the label of "cohesion". In talking about discourse or text, another term, i. e. **coherence**, is frequently applied. The terms may seem almost interchangeable. However, there is an important difference between them. Cohesion refers to the linguistic devices by which the speaker can signal the experiential and interpersonal coherence of the text, and is thus a textual phenomenon: we can point to features of the text which serve a cohesive function. Coherence, on the other hand, is in the mind of the writer and reader: it is a mental phenomenon and cannot be identified or quantified in the same way as cohesion. Cohesion and coherence are in most cases linked, in that a text which exploits the cohesive resources of the language effectively should normally be perceived as coherent. However, all language users are generally predisposed to construct coherence even from language with few recognizable cohesive signals, if they have reason to believe that it is intended to be coherent. The following pair of sentences have only one cohesive link ("Hugo" — "He"), but they make sense together, that is, they are coherent:

(37) Hugo spent all of his legacy laying down wine. He was ensuring a happy middle age.

Nevertheless, coherence is a crucial linguistic resource in the expression of coherent meanings; and the analyst may gain equally important insights into how it works from cases where a lack of cohesive devices in a text does not lead to the interactants perceiving it as incoherent.

7. 4 Discourse marker

In a lively speech, the speaker usually makes use of such linguistic elements as *you know*, *I mean*, *well*, *oh*, *you see*, etc. These elements are conventionally taken as **discourse markers**. Discourse markers are linguistic expressions used to signal the relation of an utterance to its immediate context. In most cases, they have a distinct prosodic entity, tend not to have specific semantic meaning, and contribute to scaffold the pragmatic coherence of interaction. It is generally believed that a conversation is much less lively and less personal without discourse markers signaling receipt of information, agreement and involvement.

Now, let's see some examples of discourse markers in English, and they are: *well*, *now*, *actually*, and *OK*.

Well

Well serves various functions in discourse depending on the context and its position in the utterance. *Well* at the beginning of a turn, for example, serves as a response marker to what has gone before.

(38) Well, I can also give you like Funds Transfer, Item Search, Order Statement or Change TIN.

Well at the beginning of the prompt is used in response to the user's request for another service (within a banking application). It serves to accept what the user has requested before moving on to respond to that request. In this way, it forms a cohesive tie within the dialogue.

Now

Now at the beginning of a turn is used as a transition marker, introducing a new topic and changing the direction of the discourse. In the case of automated dialogues, where the application may be very specific, *now* can be used to move from one part of the dialogue to another. Consider:

(39) Now, would you like to select another service?

This prompt would be played after a user had completed a particular transaction. One part of the dialogue is complete, and then moves on to something new.

Actually

Actually, as a discourse marker, gives processing instructions to a listener about how the particular utterance should be understood. For the hearer, the use of *actually* highlights the fact that something is now being said that might not have been expected in this context but that is relevant nevertheless.

Actually can therefore be used to signal to the hearer that although what follows is relevant to the ongoing discourse, it will contain (in the opinion of the speaker) information that the hearer is not expecting. Let's look at the following example:

(40) Actually, there is a charge of three pounds for an interim postal statement. Would you like one to be sent?

The use of *actually* in (40) signals that the information that would follow, although relevant, may not be what they were expecting.

OK

OK has a rather informal status in spoken English, but can have many uses in spoken dialogue systems, depending on the level of formality required for the service. We can assign various functions to *OK* depending on its location within an utterance. *OK* at the beginning of a turn expresses agreement, and can also indicate ack-nowledgement of the preceding utterance. *OK* in second position following *yes* emphasizes the agreement expressed by *yes*. However, that role depends on the intonation of the utterance. For example, "Yes, OK" (spoken with a sigh) potentially indicates reluctant agreement or consent. On the other hand, "Yes, OK" (spoken with stress on *OK*) in *OK* at the end of a turn asks for confirmation. For example:

(41) OK, just tell me if you want another service.

Here the *OK* serves as an acknowledgement of the user's request for help. As we can see from the above examples, discourse markers seem to clarify a text's structural relations for the reader. Though discourse markers may refer to different things in different contexts, these items share a number of formal and textual features. These features can be summed up in the following: they do not belong to the sentence elements proper (subject, verb, complements); they are typically found in the initial position of an utterance or, on the whole, in transitional locations (beginning and end of units); they do not always have a clear propositional (semantic) meaning and their propositional meaning is superseded by their discourse functions; they assume multiple roles in signaling relations (ideational, textual, interpersonal) between units at different levels.

7.5   Multimodal discourse analysis

Multimodal discourse analysis (MDA) is an emerging paradigm in discourse studies, which attempts to investigate discourse in combination with other resources, such as images, scientific symbolism, gesture, action, music, and sound. The terminology in MDA is used somewhat loosely at present as concepts and approaches evolve in this relatively new field of study. For example, language and other resources which integrate to create meaning in "multimodal" (or "multisemiotic") phenomena (e.g. print materials, videos, websites, three-dimensional objects and day-to-day events) are variously called "semiotic resources", "modes" and "modalities". MDA itself is referred to as "multimodality", "multimodal analysis", "multimodal semiotics", and "multimodal studies". In what follows, the major concerns of MDA and the reasons for the emergence of this field in linguistics will be discussed.

MDA is concerned with theory and analysis of semiotic resources and the semantic expansions which occur as semiotic choices in multimodal phenomena. **Semiotic resource** is used here to describe the resources (or modes) (e. g. language, image, music, gesture and architecture) which integrate across sensory modalities (e. g. visual, auditory, tactile, olfactory, gustatory, kinesthetic) in multimodal texts, discourses and events, collectively called multimodal phenomena. The "inter-semiotic" (or inter-modal) relations arising from the interaction of semiotic choices, known as intersemiosis, is a central area of multimodal research. MDA is also concerned with the design, production and distribution of multimodal resources in social settings, and the resemioticisation of multimodal phenomena which takes place as social practices unfold. The major challenges that MDA faces include the development of theories and frameworks for semiotic resources other than language, the modeling of social semiotic processes (in particular, intersemiosis and resemioticisation), and the interpretation of the complex semantic space which unfolds within and across multimodal phenomena.

The emergence of MDA can be accounted for by the following points. First, discourse analysts attempting to interpret the wide range of human discourse practices have found the need to account for the meaning arising from multiple semiotic resources deployed in various media, including contemporary interactive digital technologies. Second, technologies develop new methodological approaches for MDA, for example, multimodal annotation tools have become available and affordable. Lastly, interdisciplinary research has become more common as scientists from various disciplines seek to solve similar problems. From "an age of disciplines, each having its own domain, its own concept of theory, and its own body of method", the twenty first century has emerged as "age of themes" which aimed at solving particular problems. MDA is an example of this paradigm shift, and it has a key contribution to make with respect to multimodal analysis, search and retrieval of information.

7. 6   Critical discourse analysis

Critical Discourse Analysis (CDA) is a field that is concerned with studying and analyzing written and spoken texts to reveal the discursive sources of power, dominance, inequality and bias. It examines how these discursive sources are maintained and reproduced within specific social, political and historical contexts. Even though there are various models of CDA (e. g. van Dijk's social-cognitive model, Wodak's discourse sociolinguistics, and Fairclough's critical language study), some basic assumptions are held by CDA practitioners. These assumptions can be summarized as follows:

1. Language is a social practice through which the world is represented.

2. Discourse/language use as a form of social practice in itself not only represents and signifies other social practices but also constitutes other social practices such as the exercise of power, domination, prejudice, resistance and so forth.

3. Texts acquire their meanings by the dialectical relationship between texts and the social subjects: writers and the readers, who always operate with various degrees of choice and access to texts and means of interpretation.

4. Linguistic features and structures are not arbitrary. They are purposeful whether the choices are conscious or not.

5. Power relations are produced, exercised, and reproduced through discourse.

6. All speakers and writers operate from specific discursive practices originating in special interests and aims which involve inclusions and exclusions.

7. Discourse is historical in the sense that texts acquire their meanings by being situated in specific social, cultural and ideological contexts, and time and space.

8. CDA does not solely interpret texts, but also explains them.

Since CDA deals with the relationship between discourse and power, a central notion in most critical work on discourse is that of power, and more specifically the social power of groups or institutions. Summarizing a complex philosophical and social analysis, social power can be defined in terms of control. Thus, groups have (more or less) power if they are able to (more or less) control the acts and minds of (members of) other groups. This ability presupposes a power base of privileged access to scarce social resources, such as force, money, status, fame, knowledge, information, culture, or indeed various forms of public discourse and communication.

Different types of power may be distinguished according to the various resources employed to exercise such power: the coercive power of the military and of violent men will rather be based on force, the rich will have power because of their money, whereas the more or less persuasive power of parents, professors, or journalists may be based on knowledge, information, or authority. Note also that power is seldom absolute. Groups may more or less control other groups, or only control them in specific situations or social domains. Moreover, dominated groups may more or less resist, accept, condone, comply with, or legitimate such power, and even find it "natural".

The power of dominant groups may be integrated in laws, rules, norms, habits, and even a quite general consensus, and thus take the form of "hegemony". Class domination, sexism, and racism are characteristic examples of such hegemony. Note also that power is not always exercised in obviously abusive acts of dominant group members, but may be enacted in the myriad of taken-for-granted actions of everyday life, as is typically the case in the forms of everyday sexism or racism. Similarly, not all members of a powerful group are always more powerful than all members of dominated groups: power is only defined here for groups as a whole.

For our analysis of the relations between discourse and power, thus, we first find that access to specific forms of discourse, e. g. those of politics, the media, or science, is itself a power resource. Secondly, action is controlled by our minds. So, if we are able to influence people's minds, e. g. their knowledge or opinions, we may indirectly control (some of) their actions, as we know from persuasion and manipulation. This also means that those groups who control most influential discourse also have more chances to control the minds and actions of others.

In general, CDA is a type of discourse analysis that primarily studies the ways social power abuse, dominance, and inequality are enacted, reproduced, and resisted by texts and talks in the social and political contexts. With such dissident research, critical discourse analysts take explicit position, and thus want to understand, expose, and ultimately resist social inequality.

7.7 Summary

This chapter has presented an overview to discourse analysis. Discourse analysis, also known as discourse studies or text analysis, is an area of linguistics that primarily deals with the analysis of language "beyond the sentence". Information structure, cohesion, and coherence are the most discussed topics in discourse studies. Information structure, including given/new information, topic/comment, and focus/presupposition, which concerns the information distribution of an utterance, is considered the most fundamental part in carrying out discourse analysis. Cohesion and coherence are the most important factors for creating "texture". Cohesion refers to the linguistic devices by which the speaker can signal the experiential and interpersonal coherence of the text, and is thus a textual phenomenon, while coherence is in the mind of the writer and reader, which is a mental phenomenon.

Self-study Activities

1. Define the following terms briefly.

   discourse   discourse analysis   information structure   given information
   new information   topic   focus   cohesion
   coherence   discourse marker   multimodal discourse analysis
   critical discourse analysis

2. Explain in what way cohesion and coherence are related.

3. Find the links between hyponym and superordinate in the following text. And then make a comment on the cohesive devices in the text.

   Brazil, with her two-crop economy, was even more severely hit by the Depression than other Latin American states and the country was on the verge of complete collapse.

4. Compare the following text with the one in exercise 3, and tell the differences. Which text do you think is more coherent? And Why?

   The country, with her two-crop economy, was even more severely hit by the Depression than other Latin American states and Brazil was on the verge of complete collapse.

5. Identify the cohesive devices in the following texts.

   (1) They came again into their bedroom. A large bed had been left in it.

   (2) A: How old is he?

      B: Two months.

   (3) He merely laughed and said that she was imagining things. This typical male reaction resulted in a row.

   (4) A: What did she say to you?

      B: Nothing.

   (5) I haven't even met Mrs. McCaffrey. I suppose I ought to have done.

   (6) I'm looking for an Indian man with a beard, have you seen one?

   (7) I would never have believed it. They've accepted the whole scheme.

   (8) I strove with none, for none was worth my strife.

   (9) Robert seems very worried about something. I think you ought to have a talk with the boy.

   (10) A: Why does this little boy wiggle all the time?

      B: Girls don't wriggle.

Sources and Suggestions for Further Reading

Brown G. and Yule, G. 2000. *Discourse Analysis*. Beijing: Foreign Language Teaching and Research Press.

Cook, G. 1990. *Discourse*. Oxford: Oxford University Press.

Fairclough, N. 1995. *Critical Discourse Analysis*. London: Longman.

Gee, J. P. 2000. *An Introduction to Discourse Analysis: Theory and Method*. Beijing: Foreign Language Teaching and Research Press.

Georgakopoulou, A. & Goutsos, D. 1997. *Discourse Analysis*. Edinburgh: Edinburgh University Press.

Halliday, M. A. K. and Hasan, R. 1976. *Cohesion in English*. London: Longman.

Jorgensen, M. & Phillips, L. 2002. *Discourse Analysis*. London: SAGE Publications.

O'Halloran, K. L. (ed.). 2004. *Multimodal Discourse Analysis*. London: Continuum.

Renkema, J. 2004. *Introduction to Discourse Studies*. Amsterdam: John Benjamins Publishing.

Rogers, R. (ed.). 2004. *An Introduction to Critical Discourse Analysis in Education*. Mahwah: Lawrence Erlbaum Associates, Inc.

Salkie, R. 1995. *Text and Discourse Analysis*. London: Routledge.

Schiffrin, D. 1997. *Approaches to Discourse*. Oxford: Blackwell.

Scollon, R. 2001. *Mediated Discourse: The Nexus of Practice*. London: Routledge.

Stubbs, M. 1983. *Discourse Analysis*. Oxford: Blackwell.

van Dijk, T. A. 1993. *Elite Discourse and Racism*. London: Sage Publications.

Wodak, R. 1996. *Orders of Discourse*. New York: Addison Wesley Longman.

Yule, G. 2000. *The Study of Language*. Beijing: Foreign Language Teaching and Research Press.

Chapter 8　Sociolinguistics

8.1　Introduction

Shown below are two marriage certificates issued in China in 1934 and 1972 respectively. The two written documents differ strikingly in the use of language as well as the format and visual effects.

The former certificate celebrates the marriage as a household event with affectionate and poetic wishes（看此日桃花灼灼，宜家宜室，待他年瓜瓞绵绵，尔昌尔炽，谨以白头之约书向鸿笺，好将红叶之盟载明鸳谱）. By contrast, the latter certificate, via Chairman Mao's quotation（千万不要忘记阶级斗争）, alarms the newly-weds at the ongoing political clashes of the nation. Probably being elegance-proud in the 1930s, but politics-minded in the 1970s, the two certificates take quite different shapes. Whatever differences they display, the structure and use of language in general can be interpreted and explained from a social perspective, i.e. from the impact of society on the way people think, speak and write.

In such cases, when we study language in its social contexts, it is called **sociolinguistics**. In other words, sociolinguistics is the study of how social factors influence the structure and use of language. Speakers' age, gender, career, social status, ethnic identity, nationality, as well as their education background often play a role in the language behaviors, consciously or less so. In addition, speakers' solidarity with the listener (e. g. as a nodding acquaintance or a bosom friend), or the site of conversation (e. g. in private or public) also tends to shape the language they use. Above the individual level, a vast web of social factors affects how communities or nations use language, manage language varieties, encourage or accommodate to language changes. These are core issues on the mind of sociolinguists, who tend to claim "You are what you say".

8. 2   Language varieties

An unfailing example to highlight language varieties is a popular joke by the name of 洋人求学记:

一个老外为了学汉语，来到中国，拜师于一位国学教授门下。第一天，老外想挑一个简单的词学习，便向老师请教英语 "I" 在汉语中应该如何说。

老师解释道：

中国是一个官本位国家，当你处在不同的级别、地位，"I" 有不同的变化。

比如，你对普通人可以说："我、咱、俺……"；如果见到老师、长辈，则应该说："愚、鄙人、卑人……"；等你当了官，见到上级和皇帝，则应该说："卑职、下官……"；见到平级，则可以说："愚兄、为兄……"；见到下级，则可以说："爷们、老子……"；如果你去当和尚、道士，则应该说："贫道、小道……"；最后你没权没地位了，只好说："老朽、老拙……"

上面一百零八种 "I"，仅仅是男性的常用说法，更多的 "I" 明天讲。

老外顿觉冷水浇头。第二天便向老师辞行："学生、愚、不材、末学，走。" 回国去了。

As this joke indicates, Chinese boasts so many self-reference terms for *wo* (*I*) that it is frustratingly complex for the foreigner to handle. This collection, still open-ended, signals the fact that language changes over time and space, from one social group to another, and from context to context. Changes in language involve a wide range of varieties, including standard language, dialects, registers, pidgins, creoles, and so on.

8. 2. 1   Standard language

Among the huge varieties of Chinese, what is the variety taught in school, used by the mouthpiece of government, adopted by official documents, and recognized as the most prestigious by the constitution and dictionaries? It is **putonghua**—the standard language in China. In general, a **standard language** refers to the variety of a language assigned with the highest status in a community or nation.

The standard language of British English is **the Received Pronunciation (RP)**, and that of American English is **Standard American English (SAE)**. That explains why most Chinese learners of English used to start with BBC or VOA programs. They provide reliable entry to standard English which in turn offers non-native speakers a sense of new identity. Likewise, putonghua is the first choice for non-native learners of Chinese.

A standard language always comes into being with the rise of a nation to conscious unity and identity, as was the case when the United States broke away from England, or when the People's Republic of China was founded. Every standard language undergoes linguistic changes, yet it needs constant care, maintenance and adjustment in order to keep off potentially disruptive forces from dialects or foreign languages. This enterprise involves enormous efforts of language planning, a topic coming up soon.

8. 2. 2   Dialects

Although a standard language outshines other varieties in terms of constitutional status, it is by no means all-purpose. Is it likely to come across two quarreling passengers on a bus who machine-gun each other with local dirty curses but in the standard tone of putonghua? The scene must be weird and ridiculous. What if all the masters of letters in Great Britain were made to write in standard British English only? There would be no chance for the birth of masterpieces like *Canterbury Tales*, a collection of stories told in dialects.

In fact, a fully developed language contains rich varieties functioning in different regions, at different times, for different social classes, and favored by different individuals. Such sub-varieties of a single language are called **dialects**. The study of dialects is called **dialectology**. Dialects fall into the following categories:

Regional/geographical dialects: varieties of a language spoken in a geographical area, such as Lancashire dialect in Britain, or Sichuan dialect in China. Regional dialects of a country show more or less differences in terms of vocabulary, accent and sentence structures. Spoken Cantonese, for example, sounds somewhat gibberish to people in other regional dialects.

Temporal dialects: varieties of a language occurring in certain periods of time. Gaps in time often leave gaps in language. Simple words like *thou*, *thee*, *thy* in Shakespeare's plays in Early Modern English sound strange to speakers at present. Similarly, the gaps between two major temporal dialects in China, i. e. classical Chinese and modern Chinese, also produce interpretive difficulties for current readers of classics like *Lunyu* (The Confucian Analects).

Social dialects or **sociolects:** varieties of a language used by people belonging to particular social classes or groups. A speech community, due to its shared membership in certain social classes, occupations, workplaces or age groups, tend to share a lot of language behaviors in common, such as jargons, slang, topics, inside stories, or styles, in addition to some phonological or syntactical similarities. Different sociolects might stand widely apart in specific aspects. For instance, while youngsters are fond of neologisms web-borne from QQ, MSN, Facebook, Twitter, or YouTube, their grandparents' generation often frowns on and seldom utters such baffling stuff.

Idiolects: varieties of a language used by individual speakers, with identifiable peculiarities of pronunciation, grammar and vocabulary. Famous writers always win reputation for their personal styles of theme expression and techniques of diction. Terms like "Shakespeare's language", "Faulkner's language", or "Li Qingzhao's language" refer to their idiolects respectively. Among other things, Shakespeare excels in creating sharp yet profound contempt; Faulkner renders highly emotional and subtle stories; Li Qingzhao is regarded as a master of wanyue pai, "the delicate restraint".

8.2.3 Registers

It is commonplace for speakers of a language to switch ways of speaking according to different communicative situations and purposes, say, one way of speech at work, another at home, one way with superiors, another with busboys, one way playful, another serious, one way for diplomatic negotiations, another for market bargaining. Such varieties classified according to use are called **registers**.

In many cases, registers are named varieties within a culture, such as novels, memos, book reviews, lectures, TV news programs, sports announcer talks, press advertising and business letters. Typical registers for private use include love letters, baby talks, caretaker-child pretend plays, homecoming greeting, household arguments, friendship chats, dinnertime conversations, etc.

These registers differ in a number of situational characteristics, the most vital of which include the participants, their relationships and their attitudes toward the communication; the setting and the level of formality; the channel of communication; the purpose of communication; the topic or subject matter. A register can be seen as the particular combination of values for each of these characteristics. It results from choices made at every linguistic dimension for a specific purpose.

At the vocabulary level, the following bunch of reference terms "我的母亲, 我的妈妈, 我妈妈, 我妈, 我老妈", tend to be used to reflect varying degrees of formality, intimacy, or easiness scale, though they stand for the same type of entity. Moreover, these referentially equivalent terms suggest different emotions and attitudes toward the addressee, the referent in question, the event being talked about, and the speech situation. But for convenience, a thesaurus just narrows down to the degrees of formality in order to distinguish synonyms like *stop*, *quit*, *end*, *cease*, *conclude*, *suspend* and *terminate*.

Likewise, syntactic choices are also register-sensitive. They shape contexts while get shaped by contexts. Suppose a customer at a bank counter needs to break a 50 dollar note, and as he hands it in he may try the following requests to different communicative effects:

(1) Would you mind giving me two twenties and two fives?
(2) I'd like to break it into two twenties and two fives.
(3) Give me two twenties and two fives, please.
(4) Two twenties and two fives.

The first three, if spoken in a polite tone, may smooth and lighten the service encounter. The last one, by contrast, is not welcome because of its face-threatening imperative pattern.

Analyses of register have often been conducted within a M. A. K. Halliday's functional-systemic framework. Halliday's register theory is concerned with three factors, namely, **field**, **mode** and **tenor of discourse**. The **field of discourse** refers to the event in which the discourse is functioning, including subject matter, e. g. the fields of Harry Potter, bakery, classical music, the Olympic Games, and household chores. The **mode of discourse** refers to the function of the discourse in the event, including both the medium of language activity—spoken or written, extempore or prepared, and its rhetorical mode, as narrative, persuasive, phatic, etc. The **tenor of discourse** refers to the role relations among the participants involved, especially the level of formality they adopt, e. g. intimate, casual, or formal. So, in line with Halliday, a roadside movie poster for *Harry Potter and the Deathly Hallows* can be analyzed as the variety of a visual and written mode featuring the field of advertising in the casual tenor.

With register awareness, speakers may make verbal choices appropriate to contexts. A working mother will not apply the baby-directed register "Sweetie, wanna have a pee-pee or poo-poo?" to her customers at the restaurant. Nor will she address her baby the way she serves customers "Sir, bathroom, this way please". The use of right register demonstrates a speaker's overall communicative competence.

8. 2. 4 Pidgin and Creole

Countless times in human history, when people have been brought together in circumstances where they had no language in common, they created a pidgin. This happened to the workers sold from a dozen of countries to the sugar plantations of Hawaii. This also happened to Shanghai about two hundred years ago when some local speakers developed the pidgin English as a means of communication with English businessmen or employers. The locals practised the pidgin English by reciting some amusing rhymes like 来是"康姆"去是"谷",廿四铜钿"吞的福",爷要"发茶"娘"卖茶",丈人阿伯"发音落".

A **pidgin** language has no native speakers. Instead, it is created and learned on contact situations such as trade or service exchanges. Working for these simple and limited purposes, a pidgin is usually crude with a small vocabulary and poor in grammar. The pidgin English in Shanghai took on reduced Chinese grammar and somewhat English sounds in strong local accent. The process in which a pidgin develops is called **pidginization**.

Only a few pidgins survive long enough to become the native language of a social community. When more and more members adopt a pidgin language for broad purposes, they expand its vocabulary and refine its grammatical system. If eventually the pidgin grows into a normal means of communication, the children of the pidgin-bound community will acquire it as their native language. In this case, the pidgin turns into a real language, a **creole** language. The process by which a pidgin turns into a creole is called **creolization**. It appears that modern Black English took its root in the creole English used by black slaves in the South, which in turn, developed from the pidgin English of the earliest slaves.

8. 3　Language and gender

Recent decades have shown a growing preference for gender-free terms such as *sailor*, *chair*, *press agent*, *sales representative* or *birth attendant*, when it is not a must to use their gender-marked counterparts like *seaman*, *chairman*, *spokesman*, *salesman* and *midwife*. Such changes result from the feminist movement as it snowballed into a greater protest against discrimination encoded in language. Feminists try to remove sexist usages of language, for instance, to replace *Miss*, *Mrs.* with *Ms.*, or to revise (1) into (2):

(1) Sexist: To find a friend, one must close one eye; to keep him, two.

(2) Revised: To find a friend, one must close one eye; to keep a friend, two.

But how to make this sentence non-sexist *If anyone calls, tell him I'll be back later*? As far as language and gender are concerned, feminists attempt to end the long-standing social conventions of representing men and women differently. Sexism in language is widespread. The word *man*, not *woman*, is used heavily in compounding words which cover both sexes, *postman*, *nobleman*, *businessman*, *fireman* etc. It is the same case with *brotherhood*, *forefathers*, *headmaster* and *son* (e. g. *son of the soil*, *sons of modern technology*) . Besides, the male forms often serve as the root for building up the female forms *via* bound morphemes, e. g. *waiter/waitress*, *host/hostess*, *hero/heroine*. The act of feminine suffixation creates an unbalanced gender pair, since it implies that the feminine noun is derived from the masculine. It also implies that female is of triviality, of lesser or inferior status. A few exceptions are found in words related to marriage or sexuality like *bride/bridegroom*, *widow/widower*, and *prostitute/prostituierter*. More serious sexism in language occurs in the asymmetry of male/female pair words, where one gender suffers semantic derogation or social prejudice. While the term *call girl* stands for an embarrassing occupation, *call boy* does not; it just refers to the person who calls actors when it is time for them to go on stage. While most women get well along with being described as *housewives*, most men feel uneasy with the label *househusbands*.

Another aspect of sexist language lies in people's likelihood to attach terms such as *drug dealer*, *chain smoker*, *president*, *millionaire*, and *lawyer* to man, *nurse*, *secretary*, *babysitter*, *housekeeper* to woman, whenever there lacks contextual cues of gender specification. Gender prejudices also lead job applicants to sending in letters with a *Dear Sir* or *Dear Gentleman* greeting, for they assume that the addressee is a man. Nowadays, applicants prefer *Dear Sir/Madam* or *Dear Personnel Manager* in order to avoid such a taken-for-granted stereotype. Although the urge for people to use gender-fair or gender-free language becomes stronger, it is necessary to acknowledge that there can be no solution to the problem of sexism in society on the level of language alone.

In addition to the focus on how men and women are handled differently in language, many linguists examine how men and women handle language differently. In some languages, they uncover sex differences with respect to pronunciations, words, or grammatical endings. In English, all-male conversations differ strikingly from all-female ones, among other things, in their choices of non-personal topics. Linguists find that women's speech can be distinguished from that of men in a number of ways including:

(i) More hedges (e. g. *She's kind of annoyed.*)

(ii) More empty adjectives (e. g. *gorgeous*)

(iii) More tag questions (e. g. *You don't mind eating this, do you?*)

(iv) More super-polite forms (e. g. *Would you mind...?*)

Furthermore, Deborah Tannen arouses wider attention to gender-specific speech. She defines female speech and male speech as " rapport-talk " and " report-talk " respectively. Women in conversations use language mainly for intimacy and support; they are consensus-driven. Men in conversations, however, mainly for information and upper hand; they are contest-driven. Different intentions explain why in mixed-sex conversations, men interrupt more often to gain a floor, to get control of topics. Furthermore, Tannen attributes the phenomena to gender distinctions or sexism built in language. Language, through all sorts of books, movies, tales and talks, keeps passing on different, asymmetrical assumptions about men and women. For example, on a self-help book shelf, two books might stand together, *How to Be Your Daughter's Daddy*: 365 *Ways to Show Her You Care* and *How to Be Your Little Man's Dad*: 365 *Things to Do with Him*. The titles leave a great deal of message that parenting a girl is taken as a different business from parenting a boy. Hence, it makes sense that the enduring effects of gender socialization through language gradually develop male and female speech.

To sum up, language both shapes gender and reflects our ideas about gender. When society is not sexism-free, when language is not gender-fair, men and women are apt to take up gender-specific speech styles. Therefore, in this section, the two mentioned directions of studying language and gender are inherently correlated.

8. 4   Choosing a code

8. 4. 1   Diglossia

When various codes exist as alternatives, there comes the choice of codes for appropriate occasions. The term **diglossia** was first introduced in 1959 by Charles A. Ferguson. In his formulation, **diglossia** refers to a relatively stable situation where two closely related languages are used side by side in a speech community, each with a clearly defined role, one for high (H) functions in public life and one for low (L) functions in domestic life.

	H	L
Sermon	√	
Instruction to servants		√
Speech in parliament	√	
University lecture	√	
Conversation with friends		√
Newspaper editorial	√	
Etc.		

The **High (H) variety** is regarded as superior to the **Low (L) variety**. In particular, H is considered more educated, more beautiful, more logical, better able to express important thoughts, etc. While H is chiefly learnt through formal schooling and supported by institutions outside home, L is typically acquired at home as a mother tongue and used in familial and informal interactions.

Diglossic speech communities are found in Switzerland (Hochdeutsch and Schwizerdütsch), in various Arabian countries (Classical Arabic and the local dialect of Arabic), in Paraguay (Spanish and Guaraní), to name a few. Triglossia exists, for example, in the age-old three-way opposition between classical written Chinese, vernacular written Chinese, and vernacular spoken Chinese. Classical Chinese served as the H variety for official documents and for literary writings until the fall of the Qing dynasty.

8.4.2 Bilingualism and multilingualism

As a Chinese, Lin Yutang achieves international reputation through his English writings such as *My Country and My People.* He is a heavyweight bilingual. For most American-born Chinese children (nicknamed as ABC children), they learn to speak both English and Chinese as their native languages. Now, at the age of globalization and cultural openness, a trash can in Seattle "speaks" four languages: English, Chinese, Vietnamese, and Spanish. A warning sign in earthquake-stricken Wenchuan "speaks" Chinese, English, Japanese, and Korean. A Pizza Hut restaurant in Lijiang, an attractive tourist city, "hails" customers in Chinese, English, and local Dongba language.

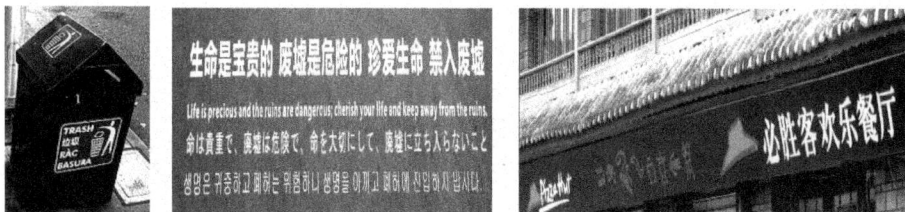

The coexistence of two and more languages used by individuals or language communities is referred to as **bilingualism** and **multilingualism**. In many parts of the world, bilingualism is the norm. Some countries are officially bilingual, such as Switzerland, Belgium, and Canada. In a bilingual society, when two languages have equivalent status in the official, cultural and family life, the situation is called **horizontal bilingualism**. A case in point is the Macau Special Administrative Region of China which takes both Portuguese and Chinese as its official languages.

People may become bilingual either by acquiring two languages at the same time in childhood or by learning a second language sometime after acquiring their first language. To acquire two languages, the children of immigrants in America are consistently exposed to their parents' native language at home and to English at school or neighborhood. To learn a L2, children and adults aim at various goals. Some minority speakers learn the majority language to function in both languages; some foster a L2 for access to higher education, for travel, study or work abroad; others take up a L2 as an academic subject, or as a means for cognitive training or understanding foreign cultures.

Multilingualism is no less the norm than bilingualism around the world. In parts of India, for example, a small child usually knows several languages. It is not surprising for researchers to find an India businessman living in a suburb of Bombay who switches among half a dozen of languages. His mother tongue and home language is Kathiawari; his daily newspaper is in standard Gujarati; in the market he uses a variety of Marathi; at the railway station he speaks Hindustani; the language of his work is Kachchi; he watches English films and listens to a sports commentary in English.

Under the pressure of having many different languages within its boundaries, a multilingual state has to exercise great political power to maintain the status of its official language (s). In 1907, US President Theodore Roosevelt wrote, "We have room for but one language in this country, and that is the English language, for we intend to see that the crucible turns our people out as Americans, of American nationality, and not as dwellers in a polyglot boarding house."

8. 4. 3   Code-switching

In diglossic speech communities, people choose between the H code and the L code, two varieties which hardly overlap in one situation. But on enormous occasions, bilinguals and multilinguals alternate between languages or dialects within a single interaction or discourse. For instance, the lyrics of the FIFA World Cup 2010 official anthem *Waka Waka* (This Time for Africa) are composed of the juxtaposition of English and Kiswahili. See the excerpt (1) below:

(1) You're a good soldier

　　 Choosing your battles

　　 Pick yourself up

　　 And dust yourself off

　　 ...

　　 Tsamina mina

　　 Zangalewa

　　 Cus this is Africa

Literary works also make use of switching. Qian Zhongshu's masterpiece *Fortress Besieged is rich in utterances produced by means of alternations between Chinese, English, and French.* Two examples are cited:

（2）到了张先生家，张先生热情地欢迎道："Hello! Doctor 方，好久不见！"

（3）苏小姐道："时间早呢，忙什么？再坐一会儿。"指着自己身旁……苏小姐胜利地微笑，低声说："Embrasse-moi！"说着一边害羞……

These instances demonstrate a phenomenon called **code-switching**, which, in a narrow sense, refers to the use of two or more languages (or dialects) within a sentence or discourse. The code-switching in Example (2) occurs at both the intersentential level and the intra-sentential level. If the term **code** is taken broadly to include register, then most of us are code-switchers in our first language, capable of switching properly on different grounds of formality. We would, for example, greet our boss in the lift with courtesy "Good Morning! Mr Jobs." At the next moment, however, we would hello our colleagues quite casually, "Yo!", or "So, how're ya doin?" In our everyday life, a good command of various codes and a timely switch can keep our social networks well-oiled.

Code-switching can be both metaphorical and situational. **Metaphorical code-switching** refers to the tendency to switch codes in conversation in order to discuss a topic that would normally fall into another conversational domain. It involves topic changes. For example, at a family dinner (where the L variety is expected), family members might switch from L to H in order to discuss school or work. At work (where the H variety is expected), interlocutors may switch from H to L when discussing family. **Situational code-switching**, however, does not involve any topic change. It occurs when the codes are used depending upon the situations. In the lyrics of *Waka Waka*, the alternation between the codes of English and Kiswahili tries to celebrate the World Cup as a big event both for the entire world and for African countries in particular. The use of two codes contributes to the same topic, but each foregrounds a specific situation.

8.5 Language planning

In China, most undergraduates in the 1950s learnt Russian as their foreign language. In the 1980s, English took the place and became crazy nationwide ever since.

Both fashions emerged neither as the result of personal preference nor of historical incidents. They were determined politically at the state level as part of language planning in general.

Primarily, language planning carries out official language policies. First of all, it is urgent for every newly-founded nation to decide on a national language among numerous languages and dialects on its territory. Then governments launch political and educational programs to standardize the national language and develop it substantially for social needs. Meanwhile, governments regulate the status and use of other languages and dialects. But at a non-government level, many ethnic, religious or occupational groups may also make bottom-up efforts to influence language policies. This package of work is called **language planning**.

Language planning deals with both **status planning** and **corpus planning**. Status planning determines the status and scope of the functions of a language or a variety of language with regard to other languages or varieties. It involves status choices, making a particular language or variety an official language, national language, etc. as English in the USA, Swahili in Kenya, or *putonghua* in China.

Corpus planning promotes the forms of a language into an appropriate medium of communication. This may be achieved by creating new words or expressions, modifying old ones, developing or reforming grammar, spelling and writing system, and compiling dictionaries. In this sense, corpus planning is often related to the standardisation of a language.

Because status planning and corpus planning demand laborious and enduring efforts, language planning is also called **linguistic engineering**. It needs to maintain, revive, reform, or update the national language, to handle tensions between languages or dialects, to enrich or reduce linguistic diversity for the sake of cultural preservation or dominance. Many nations, therefore, have language regulatory bodies in charge of formulating and implementing language planning policies, as well as releasing annual reports on various aspects of social life in language.

Planning decisions lead to changes especially vital on the part of minority ethnic languages. A minority language is often put at risk, for it lives in the shadow of a culturally dominant language, for example, Irish in that of English and Frisian in that of Dutch. Out of political motives, a minority language might be meant to die, or let die, or rescued and protected.

Chinese government has been helping many lesser-known or endangered ethnic languages survive, while strengthening more influential minority languages, e. g. Mongolian and Tibetan, by introducing *putonghua* and English as the second and third language to those ethnic speakers.

8. 6 Methods for sociolinguistic investigation

Although contemporary sociolinguistics comprises a great many different traditions of research, all sociolinguists share a common orientation to language data, believing that analyses of linguistic behavior must be based on empirical data. Thus, the methodologies employed in current sociolinguistics are field-based. Research methods in interactional sociolinguistics (IS) involve several stages: a preliminary period of ethnography; the main processes of data collection, transcription and analysis; and a final effort of confirming the findings.

For sociolinguists, the basic principle of speaker selection is the impartial choice of informants. No preference is given to older, male, or rural speakers. The choice of informants must be random and thus unbiased by the field worker. To ensure that one's data is obtained from observed sources, random and objective, sociolinguistics has developed various methods, including sociolinguistic interview, participant observation, and questionnaire.

When sociolinguists need to collect data directly from speakers, they may conduct one-on-one sociolinguistic interviews lasting at least an hour, in which different tasks or activities are used to elicit different styles of speech. In some situations, informants will be asked by the investigator to narrate stories or give anecdotes and to talk about their interests in various subjects e. g. about their daily activities. Participant observation refers to the practice of spending longer periods of time with speakers, observing how they use language and react to others' use of it.

The procedure of interviewing and observing, however, has the disadvantage that the field worker very often has a negative effect on the informants. This is called the observer's paradox, namely the double-bind that researchers encounter when what they are interested in is how people behave when not being observed, but the only way to find out how they behave is to observe them. Labov's answer to this problem was to develop the in-person rapid and anonymous interview in which data are gathered quickly from informants who are not made aware they are being interviewed by a linguist in the public domain. This situation, whether elicited or not, is much more favorable and less likely to distort the results. Informants can be recorded on tape or researchers can recall what informants said later by memory.

Polling questionnaire is quite effective in sociolinguistic projects. A questionnaire needs to be well-prepared in order to collect, for example, the social and linguistic background of the informants, or various kinds of information related to language variations. Questionnaire can be conducted through conventional or modern channels, in forms of postal questionnaire, telephone questionnaire, email questionnaire, and mobile phone questionnaire.

Sociolinguistic researches employ both qualitative and quantitative methods widely. Qualitative method is dominant in interactional traditions, while quantitative method is strongly associated with variationist traditions established by William Labov. Sometimes, a sociolinguistic study calls for a combination of quantitative and qualitative methods using data from several independent tests to confirm its results, for example, from sociolinguistic interviews, personal narratives together with postal questionnaire. Such practice consists with the principle of triangulation for enhancing the overall accountability of the study.

8.7 Summary

Like all fields of enquiry, sociolinguistics has developed a distinctive orientation to the study of human language. It focuses on the relationship between language and society, on how social factors influence the structure and use of language. It shows enduring interest in a set of issues, such as language variation, language contact, language and gender, language planning, etc. Sociolinguists do not of course operate independently of other branches of linguistic science. It keeps absorbing new trends and latest findings from neighboring areas, while making exciting contributions to the study of language as a whole.

Self-study Activities

1. Define the following terms briefly.

   (1) sociolinguistics   (2) code-switching   (3) dialects   (4) registers
   (5) diglossia

2. When writing business letters for application or information, how to greet an unknown addressee in the salutation? Offer three types of commonly used greetings and discuss what social factors are taken into consideration in order to sound appropriate.

3. How do people become bilingual? Find out three typical situations where people come to acquire or learn two languages.

4. The following excerpt of the novel, *The Joy Luck Club*, vividly reveals both the mother-daughter generation tension and Chinese-American cultural conflicts. Can we identify the mother's strange-sounding English (boldfaced utterances) as Chinglish or a kind of pidgin English? What are the distinctive characteristics of each of them?

> "Why don't you like me the way I am? I'm not a genius! I can't play the piano. And even if I could, I wouldn't go on TV if you paid me a million dollars!" I cried.
>
> My mother slapped me. "**Who ask you be genius?**" she shouted. "**Only ask you be your best. For your sake. You think I want you be genius?** Hnnh! What for! **Who ask you!**"

Sources and Suggestions for Further Reading

Coulmas, F. 1997. *The Handbook of Sociolinguistics*. Oxford: Blackwell Publishing Ltd.

Coupland, N. & Jaworski A. 2009. *The New Sociolinguistics Reader* (2nd ed.). New York: Palgrave Macmillan.

Holmes, J. & Meyerhoff, M. 2003. *The Handbook of Language and Gender*. Oxford: Blackwell Publishing Ltd.

Labov, W. 2010. *Principles of Linguistic Change* (3 vols). Oxford: Blackwell Publishing Ltd.

Lakoff, R. 1991. You are what you say. In AshtonJones, E. & Olson, G. A. (eds.) *The Gender Reader*. Boston: Allyn & Bacon. 292-298.

Meschrie, R. 2001. *Concise Encyclopedia of Sociolinguistics*. Amsterdam: Elsevier Publishing House.

Tannen, D. 1991. *You Just Don't Understand*: *Women and Men in Conversation.* New York: Ballantine Books.

Wardhaugh, R. 2010. *An Introduction to Sociolinguistics* (6th ed.) . Malden: Wiley-Blackwell.

Chapter 9   Stylistics

9.1   Introduction

As a branch of linguistics, **stylistics** refers to the study of style. Although **style** is used very frequently in literary criticism and especially in stylistics, it is very difficult to define. Firstly, it refers to the distinctive manner of expression in writing or speaking. For example, we may talk of someone writing in an "ornate" style, or speaking in a "comic style". In this sense, style has evaluative connotations: we may praise someone for writing in a good style or criticize him or her for speaking in a bad style.

Secondly, style can be seen as variation in language use, whether literary or non-literary. On the one hand, there are different styles in different situations, and on the other hand, the same activity can produce stylistic variation. For example, a policeman may report to the magistrate in the law court that "I apprehended the alleged perpetrator", but he may talk to his colleague in the bar that "I collared this creep."

Style variation occurs not only from situation to situation but also according to medium and degree of formality. For example:

(1) a. You've got to pay fines for overdue books.

b. Penalties for overdue books will be strictly enforced.

These two sentences express the same library rule, but in different styles. While (1a) is colloquial and informal and thus can be uttered orally, (1b) is formal and is more likely to be written as a library regulation.

Style may vary in literary language within or between texts, genres and periods. So we may talk of the stylistic differences between Petrarchan and Shakespearean sonnets, or the stylistic features of the Victorian fiction. In this sense, style should be seen against a background of larger or smaller domains or contexts.

9.2 Dimensions of variation

In essence, style can be seen as a set or sum of distinctive linguistic features, which are characteristic of a certain register, genre or period. Stylistic variation may occur on different linguistic levels.

9.2.1 Lexical variation

Different styles may involve different lexical choices. For example:

(2) a. The price of meat has been going down steeply.

b. The price of meat has been declining alarmingly.

(3) a. They made a decision to walk out on the project.

b. They decided to abandon the project.

The above two pairs of sentences can be seen respectively as synonymous, but they are different in formality, with (2a) and (3a) being more informal than the corresponding (2b) and (3b). Such stylistic variation is realized by different lexical choices:

formal	informal
decline	go down
alarmingly	steeply
decide	make a decision
abandon	walk out on

In English poetry, the poets may attribute some new usage and meanings to existing lexical items to achieve a particular artistic effect:

(4) And storms *bugle* his fame. (Gerard Manley Hopkins, The Wreck of the *Deutschland*)

(5) Let him *easter* in him. (ibid)

In some situations, the poet may even coin some novel neologisms to achieve similar effects:

(6) the *widow-making unchilding unfathering* deeps (ibid)

Sometimes, the poet may juxtapose expressions of different registers or periods in a single poem for some special effect:

(7) Today we have *naming of parts*. Yesterday,

    We had *daily cleaning*. And tomorrow morning,

    We shall have what to do after *firing*. But today,

    Today we have *naming of parts*. Japonica

    Glistens like coral in all of the neighboring gardens,

    And today we have *naming of parts*.

                   (Henry Reed, *Lessons of the War*: 1. *Naming of Parts*)

(8) The association of man and woman

    In *daunsinge*, signifying *matrimonie* –

    A dignified and commodious sacrament,

    Two and two, *necessarye* conjunction

    Holding *eche* other by the hand or the arm

    Which *betokeneth concorde*.

                       (T. S. Eliot, *East Coker*)

In (7), the poet uses the italicized expressions for rifle instruction and the register of lyrical description to ridicule the theme of war and peace, whereas in (8), the author alternates between the italicized ancient spelling (e. g. daunsinge = dancing, matrimonie = matrimony, necessarye = necessary, eche = each, betokeneth = betokens, concorde = concord) and modern spelling of the English language to express the eternal nature of "the association of man and woman".

9. 2. 2 Grammatical variation

Stylistic variation may also involve, more often than not, some distinctive grammatical structures. Take the following poem for example:

(9) Shall I compare thee to a summer's day?

    Thou art more lovely and more temperate:

    Rough winds do shake the darling buds of May,

    And summer's lease hath all too short a date:

    Sometime too hot the eye of the heaven shines

    And often is his gold complexion dimmed;

    And every fair from fair sometime declines,

    By chance or nature's changing course untrimmed;

But thy eternal summer shall not fade,

Nor lose possession of that fair thou ow'st;

Nor shall death brag thou wander'st in his shade,

When in eternal lines to time thou grow'st:

So long as a man can breathe, or eyes can see,

So long lives this, and this gives live to thee.

(William Shakespeare, *Sonnet* 18)

In this poem, the author on one hand uses some lexical items characteristic of his period, i. e. Early Modern English, such as "sometime" (= sometimes), the second-person pronouns "thou", "thee", "thy", third-person singular predicates, such as "hath" (= has), and second-person singular predicates, such as "art" (= are), "ow'st" (= own), "wander'st" (= wander), "grow'st" (= grow), and on the other hand rearranges some lines for the sake of rhyming or rhythm:

And often is his gold complexion dimmed = And his gold complexion is often dimmed

And every fair from fair sometime declines = And every fair sometimes declines from fair

When in eternal lines to time thou grow'st = When thou grow'st in eternal lines to time

In fiction, essays, or public speeches, the author may use the same expressions or sentence patterns repeatedly for emphasis, contrast or some other artistic effects:

(10) Studies serve for delight, for ornament, and for ability. Their chief use for delight, is in privateness and retiring; for ornament, is in discourse; and for ability, is in the judgment, and disposition of business. (Francis Bacon, *Of Studies*)

(11) It was the best of times, it was the worst of times, it was the age of wisdom, it was the age of foolishness, it was the epoch of belief, it was the epoch of incredulity, it was the season of Light, it was the season of Darkness, it was the spring of hope, it was the winter of despair, we had everything before us, we had nothing before us, we were all going direct to Heaven, we were all going direct the other way – in short, the period was so far like the present

period, that some of its noisiest authorities insisted on its being received, for good or for evil, in the superlative degree of comparison only. (Charles Dickens, *A Tale of Two Cities*)

9.2.3 Phonological variation

Stylistic variation can also be realized phonologically. Firstly, the same wording may take on different patterns of tonality to express different meanings. For example:

(12) a. My brother who lives in Nai'robi has just arrived.

b. My 'brother who lives in Nai'robi has just arrived.

The two sentences are identical in wording but differ in tonality, which in turn changes the syntactical structure and semantic meaning. In (12a), the stress falls on "Nairobi" and thus the relative clause defines which brother is meant, i.e. not the one who lives anywhere else; it restricts the reference. In (12b), the stress falls on "brother" and "Nairobi" and thus the relative clause does not define which brother is meant; it adds extra information; it does not restrict the reference, and we may justifiably assume that there is in fact only one brother to refer to. In written discourse, we may insert commas to indicate that the relative clause functions as an "adding clause", as in (12c):

(12) c. My brother, who lives in Nairobi, has just arrived.

Similarly, we may change the tonic of a sentence to change the focus of information. For example:

(13) a. Can you break the apple in *two*?

b. Can you break the *apple* in two?

In this case, the tonic syllable falls on different parts of the clause and thus changes the focus of information. In (13a), *two* is the tonic and is made prominent. In (13b), the focus of attention switches to *apple*; the sentence could really only make sense if people had already been talking about breaking things in two, and the new focus of information is on a new item being offered for consideration.

In poetry, sometimes we may vary the pronunciation of some lexical items for the sake of rhythm. For example:

(14) The curfew tolls the knell of parting day,

The lowing herd winds slowly *o'er* the lea,

The ploughman homeward plods his weary way,

And leaves the world to darkness and to me.

(Thomas Gray, *Elegy Written in a Country Church Yard*)

In this poem, the author uses *o'er* (= over) to shape the line into iambic pentameter.

In some cases, lexical items typical of the poetic style are needed for the sake of prosody. For example:

(15) You think I'll weep:

No, I'll not weep.

I have full cause of weeping, but this heart

Shall break into a hundred thousand flaws

Or ere I'll weep.

(William Shakespeare, *King Lear*)

In the last line, the poetic word *ere* is used instead of *before*, which is its counterpart in Modern English commonly used in daily communication.

9.2.4　Graphological variation

In some cases, the author may specially design the text so as to achieve some particular effect. Take the following poem by E. E. Cummings for example:

(16) ... and break *onetwothreefourfivepigeons-justlikethat*

In this line, the poet writes a number of words in succession as if to portray the shooting of five pigeons without any break.

What is often debatable, however, is the extent to which such stylistic choice involves variation in meaning. For many people, stylistic meaning or variational value is what distinguishes propositions that on the deep level express the "same" meaning. In other words, there is always more than one way to say anything, but different expressions often render different stylistic effects. In this sense, all utterances have a style, even if they might seem relatively "plain" or "unmarked": a plain style is itself a style. For example:

(17) a. His dad *died* last summer.

b. His dad *passed away* last summer.

c. Jack *kicked the bucket* last summer.

In this example, the same proposition is expressed in three different ways and thus produces different stylistic effects. While (17a) is in a "plain" style, (17b) uses the euphemism "passed away" to connote respect for the father and (18c) uses the slangy expression "kicked the bucket" in a humorous tone.

9.3 Stylistic codification

9.3.1 Style markers

As discussed above, stylistic features are basically features of language. They may reflect the language habits or idiolect of the author. The set of features peculiar to, or characteristic of an author is called **style markers**. For example, Ernest Hemingway's fiction *The Old Man and the Sea* is noted not only for its unique theme and characters, but also for its economical writing style, and the effective use of symbolic images and contrasts. Similarly, O'Henry's short stories are generally characterized with surprising endings; James Joyce's *Ulysses* is peculiar in the employment of the technique of stream of consciousness. All these can be seen as the style markers of the individual authors.

9.3.2 Dictionaries

A good dictionary should provide stylistic labels so that the users can be equipped with adequate knowledge to use the language appropriately. For example, in *Merriam Webster's Collegiate Dictionary*, the following usage labels are used to code the stylistic features of the entries concerned:

Archaic: meaning that a word or sense once in common use but is found today only sporadically or in special contexts.

Obs: for "obsolete", meaning that there is no evidence of use since 1755.

Slang: showing that the word or sense is especially appropriate in contexts of extreme informality.

Nonstand: for "nonstandard", indicating a word or sense that is disapproved of by many but has some currency in reputable contexts.

Substand: for "substandard", used for a word or sense which differs from that of the prestige group of the community.

Bri: for "Britain", suggesting that a word or sense is limited in use to Great Britain.

Chiefly Scot: suggesting that a word or sense is chiefly used in Scotland.

Chiefly Irish: suggesting that a word or sense is chiefly used in Ireland

Scot & Irish: suggesting that a word or sense is chiefly used in Scotland and Ireland.

Canad: suggesting that a word or sense is chiefly used in Canada.

Chiefly Austral: suggesting that a word or sense is chiefly used in Australia.

Austral & NewZeal: suggesting that a word or sense is chiefly used in Australia and New Zealand.

Chiefly SoAfri: suggesting that a word or sense is chiefly used in South Africa.

Dial: for "dialect", indicating that the pattern of use of a word or sense is limited to some regional varieties of American English or British English.

NewEng: for "New England", indicating that a word or sense is limited in use to New England.

Southern: indicating that a word or sense is limited in use to the Southern States of U. S.

Southern & Midland: indicating that a word or sense is limited in use to the Southern States and Midland of U. S.

Northwest: indicating that a word or sense is limited in use to the Northwest part of U. S.

Chiefly Southwest: indicating that a word or sense is chiefly used in the Southwest part of U. S.

Chiefly West: indicating that a word or sense is chiefly used in the West part of U. S.

9. 3. 3 Grammars

Stylistic variation may also involve grammatical variation. Thus information concerning stylistic variation should also be coded in grammar books. For example, in *A Comprehensive Grammar of the English Language* by Randolph Quirk, et al. (1985), the various varieties of English are discussed in Chapter One, including such detailed stylistic information as types of variation (including regional variation, social variation, varieties according to field of discourse, medium, attitude, and interference), relationship among variety types, variation within a variety, and attitudes to variation.

9.3.4　Figures of speech

Effective communication depends not only on the correctness of, but also on the appropriateness and effectiveness of, linguistic expressions. In other words, to communicate in a proper style, especially in literary texts, often involves the effective use of some figures of speech, which, according to the American linguists Brooks and Woolen, refer to "the art of using language effectively", namely, the linguistic expressions that make verbal communication more precisely, vividly and lively. The following are some of the major figures of speech:

1）**Simile**

   （18）*Just as the waves make towards the shore, so do our minutes hasten to their end.*

   （19）So compared with any ordinary beam of light, the laser beam is a very orderly affair indeed. It's *like a military march — everyone in step.* In an ordinary beam, the waves are *like the people in a crowd going to a football match, jostling and bumping into one another.*

2）**Metaphor**

   （20）*She was strangled in the net of gossip.*

   （21）When I was indicted on May 7, no one, least of all I, anticipated that my case would *snowball* into one of the most famous trials in U. S. History. (John Scopes, *The Trial That Racked the World*)

3）**Metonymy**

   （22）*The pen* is mightier than *the sword.*

   （23）He must have been spoilt from *the cradle.*

4）**Synecdoche**

   （24）The poor man had six *mouths* to feed.

   （25）*China* beat *Japan* at volleyball.

5）**Transferred epithet**

   （26）He climbed up the crane to a *dizzy* height.

   （27）"Don't worry, son, we'll show them a few tricks," Darrow had whispered throwing a *reassuring* arm round my shoulder as we were waiting for the court to open. (John Scopes, *The Trial That Rocked the World*)

6）**Personification**

   （28）The sun *kisses* the green fields.

(29) Bitterness *fed on the man* who had made the world laugh.

7) **Pun**

(30) One *swallow* doesn't make a summer, but it sure warms you on a cold winter day. (*Reader's Digest*)

(31) Ben Battle was a warrior bold,

And used to war's alarms:

But a cannon-ball took off his legs,

So he laid down his *arms*. (Thomas Hood)

8) **Hyperbole**

(32) *I'm dying to see you.*

(33) Belinda smiled, and *all the world was gay*. (Alexander Pope)

9) **Understatement**

(34) That's *no laughing matter*. (*cf.* That's a serious matter.)

(35) "Don't worry. It's *only a little scratch*," he said, though he had been badly mauled by the tiger.

10) **Irony**

(36) "Oh, how I *enjoy* the freezing weather!" (Actually the speaker hates the freezing weather)

11) **Paradox**

(37) The child is father of the Man. (Wordsworth)

(38) I can resist anything but temptation. (Oscar Wilde)

12) **Oxymoron**

(39) She received him *in a cold pleasant manner*.

(40) At this, she burst into *a tearful laughter*.

13) **Euphemism**

(41) His wife *is expecting another child*.

(42) I have to *powder my nose*.

14) **Parallelism**

(43) *We will never* parley, *we will never* negotiate with Hitler or any of his gang. *We shall fight him* by land, *we shall fight him* by sea, *we shall fight him* in the air, until, with God's help, we have rid the earth of his shadow and liberated its people from his yoke. (Winston Churchill)

15) **Antithesis**

(44) Marry in haste, repent in leisure.

(45) To err is human, to be perfect is divine.

16) **Climax and anti-climax**

(46) Reading maketh a full man; conference a ready man; and writhing an exact man. (Francis Bacon, *Of Studies*)

(47) Golf does queer thing to the players. The average man will show greater distress more openly over the loss of a golf ball than over a loss of his business, his home or a close relative. (H. I. Phillipes)

17) **Rhetorical question**

(48) Shylock: I am a Jew. Hath not a Jew eyes? Hath not a Jew hands, organs, dimensions, senses, affections, passions fed with the same food, hurt with the same weapons, subject to the same winter and summer, as a Christian is? If you prick us, do we not bleed? If you tickle us, do we not laugh? If you poison us, do we not die? And if you wrong us, shall we not revenge? (William Shakespeare, *The Merchant of Venice*)

9.4   Linguistic approaches to stylistic analysis

Due to the influences of different branches of linguistics and literary criticism, there are different stylistic approaches. The following are two of the major contemporary stylistic approaches.

9.4.1   Functional stylistics

In linguistics, a broad distinction is sometimes made between the two approaches of formalism and functionalism. The former, as illustrated in Chomsky's generative grammar in the 1960s, studies language as an autonomous system, focusing on grammatical forms and the propositional meaning of sentences; the latter, as illustrated in systemic functional grammar developed by Michael Halliday since the 1970s, emphasizing the pragmatic function of language in its communicative context.

A similar distinction can also be made between **formalist stylistics** and **functional stylistics**. Whereas formalistic stylistics lays heavy reliance on the study of formal features, functional stylistics takes particular notes of the stylistic functions or effects or thematic significance of linguistic features in literary and non-literary texts.

In systemic functional linguistics, **lexicogrammar** is utilized to realize the three metafunctions of language (i. e. **ideational**, **interpersonal**, and **textual**), which are in turn respectively related to the three factors of the context of situation (including the field of discourse, the tenor of discourse and the mode of discourse). The relationship between the context of situation and the metafunctions and lexicogrammar of language can be summarized as follows:

Table 9. 1   Metafunctions, lexicogrammar and the context of situation

Context of Situation	Metafunctions	Lexicogrammar
Field of discourse ——→	Ideational: Experiential ——→	Transitivity Nominalization
Tenor of discourse ——→	Interpersonal ——→	Mood Modality
Mode of discourse ——→	Textual ——→	Thematic structure Information structure

Thus in functional stylistics, language is classified into different varieties according to the three factors of the context of situation. For example, according to the field of discourse (i. e. the content of discourse), English can be categorized as journalistic English, advertising English, forensic English, English for science and technology, etc. ; according to the tenor of discourse (i. e. the interpersonal relationship between the participants), English can be classified into formal and informal varieties in terms of formality; according to the mode of discourse (i. e. the medium of communication), we can make a distinction between written English and spoken English. Then we can characterize the linguistic features of such varieties by contextualizing the lexicogrammar in relation to metafunctions.

Following the tradition of structural stylistics, functional stylistics also lays emphasis on the stylistic effect of deviation. According to Leech (1969: 42-51), deviation falls into two categories: qualitative deviation and quantitative deviation. The former refers to the breaking of the normal rules of linguistic structure, whether phonological, graphical, lexical, grammatical, semantic, dialectal, registeral, or historical, whereas the latter refers to the breaking of the normal frequency of distribution of some linguistic structures in a certain text type. Halliday (1988) makes a similar distinction, labeling the first category of deviation as "incongruity" and the second category of deviation as "deflection". For example:

(49) Description, as the ultimate goal of linguistic science, *digs its own grave*.

(50) *To complain of the age we live in, to murmur at the present possessors of power, to lament the past, to conceive extravagant hopes of the future,* are the common disposition of the greatest part of mankind.

In (49), the collocation of the nominal subject "description" and the verbal predicate "digs its own grave" is not congruent with the normal usage of the English language and thus makes the theorizing sentence more lively and light-toned. In (50), four *to*-infinitive phrases are used successively as the subject. This over-use of infinitive phrases deviates from the normal distribution pattern of the English language and thus constitutes a deflected parallelism to portray the disposition of great mankind.

9.4.2 Cognitive stylistics

Cognitive stylistics is a new perspective on style as one of the aftermaths of the rapid development and prosperity of cognitive linguistics since the 1980s. As a cross-disciplinary approach, cognitive stylistics is theoretically rooted in cognitive linguistics.

By adopting the **figure-ground theory**, cognitive stylistics offers a new interpretation of deviation in literature in terms of **foregrounding**. Thus, the literary innovations and creative expressions are seen as foregrounding against the background of everyday non-literary language. In this view, one of the main functions of literature is to defamiliazize the subject matter, to estrange the reader from aspects of the world in order to present the world in a creative and newly figured way. Foregrounding within the text can be achieved by a variety of devices of deviation, such as repetition, unusual naming, innovative descriptions, creative syntactic ordering, puns, rhyme, alliteration, metrical emphasis, the use of creative metaphor, and so on. For example:

(51) I slip, I slide, I gloom, I glance,

Among my skimming swallows;

I make the netted sunbeam dance,

Against my sandy shallows.

(Alfred Tennyson, *The Brook*)

In the first line of this stanza, the author uses two pairs of words in alliteration (i. e. *slip* and *slide*, *gloom* and *glance*) to describe the "action" of the brook vividly and strikingly.

Another cognitive theory adopted in cognitive stylistics is **prototype theory**. According to this theory, our cognitive system for categorization is not like an "in or out" filling cabinet, but an arrangement of elements in a radial structure or network with central good examples, secondary poorer examples, and peripheral examples. The boundaries of the category are fuzzy rather than fixed. This kind of phenomenon is called **prototypicality**, which is the basis of categoricalization. Prototype theory can be applied to stylistic analysis to specify linguistic deviation. For example:

(52) *Folded away in the memory of nature with her toys.* Memories beset his brooding brain. *Her glass of water from the kitchen tap when she had approached the sacrament. A cored apple, filled with brown sugar, roasting for her at the hob on a dark autumn evening.* Her shapely fingernails reddened by the blood of squashed lice from the children's shirts. (James Joyce, *Ulysses*)

In this passage, the author uses a number of sentence fragments, which are some distance away from prototypical sentences. James Joyce does not state the matter in clear asserted prototypically actualized propositions. This renders the text to be reasonably open to readerliness in interpretation. In general, as Stockwell (2002: 36) observes, the less prototypical the style, the more potentially open the text is for readerly intervention.

Mental space theory is one more cognitive theory that is applied to cognitive stylistic analysis of literary works to consider the way in which texts project complex sets of states of affairs that can stand in different ontological relations to each other. This theory aims to account for the online production and comprehension of language. According to mental space theory, text processing involves the incremental construction of networks of interconnected mental spaces. Mental spaces are defined as short-term cognitive representation of states of affairs, constructed on the basis of the textual input on the one hand, and the comprehender's background knowledge on the other (Fauconnier, 1997). In cognitive stylistics, mental space theory has been used to account for the incremental understanding of short narrative texts. Take the following sentence for example:

(53) *Maybe Romeo is in love with Juliet.*

The comprehension of this sentence, according to Fauconnier, involves the construction of two mental spaces. The first mental space, the "Base" (B), includes two elements "a" and "b", which are accessed by the names "Romeo" and "Juliet". This space is linked with information about the two entities which is part of background knowledge or has been derived from the proceeding co-text. The Base functions as the starting point of each network of spaces, and is always accessible for the addition of further material or for the construction of new spaces.

The second mental space is derived from the Base via the word "maybe", which functions as a **"space builder"**. The word "maybe" sets up the new space (M) as a "possibility" space, i. e. as corresponding to a state of affairs that may or may not be true in relation to the Base. The possibility space contains two entities "a^i" and "b^i", which are counterparts of "a" and "b" in the Base, and are accessed by means of the same names. In the possible space, "a^i" is in love with "b^i". This space is also structured by background knowledge triggered by the expression "in love with". This can be diagramed in Figure 9. 1.

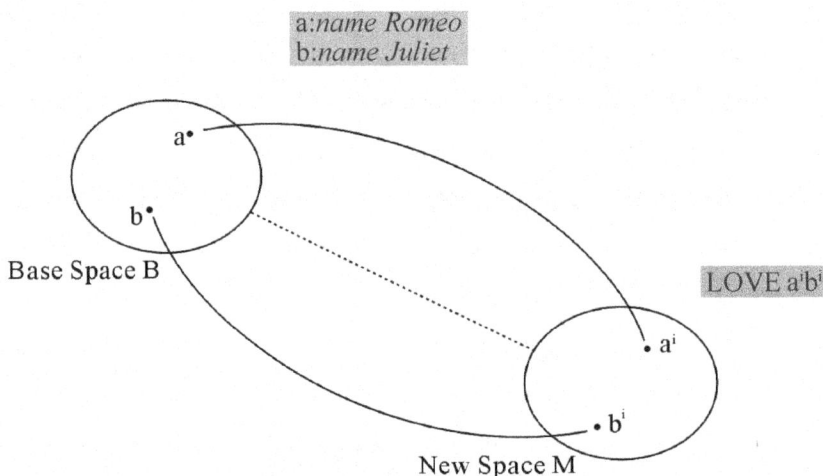

Figure 9. 1   Adapted from Fauconnier (1997: 43)

In this figure, B functions as "Viewpoint" space, i. e. the space from which the new one is set up and accessed, whereas M functions as the "Focus" space", i. e. the space to which material is being added by the sentence. In this way, the comprehension of the sentence "Maybe Romeo is in love with Juliet" is interpreted on the one hand by relating the structure of the sentence to the comprehender's background knowledge and on the other hand by illuminating how the comprehender's mentality is reconstructed after the sentence is comprehended.

9. 5　Practical stylistics

Practical stylistics in the narrow sense refers to the stylistic analysis of texts as teaching aids for literature and language study by native and foreign speakers of English (Widdowson, 1992). This is also called "pedagogical stylistics". Such analysis may cover poetry, prose, fiction, and drama. In a broad sense, practical stylistics may refer to stylistic analysis of both literary and non-literary texts in language study, translation, natural language processing, etc. In translation, for instance, the translator must develop a good stylistic awareness and have a profound understanding of the source text so as to produce a functionally equivalent target text. Similarly, in computerized natural language processing, an effective stylistic module must be designed so that the stylistic features of the data in question can be properly processed in language production and comprehension. All this presupposes a comprehensive analysis and understanding of stylistic features of language, for which we still have a long way to go ahead.

9. 6　Summary

In this chapter we have provided a basic introduction to the field of stylistics. Stylistics is concerned with the description and analysis of the variability of linguistic forms in actual language use. We began by introducing four types of stylistic variations, namely lexical variation, grammatical variation, phonological variation and graphological variation. The concept of "stylistic variation" in language implies that within the language system, the same content can be encoded in more than one linguistic form. Then we discussed "stylistic codification" in stylistics, including style markers, dictionaries, grammars and figures of speech. In the second part of the chapter, we introduced two major contemporary stylistic approaches, i. e. , functional stylistics and cognitive stylistics. The former takes particular notes of the stylistic functions or effects or thematic significance of linguistic features in literary and non-literary texts, while the latter is theoretically rooted in cognitive linguistics, which uses cognitive apparatuses such as figure-ground theory, conceptual metaphor theory and mental space theory to analyze literary texts.

Self-study Activities

1. Compare the following two passages and tell the stylistic differences between them.

   (1) The Federal Government have decided to ask the Arbitration Commission to determine whether the BLF have seriously misbehaved in the industry, as they are intending to deregister the BLF in certain states; no government has ever acted more weakly when people have behaved like thugs.

   (2) The Federal Government's decision to ask the Arbitration Commission to determine whether the BLF has engaged in serious industrial misconduct, as part of its move to deregister the BLF in certain states, is one of the weakest actions ever taken by a government in the face of industrial thuggery. "Their guerrilla tactics and use of thuggery, violence and intimidation have had a disastrous impact not only on building employers but also on fellow workers in the industry." Obviously the Government is frightened of union reaction to its move to impose proper behavior on unions.

2. Analyze the stylistic features of the following passages.

   (1) Dear white fella

   Couple things you should know

   When I born, I black

   When I grow up, I black

   When I go in sun, I black

   When I cold, I black

   When I scared, I black

   When I sick, I black

   And when I die, I still black.

   You white fella

   When you born, you pink

   When you grow up, you white

   When you go in sun, you red

   When you cold, you blue

   When you scared, you yellow

   When you sick, you green

   And when you die, you grey.

And you have the cheek to call me colored?

(African Shakespeare, *Coloured*)

(2) The United Nations shall establish under its authority an international trusteeship system for the administration and supervision of such territories as may be placed thereunder by subsequent individual agreements. These territories are hereafter referred to as trust territories.

(From *Charter of the United Nations*)

3. Point out the rhetorical devices used in the following sentences and then interpret the possible stylistic effect of such linguistic choices.

(1) We almost died laughing.

(2) The *grey hair* should be respected.

(3) Greece was the *cradle* of Western culture.

(4) The professor's desk is always in *disorderly chaos*.

(5) It takes a great deal of history to produce a little literature.

(6) I see the Russian soldiers standing on the *threshold* of their native land.

(7) It must be delightful to find oneself in a foreign country without a penny in one's pocket.

(8) In fact, it appears that the teacher of English teach English so poorly largely because they teach grammar so well.

(9) As London increased, however, rank and fashion rolled off to the west, and trade, creeping on at their heels, took possession of their deserted abodes.

(10) He commented with a crushing sense of despair on *man's final release from earthly struggles*.

Sources and Suggestions for Further Reading

Leech, G. N. 2001. *A Linguistic Guide to English Poetry*. Beijing: Foreign Language Teaching and Research Press.

Leech, G. N., and Short, M. H. 2000. *Style in Fiction: A Linguistic Introduction to English Fictional Prose*. Beijing: Foreign Language Teaching and Research Press.

Verdonk, P. 2002. *Stylistics*. Oxford: Oxford University Press.

Wales, K. 2001. *A Dictionary of Stylistics*. Harlow, England: Longman.

Widdowson, H. G. 1992. *Practical Stylistics*. Oxford: Oxford University Press.

Chapter 10   Psycholinguistics

10. 1   Introduction

Before we pick up the academic stuff, let us think about the following questions: Firstly, they say you can teach an old dog a new trick, because the dog, no matter how old he is, is intelligent enough to learn tricks. However, can you talk Shakespeare to a dog? Obviously, you would say "no" to the question for the reason that talking Shakespeare to a dog is just the same as playing the music to a herd of cattle. Secondly, you may have such a belief that your dog is much cleverer than your chicken. Without doubt, both of your dog and your chicken can produce sounds, but whose sound-making bears more resemblance to human's sound-making: your dog's or your chicken's? The third question goes as follows: Why does the damage to a certain part of the brain inevitably result in a loss of language?

Thinking about questions of this type in an analytical manner, you are absolutely engaged in a psychological analysis of language production, language comprehension, and language acquisition. In a word, you are doing what a psycholinguist is supposed to do in the field of psycholinguistics.

Psycholinguistics, also named as the **psychology of language**, is an interdisciplinary field of study of which the goals are to understand how people acquire language, how people use language to speak and understand one another, and how language is represented and processed in the brain. Psycholinguistics is primarily a sub-discipline of psychology and linguistics, but it is also related to developmental psychology, cognitive psychology, neurolinguistics, and speech science. This chapter is just to introduce some of the central ideas in contemporary psycholinguistics, with an attempt to reveal the mechanisms of language processes. It will center on questions of the following: how language is produced, comprehended, and acquired, and what approaches to psycholinguistics are.

10. 2　Language production

The British philosopher Bertrand Russell once said, "No matter how eloquently a dog may bark, he cannot tell you his parents were poor but honest!" Why? A dog does not know how to produce human sound in a creative manner, let alone to produce language. In sound making, a dog is less skillful than a chicken because a chicken is able to control the air stream to modify its sound production within one breath, while the dog can only bark once within one breath, unable to modify its sound within one bark. Sound-making is the most fundamental of all in language production. Any damage to any part of speech organs will definitely result in corresponding damage to language production. This shows that language production has biological foundations.

10. 2. 1　Biological foundations of language production

The biological foundation of language production includes the operation of speech organs, the modification of air stream, and more importantly, the function of human brain. It has been found in neuroscience that the human brain has two important areas: the **Broca's area** and the **Wernicke's area**. Language production is related to the Broca's area, while the Wernicke's area is involved in language comprehension. Some researchers also discovered that human's left brain and right brain have different functions. The left brain is in charge of language production, logic thought, analytic thought, and scientific reasoning, while the right brain is characterized by holistic thought, intuition, creativity, art and music. Since language production involves creativity, both of the left brain and right brain are indispensible.

When talking about human brain, psychologists tend to associate it with human mind, and in some researches, the human brain is treated as the human mind. Language production belongs to human mind. Therefore, it's not an easy job to reveal how human beings produce language. What we have found about language production is some observations and some assumptions that are based on the corresponding observations.

10. 2. 2　Steps of language production

Language production is logically divided into three major steps: deciding what to express (**conceptualization**), determining how to express it (**formulation**), and expressing it (**articulation**). Although achieving goals in conversation, structuring narratives, and modulating the ebb and flow of dialogue are inherently important to understand how people speak, psycholinguistic studies of language production have primarily focused on the formulation of single, isolated utterances. Language production research relied to a large extent on an indirect view of the production process: inferring the normal processes of operation from observation of the breakdown of those processes. Thus the major study of language production includes views from slips of the tongue and language breakdown in aphasia. In this section, we describe the basic steps of word production.

The simplest meaningful utterance consists of a single word. Generating a word begins with specifying its semantic and pragmatic properties. That is, a speaker decides upon an intention or some content to express (e. g. a desired outcome or an observation) and encodes the situational constraints on how the content may be expressed (e. g. polite or informal speech, monolingual or mixing languages). This process, termed **conceptualization** or message planning, is traditionally considered prelinguistic and language neutral. However, speakers may include different information in their messages when preparing to speak different languages.

The next major stage is **formulation**, which in turn is divided into a word selection stage and a sound processing stage. Deciding which word to use involves selecting a word in one's vocabulary based on its correspondence to semantic and pragmatic specifications. The relevant word representation is often called a lemma, lexical entry, lexical representation, or simply a word, and it marks the presence of a word in a speaker's vocabulary that is capable of expressing particular semantic and pragmatic content within a particular syntactic context. Sound processing, in contrast, involves constructing the phonological form of a selected word by retrieving its individual sounds and organizing them into stressed and unstressed syllables (phonological encoding) and then specifying the motor programs to realize those syllables (phonetic encoding).

The final process is **articulation**, that is, the execution of motor programs to pronounce the sounds of a word. This sequence of stages is illustrated in Figure 10. 1.

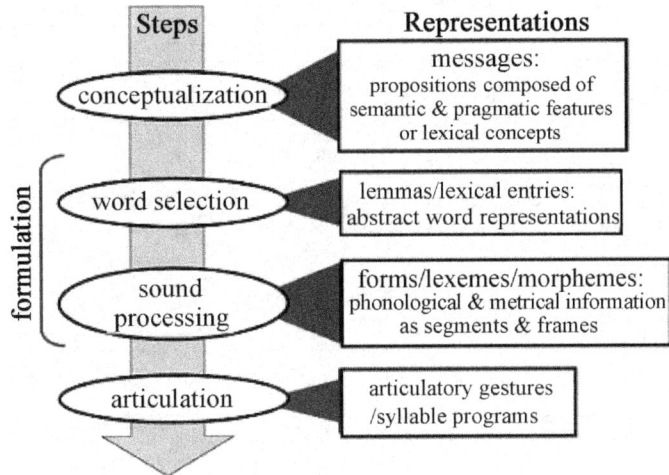

Figure 10. 1 Major steps and representations in language production

(Cited from Griffin & Ferreira, 2006: 22)

Generally, language production contains three successive steps: conceptualization, formation, and articulation. However, some psycholinguists claim that there are four steps of language production. In addition to the three steps mentioned here, the fourth step is **regulation, self-regulation,** or **self-monitoring**. The step of regulation is marked with speech errors. In other words, psycholinguists have regarded the speech errors as the typical linguistic evidence of self-regulation or self-monitoring.

10. 2. 3 Speech errors

When the language production system is working correctly, it is easy to underestimate its complexity. Every now and then, however, the system slips up and produces an error, and errors in any system can have a tremendous explanatory value. They can tell us, for example, whether apparently separate functions fail separately or together, and thus whether they probably derive from one or more modular processes. With further analysis, they can also tell us which modules communicate with other modules, what form of encoding is being passed back and forth, and how well protected the communication links are against damage or interference. In Table 10. 1, we can find the common types of speech errors.

Table 10.1 Types of speech errors

Type	Definition	Example
Addition	Additions add linguistic material.	Target: We Error: We and I
Anticipation	A later segment takes the place of an earlier segment.	Target: reading list Error: leading list
Blends	Blends are a subcategory of lexical selection errors.	Target: person/people Error: perple
Deletion	Deletions or omissions leave some linguistic material out.	Target: unanimity of opinion Error: unamity of opinion
Exchange	Exchanges are double shifts. Two linguistic units change places.	Target: getting your nose remodeled Error: getting your model renosed
Lexical selection error	The speaker has "problems with selecting the correct word".	Target: bake the cake Error: cake the bake
Malapropism	The speaker has the wrong beliefs about the meaning of a word. Consequently, he produces the intended word, which is semantically inadequate. Therefore, this is rather a competence error than a performance error. Malapropisms are named after a character from Richard B. Sheridan's eighteenth-century play "The Rivals".	Target: The flood damage was so bad they had to evacuate the city. Error: The flood damage was so bad they had to evaporate the city.
Metathesis	Switching of two sounds, each taking the place of the other.	Target: pus pocket Error: pos pucket
Morpheme stranding	Morphemes remain in place but are attached to the wrong words.	Target: He has already packed two trunks. Error: He has already trunked to packs.
Perseveration	An earlier segment replaces a later item.	Target: black boxes Error: black bloxes
Shift	One speech segment disappears from its appropriate location and appears somewhere else.	Target: She decides to hit it. Error: She decide to hits it.
Sound-exchange error	Two sounds switch places.	Target: Night life [nait laif] Error: Knife light [naif lait]
Spoonerism	A spoonerism is a kind of metathesis. Switching of initial sounds of two separate words. They are named after Reverend William Archibald Spooner, who probably invented most of his famous spoonerisms.	Target: I saw you light a fire. Error: I saw you fight a liar.

Continued

Type	Definition	Example
Substitution	One segment is replaced by an intruder. The source of the intrusion is not in the sentence.	Target: Where is my tennis racquet? Error: Where is my tennis bat?
Word-exchange error	A word-exchange error is a subcategory of lexical selection errors, in which two words are switched.	Target: I must let the cat out of the house. Error: I must let the house out of the cat.

Speech production is a highly complex and extremely rapid process so that research into the involved mental mechanisms is very difficult. Investigating the audible output of the speech production system is a way to understand these mental mechanisms. Therefore, speech errors are of an explanatory value with regard to the nature of language and language production.

10. 3 Language comprehension

One of the primary aims of psycholinguistics is to understand how people create and understand language. **Language comprehension** is an important aspect of day to day functioning in adulthood. Comprehension of written and spoken language relies on the ability to correctly process word and phrase meanings, sentence grammar, and discourse or text structure.

Language comprehension cannot be separated from language production because understanding language, like producing it, is such an automatic task that it may appear to be a relatively straightforward process. Sounds or letters strike our ears or eyes in a swift and linear fashion creating words, which in turn very quickly form phrases, clauses, and sentences so that comprehension seems to be nothing more than the recognition of a sequential string of linguistic symbols. Language comprehension is a process of decoding what has been encoded in a particular linguistic form. Figure 10. 2 shows the process of comprehension.

Clearly language comprehension and production are closely connected in the speaker-hearer model of language use. However, for many, in fact most of the years that psycholinguistics has existed, the research on comprehension predominates over the research on production. The reason for this asymmetry is obvious: in any experimental

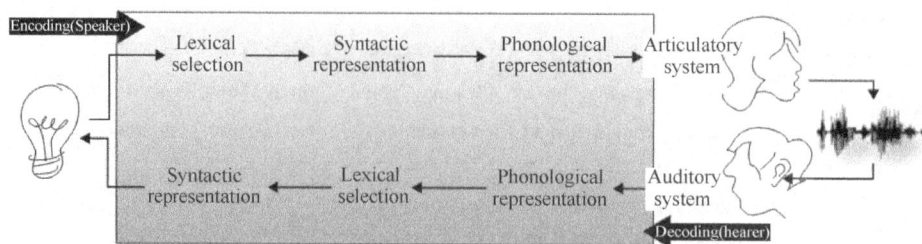

Figure 10.2 Processes of language comprehension
(Cited from Fernández & Cairns, 2010: 16)

science, control over the conditions in which an experiment is conducted is paramount, and control over stimuli presented for comprehension is trivially easy to achieve while control over language production nearly seems at first glance impossible. So dominant is comprehension research in psycholinguistics that some psycholinguists claim that the fundamental problem in psycholinguistics is simple to formulate: What happens when we understand sentences?

Systematically, language comprehension contains **sound comprehension**, **word comprehension**, **sentence comprehension**, and **text comprehension**.

10.3.1 Sound comprehension

Sound comprehension is not a passive process. It often depends on context from which listeners expect to hear. People understand the meaning as a whole, but not in isolation. They do not listen to each word individually. For example, when hearing the two phrases *the _ eel on the shoe* and *_ eel on the orange*, listeners can restore the phonemes according to the information provided in the context without any listening activities (the first answer is *heel*, second answer is *peel*). So we can see that understanding language is greatly influenced by slight changes in discourse which listeners attend to, and that listeners do not understand the information word by word.

Distinguishing similar sounds, such as /b/ and /p/, /t/ and /d/ in English, is another sound comprehension. People often recognize the differences of the sounds based on the length of producing time. Psycholinguists have found that humans are born with the ability to distinguish different sounds.

In a word, the successful comprehension of speech sounds is a combination of the innate ability of humans to distinguish minute differences between speech sounds, and the ability to adjust the acoustic categories of the language they are exposed to.

10. 3. 2　Word comprehension

Word comprehension is a very complex psycholinguistic process and is much more complex than the processing of speech sounds. That is because there are mountains of words which do not only consist of sounds, but also convey meanings.

Psycholinguists use **parallel distributed processing (PDP)** to explain the complex process of word understanding. PDP is a model of cognition developed from research in neurology, computer science and psychology. It is a way in which people use several separate and parallel processes at the same time to understand spoken or written language. In understanding words, for example, when people try to remember a word, they search for its meaning, spelling and pronunciation at the same time.

A PDP model of comprehension can be used to explain lexical access. In our mind we have stored many words, some of which are easy to be accessible, but some of which are not. As a rule, high-frequency words, such as *book*, are rapidly and frequently activated, and low-frequency words, such as *logogen*, take longer time to be incorporated into a system of understanding. All this is based on logogen model of comprehension. Logogens, or lexical detection devices, are like individual neuros in a gigantic neuronal network. When they are activated, they would co-operate with many other logogens to create comprehension. Considering another factor about word access, the words with semantic association are easily accessible. For example, in the pairs *teacher—student* and *teacher—office*, we find that the former is more accessible than the latter. So we do not access words in an alphabetical order.

The PDP approach is able to explain tip-of-the-tongue (TOT) phenomenon. In our daily life many of us have had the experience that we knew the word, but could not access the whole word. For many times, we could only get part of the words vaguely, such as the beginning or the ending of the words. This is called *bathtub effect* because when we submerge ourselves in a bathtub, we can only see our heads and feet.

In the comprehension of words, people do not understand words by only one strategy. They have some other strategies to understand words, such as by top-down data involving context and meaning, and by bottom-up information involving pronunciation and spelling. The comprehension of words is a very complex process indeed.

10. 3. 3　Sentence comprehension

Besides the decoding of sounds and lexical meanings, comprehension also includes the untangling of the meanings of sentences. At first, psycholinguists made use of Chomsky's TG grammar to explore the process of sentence understanding. They claimed that the more transformation the sentence has, the more complicated the sentence is. But according to the results of experiments, transformational complexity does not affect comprehension greatly and the greatest influence on sentence comprehension is meaning.

There are a couple of factors influencing the comprehension of sentences. The first is the ambiguity of word meaning that leads to difficulties in sentence understanding. If the word has more complex information, the sentence is more difficult to understand. In sentences (1) and (3), the meanings of the words *drill* and *straw* are ambiguous. *Drill* has two meanings: drill by using an instrument; drill by rehearsing marching formations. *Straw* has two meanings here too: dried grass; a tube used for sipping liquids. In contrast, sentences (2) and (4) do not use ambiguous words and are easier to understand.

(1) The men started to drill *before* they were ordered to do so.

(2) The men started to march *before* they were ordered to do so.

(3) The merchant put his straw *beside* the machine.

(4) The merchant put his oats *beside* the machine.

The second factor is the linguistic structure of the sentence that affects the processing time. If the sentence structure is what readers or hearers expect to read or hear, the processing time is short, and the sentence is easy to understand. If the sentence structure is not what readers or hearers expect, the comprehension is disrupted and sentence comprehension becomes slow. This is so-called *garden-pathing*, a natural comprehension of strategy. In understanding sentences, the point is whether readers or hearers choose the right path or wrong path. Perhaps the most famous *garden path sentence* is the following one:

(5) The horse raced past the barn fell.

This sentence is perfectly grammatical, but almost impossible to understand. The reason for this is that, as we read the sentence, we build up a syntactic structure in which *The horse* is the subject of the sentence and *raced past the barn* is the main VP of the sentence. When we get to the word *fell*, we are surprised because the sentence we have built up has no room for an extra VP. In the correct interpretation for the sentence, *fell* is the head of the main VP and *raced past the barn* is a clause that attaches to the NP *the barn*.

10. 3. 4   Text comprehension

Text comprehension is the largest unit compared with the comprehension of sounds, words and sentences. According to the research on text understanding, people tend to comprehend or memorize the content but not the structure. Therefore in the process of understanding texts, background information plays a very important part in understanding, and greatly affects the way in which people remember a piece of discourse. Background knowledge can activate people's mental association which can help the comprehension of texts. For example, if people are given the title of the text, the text is easier or more quickly to remember. Now, let's make a little experiment: Read the following passage first, then close your book, and attempt to write down as much as possible of what you have just read.

With hocked gems financing him, our hero bravely defied all scornful laughter that tried to prevent his scheme. Your eyes deceive you, he had said, an egg not a table correctly typifies this unexplored planet. Now three sturdy sisters sought proof, forging along sometimes through calm vastness, yet more often over turbulent peaks and valleys. Days became weeks as many doubters spread fearful rumors about the edge. At last, from nowhere, welcome winged creatures appeared, signifying momentous success.

You may have difficulty in recalling the exact wording and the sequence of sentences in this seemingly incoherent account, and you may also have wondered what it was all about. Now give this passage to one of your friend to read and to recall, but before you do so, point out that this is the story of "Christopher Columbus discovering America".

10. 4　Language acquisition

When you come across a person who complains about himself for being unable to have a good command of a foreign language, what will you say to pump her up? Have you found any logic problem hidden in this person's complaints? You can find some good answers both from philosophy and theories of language acquisition.

On the one hand, according to Aristotle's logic, all human beings are able to master linguistic tools to perform their life tasks. A foreign language is one kind of linguistic tools and you are a human being. Therefore, you are able to master the foreign language you want to acquire. On the other hand, according to Chomsky, since you have mastered your native language, it shows that you have the ability to acquire any one of the foreign languages. That is, a child growing up in China speaks Chinese very well whereas the same child brought up in England would be able to speak English very well. Why? Human beings have the ability of acquiring language.

Language acquisition refers to the process of learning a native or a second language. The learning of a native or first language is called **first language acquisition**, and the learning of a second or foreign language is called **second language acquisition**. The term **acquisition** is often preferred to **learning** because the latter is sometimes connected to a behaviorist theory of learning. Language acquisition is studied by linguists, psychologists and applied linguists to enable them to understand the processes, and to give a better understanding of the nature of language. Techniques used include longitudinal studies of language learners as well as experimental approaches, and focus on the study of the development of phonology, vocabulary, grammar, and communicative competence. Here, we only introduce two basic notions in first language acquisition: **overgeneralization** and **undergeneralization**.

It is shown by psycholinguistics that children's use of language is rule-governed. For example, children frequently say *tooths* and *mouses*, instead of *teeth* and *mice*, and *holded* and *finded*, instead of *held* and *found*. These are examples of **overgeneralization** or **overextension**: the extension of a rule beyond its proper limits. In these cases the child knows the regular rules for forming the plural and the past tense but doesn't know that these particular words are irregular.

Overgeneralization is a frequent phenomenon in language development. It can be found not only in syntactic usage but also in word meanings. Many young children will sometimes refer to all four-legged animals as *dogs* or all round objects as *moon*, or call all vehicles *cars*, and perhaps more disconcertingly, all men *dad*. Researchers have found that some, like the examples given here, are based on perceptual similarities between objects. Others are based on other kinds of similarity, such as functional (a child referring to a shirt stuck on a person's head as a *hat*), contextual (calling a crib blanket a *nap*), and affective (referring to a forbidden object as *hot*). Discovering the limits of these words, what they do, and do not, apply to, is a useful way of penetrating the child's semantic system. It can take time, for example, for children to learn that words can refer to separate things. When a child refers to *milk*, for instance, does he or she mean the whole process of pouring it into a mug and placing it down, or does it have the restricted meaning we are used to? Most psycholinguists believe that the intonational, gestural, and contextual clues make it clear that children are using single-word sentences, exactly as adults often do in conversation. *Milk* is often used as a shortened form of "Do you have any milk?", but given an appropriate context, "Milk!" is just as obviously an abbreviated version of "I'd like some milk".

Children also undergeneralize. When a child uses a word in a more limited way than adults do (e.g. refusing to call a taxi a car), this phenomenon is called *undergeneralization* or *underextension*. Indeed, undergeneralization is also a frequent phenomenon in first language acquisition. A child may often only be able to use words in a particular context. It's not uncommon for children to call their own shoes *shoes* but unfortunately, they do not know what someone else's are called. Reich (1986) provides a very interesting example. When his son, Quentin, was asked "*Where's the shoes?*", when he was in his parent's bedroom, he would crawl to his mother's closet and play with her shoes. If other shoes were between Quentin and the closet, he would crawl around them to get to his mother's shoes. Similarly, his father's shoes did not count. Reich found that Quentin's notion of shoes gradually expanded to coincide with adult usage.

There are some reasons why children use overgeneralization and undergeneralization. On some occasions, children's conceptual categories may actually differ from those of adults; children may, for instance, initially regard cows and dogs as part of the same category until being told otherwise. On other occasions, they may know perfectly well that a cow is not a dog but not know what it is called. In this case, a child may deliberately mislabel an object to be corrected and thus hear the appropriate name.

10. 5 Summary

This chapter deals with the psychology of language, i. e. psycholinguistics. Psycholinguistics is concerned with how people acquire language, how people use language to speak and understand one another, and how language is represented and processed in the brain. Three most discussed topics in psycholinguistics are: language production, language comprehension and language acquisition. Language production has biological foundations, which is logically realized by three steps: conceptualization, formulation and articulation. Language production, which concerns the creating of language, cannot be separated from language comprehension, i. e. the understanding of language.

This chapter also discusses four types of language comprehension: sound comprehension, word comprehension, sentence comprehension and text comprehension. Language comprehension and language production are considered, undoubtedly, the most important part of psycholinguistics. Language acquisition refers to the process of learning a native or a second language. Overgeneralization and undergeneralization are two commonest problems encountered in language acquisition.

Self-study Activities

1. Define the following terms.

   (1) psycholinguistics   (2) linguistic determinism   (3) linguistic relativity

   (4) undergeneralization   (5) overgeneralization   (6) conceptualization

   (7) language comprehension   (8) language acquisition

2. Decide whether each of the following statements is *True* or *False*.

   (1) According to researches, the left hemisphere of human brain is responsible for language use.

   (2) Speech error analyses suggest that the most common error in word selection occurs when a speaker substitutes a semantically related word for the intended one, such as calling a van bus.

   (3) Although all human languages do not share some universal syntactic properties, the constraints on how constituents may be generated vary substantially.

   (4) According to research on text understanding, people tend to comprehend or memorize the structure but not the content. Therefore, background information

does not play a very important role in text understanding.

(5) There's nothing critically different between the first language acquisition and the second language acquisition.

3. Children have been found easy to commit the mistakes of overgeneralization. Do you think adults are immune to the problem of this kind? Why or why not?

4. What implication can you get from the following expressions? A room without light. A river without lighthouse. A professor without skill. A stick without length.

5. Read carefully the following sentences produced by George W. Bush and analyze the mistakes in light of psycholinguistic theories.

(1) You know, I'm the President during this period of time, but I think when the history of this period is written, people will realize a lot of the decisions that were made on Wall Street took place over a decade or so, before I arrived in President, during I arrived in President.

(2) Make no mistake about it; I understand how tough it is, sir. I talk to families who die.

(3) Our enemies are innovative and resourceful, and so are we. They never stop thinking about new ways to harm our country and our people, and neither do we.

(4) Rarely is the question asked: Is our children learning?

Sources and Suggestions for Further Reading

Cairns, H. S. 1999. *Psycholinguistics: An Introduction.* Texas: Proed.

Carroll, D. W. 2000. *Psychology of Language* (3rd ed.). Beijing: Foreign Language Teaching and Research Press.

Cutler, A. 2005. *Twenty-First Century Psycholinguistics.* New Jersey: Lawrence Erlbaum.

Field, J. 2004. *Psycholinguistics: The Key Concepts.* London: Routledge.

Forrestor, M. A. 1996. *Psychology of Language: A Critical Introduction.* London: SAGE Publications.

Garman. M. 2000. *Psycholinguistics.* Cambridge: Cambridge University Press.

Scovel, T. 2000. *Psycholinguistics.* Shanghai: Shanghai Foreign Language Education Press.

Taylor, I. & Taylor, W. M. M. 1990. *Psycholinguistics: Learning and Using Language.* New Jersey: Prentice Hall.

Chapter 11   Cognitive Linguistics

11.1   Introduction

Cognitive linguistics is a modern school of linguistic thought and practice. It is concerned with investigating the relationship between human language, the mind and socio-physical experience. It originally emerged in the 1970s and arose out of dissatisfaction with formal approaches to language which were dominant, at that time, in the disciplines of linguistics and philosophy. It began to flourish in the 1980s. Cognitive linguistics is best described as a movement or an enterprise, precisely because it does not constitute a single closely-articulated theory. Instead, it is an approach that has adopted a common set of core commitments and guiding principles, which have led to a diverse range of complementary, overlapping theories.

It is believed that natural language is a product of the human mind, based on the same organizing principles that operate in other cognitive domains. As one domain of human cognition, language is intimately linked with other cognitive domains, and as such mirrors the interplay of psychological, cultural, social, ecological, and other factors. Language is not just a system consisting of arbitrary signs, and its structures are related to and motivated by human conceptual knowledge, bodily experience, and the communicative functions of discourse.

Cognitive linguistics approaches language as an integrated part of human cognition which operates in interaction with and on the basis of the same principles as other cognitive faculties. It is therefore defined as a linguistic approach which analyzes language in relation to other cognitive domains and faculties such as bodily and mental experiences, image schemas, perception, attention, memory, viewing frames, categorization, abstract thought, emotion, reasoning, and inference.

Cognitive linguistics is a relatively new framework and one of the most exciting approaches to the study of language and thought that has emerged within the modern interdisciplinary framework of cognitive science. Because it sees language as embedded in the overall cognitive capacities of mankind, topics of special interest for cognitive linguistics include the structural characteristics of natural language categorization, the functional principles of linguistic organization, the conceptual interface between syntax and semantics, the experiential and pragmatic background of language in use, and the relationship between language and thought.

The three founding fathers in cognitive linguistics are George Lakoff, Ronald Langacker and Leonard Talmy.

11. 2   Categories and categorization

Every time we see something as a *kind* of thing, for example, a bird, we are categorizing. Usually for some specific purpose, we group objects into categories. For example, we may classify birds into robin, dove, sparrow, cuckoo, canary, owl, pheasant, parrot, eagle, peacock, crane, penguin, swan, etc. , and classify college students into freshman, sophomore, junior, senior, or group them according to their specialties. This mental process of classification is commonly called **categorization**, and its products are the **categories**, or **cognitive categories**. We put things in the same categories because they are similar to each other. A *dove* and a *cuckoo* (both birds) seem obviously more similar than a *dove* and an *elephant* (not a bird). Elephants are not identified as birds in respect that they are not sufficiently similar to any individual in the bird category.

Categorization is one of the most fundamental human cognitive activities. Suffice it to say that there is nothing more basic than categorization to our thought, perception, act and speech. In the following part we are going to deal with two most influential theories of categorization, namely, the **classical theory** and **prototype theory**.

In speaking of categorization, we have to mention the classical theory. This approach is " classical " not only because it can trace back to Greek antiquity (Aristotle), but because it has dominated philosophy, psychology and linguistics for more than 2000 years. According to the classical theory, an entity represents a category member by virtue of fulfilling a set of necessary and sufficient conditions for a category membership. For example, if we assume that the category SPINSTER is defined by the conditions of being human, adult, female and unmarried, each one is necessary. If someone is lacking in any of the four features, she is not a spinster. Thus we can say that the conditions of being human adult, female, and unmarried are sufficient for membership in the category SPINSTER. It does not matter what other conditions someone or something may fulfill. Being a spinster or not depends on these four conditions. The classical theory exhibits the following basic assumptions:

(i) Categories are defined in terms of a set of necessary and jointly sufficient conditions.

(ii) Features are binary.

(iii) Categories have clear boundaries.

(iv) All members of a category have equal status.

The claim that categories have clear boundaries is mainly due to the fact that features are binary. Everything either fulfils this set of conditions or does not. If it does, it belongs to the category, otherwise it does not. Consequently, categories have clear boundaries, and within their boundaries all members have the same status of full members. However, these arguments are untenable in the following circumstances. First, it is difficult or impossible, in most cases, to identify the set of necessary and sufficient conditions to define a category. Wittgenstein's discussion of GAME provides a good example. We have the following games: board-games, card-games, ball-games, Olympic Games, and so on. Is there a single set of features that is shared by every member of the GAME category? Is there a clear boundary between the games? Second, the classical theory can not explain the concepts that are graded. In such cases the denial of one is not necessarily the assertion of the other. Something that is not "big" does not necessarily mean that it is "small". It may simply be "so-so" or "average". This is a violation of the assumptions (ii) and (iii) . Third, not all of the members of a category have equal status. Members in a category may differ in terms of their typicality. For example, TABLE and CHAIR are "good examples" or "typical examples" of the category FURNITURE, while CARPET and BROOM are judged as "peripheral examples" or "bad examples". In this regard, the assumption (iv) of the classical theory also doesn't work.

However, these problems can be ideally dealt with in prototype theory. During the 1970s, experimental findings which emerged under the banner of **Prototype Theory**, given by the psychologist Eleanor Rosch and her colleagues, showed that the classical theory of category was implausible as a model of human categorization. In the experiments when people were asked to select "good examples" of a particular

category. **Prototype effects** were found in all cases. For example, chairs, tables, beds and sofas were generally regarded as prototypical or good examples of "furniture", while radios, vases and ashtrays were deemed to be peripheral or bad examples. Armstrong *et al.* (1983) presented another world-famous experiment to show the existence of **family resem-blance**. See Figure 11. 1.

Figure 11. 1   The picture of "Smith brothers"

As shown in the figure, all other faces of "Smith brothers" are arranged around the face in the center (prototype). In other words, other faces are more or less similar to the face in the center. Yet there are no features common to all the faces. Some faces have practically nothing in common with others. This further implies that category membership is a gradient phenomenon, that is, some members of a category are more central than others. Prototype theory is characterized by the following points:

(i) Categories are not defined by virtue of shared criterial features but organized in terms of their family resemblances.

(ii) The boundary of the category is not clear but fuzzy.

(iii) Not all members of a category have the same status within a category, which vary according to their prototypicality.

(iv) Categories are radial, organized around prototypes.

11. 3   Conceptual metaphors

For over 2, 000 years, metaphor was studied within the discipline known as rhetoric, since metaphor used to be thought of as a rather unusual form of discourse, characteristic of the literary language. Within this approach, metaphor was organized by the schematic form: A is B, as in *Achilles is a lion*. Thus, metaphor has been identified since the time of Aristotle with "implicit comparison", in which the comparison is not explicitly marked. This contrasts with **simile**, where the comparison is explicitly expressed by the word *as* or *like*: *Achilles is as brave as a lion*, or *Achilles is brave*, *like a lion*.

However, the important pioneering work by Lakoff and Johnson (1980) showed that metaphor is not simply a figurative use of language, but a cognitive tool for our organizing and understanding the world, since human thought itself is metaphorical in nature. Within the domain of cognitive linguistics, metaphor is defined as understanding one conceptual domain in terms of another conceptual domain, which can be schematized as: **CONCEPTUAL DOMAIN (A) IS CONCEPTUAL DOMAIN (B)** . This is known as **conceptual metaphor**. We see that a conceptual metaphor consists of two conceptual domains, in which one domain (**the target domain**) is understood in terms of another (**the source domain**) . In other words, a conceptual metaphor is essentially a device that involves conceptualizing one domain of experience in terms of another. Source domains tend to be relatively concrete areas of experience and target domains to be more abstract. For instance, we can talk about and think about QUANTITY in terms of VERTICAL ELEVATION, as in *John has got a high mark in the final exam*, in which *high* refers not to physical height but to a good mark. This is because the conceptual domain QUANTITY is conventionally structured and understood by virtue of the conceptual domain VERTICAL ELEVATION.

In Lakoff and Johnson's book *Metaphors We Live by* (1980), they mentioned an important conceptual metaphor TIME IS MONEY. In this metaphor, TIME as the target domain is understood in terms of the source domain MONEY. Time, as is known to all, is a valuable commodity. The metaphor TIME IS MONEY suggests that we understand and experience time as the kind of thing that can be spent, wasted, budgeted, invested, or saved.

TIME IS MONEY

You are *wasting* my time.

This gadget will *save* your hours.

I don't *have* the time to give you.

How do you *spend* your time these days?

The flat tire *cost* me an hour.

I've *invested* a lot of time in her.

I don't have *enough* time to *spare* for that.

You're *running out* of time.

You need to *budget* your time.

Put aside some time for ping pong.

Is that *worth your while*?

Do you *have much* time left?

He's living on *borrowed* time.

You don't use your time *profitably*.

I *lost* a lot of time when I got sick.

Here, it should be noted that conceptual metaphors differ from **linguistic metaphors** or **metaphorical linguistic expressions**. Generally speaking, conceptual metaphors relate to "ways of thinking", thus are schematic or abstract such as TIME IS MONEY; in contrast, linguistic metaphors are manifestations of conceptual metaphors, which reveal the existence of conceptual metaphors. In the above examples, these concrete expressions listed beneath the conceptual metaphor TIME IS MONEY are linguistic metaphors. Further examples of conceptual metaphors are LOVE IS A JOURNEY, ARGUMENT IS WAR, HAPPY IS UP, SAD IS DOWN, MORE IS UP, THE MIND IS A BRITTLE OBJECT, etc. The following part will exemplify how these conceptual metaphors are realized by linguistic metaphors:

LOVE IS A JOURNEY

Our relationship had hit a dead-end street.

We are going in different directions.

The marriage is on the rocks.

ARGUMENT IS WAR

His criticisms were right on the target.

I demolished his argument.

He attacked every weak point in my argument.

HAPPY IS UP

We're in high spirits.

Thinking about her always gives me a lift.

I'm feeling up today.

SAD IS DOWN

He's really low these days.

My spirit sank.

MORE IS UP

Speak up, please.

My salary rose last year.

The number of books printed each year keeps going up.

THE MIND IS A BRITTLE OBJECT

He broke under cross-examination.

You have to handle him with care since his wife's death.

In short, as a central concept in cognitive linguistics, conceptual metaphor is in fact a prime manifestation of the cognitive view that language and thought are inextricably intertwined.

11. 4　Conceptual metonymies

Metonymy, like metaphor, is not a purely linguistic device but is central to human thought. In other words, metonymy is conceptual in nature, which is fundamental to conceptual organization. Take the utterance *There are a lot of good heads in the university* for example, in this expression the use of *good heads* is an instance of the conceptual metonymy THE PART FOR THE WHOLE. The expression *good heads* refers to *intelligent people* rather than the physical heads. Two entities are associated (brilliant people having good heads) so that one entity (good heads) can be applied to stand for the other (intelligent people). This feature thus distinguishes conceptual metonymies from conceptual metaphors. The former reveals the conceptual relation "X stands for Y", while the latter reflects the conceptual relation "X is understood in terms of Y". This distinction gives rise to another difference between conceptual metonymies and metaphors: both can be understood as mapping processes, but metonymy is a mapping within one cognitive domain, whereas metaphor is a cross-domain mapping.

A crucial feature of metonymy is that metonymy is always motivated by physical or causal associations. This is traditionally understood as **contiguity**: a close or direct relationship between two entities. *Good heads* can metonymically refer to *intelligent people* mainly because intelligent individuals always have *good heads*, that is, there is a natural association between *good heads* and *intelligent people*. In order to see how conceptual metonymies function in everyday language, let's have a look at some common examples given below:

THE PART FOR THE WHOLE

We don't hire *longhairs*.

My *wheels* are parked out the back.

Lend me *a hand*.

THE PRODUCER FOR THE PRODUCT

I bought a *Ford*.

Pass me the *Shakespeare* on the top of the shelf.

He's got a *Picasso* in his den.

THE OBJECT FOR THE USER

The *buses* are on strike.

We need a better *glove* at third base.

The *pen* is mightier than the *sword*.

THE CONTROLLER FOR THE CONTROLLED

Napoleon lost at Waterloo.

Nixon bombed Hanoi.

THE PLACE FOR THE INSTITUTION

Wall Street is in a panic.

Paris and *Washington* are having a spat.

Hollywood is putting out terrible movies.

THE PLACE FOR THE EVENT

Watergate changed American politics.

American public opinion fears another *Vietnam*.

THE EFFECT FOR THE CAUSE
Tom's *face is beaming*.
It's a *slow* road.
He *has a spring in his step* today.

In these examples, the source concepts and target concepts are linked through contiguity relations (part for whole, producer for product, object for user, place for institution, place for event, etc.) All these metonymic concepts are grounded in our experience, thus we have reason to say that metonymic concepts structure not just our language but our thoughts, attitudes and actions.

11.5   Image schemas

Performing a trivial activity, such as walking to a supermarket, selecting some fruits and eggs, bringing them to the check-out counter, checking them out, and taking them home, is not a simple matter. This experience involves the connection of multiple acts of sensing, perceiving, moving and conceptualizing in a three-dimensional world. Importantly, it is these trivial activities that are most likely to reflect the basic features of human language and thought. In order for us to have meaningful, connected experiences that we can comprehend and reason about, there must be patterns or structures that represent our recurrent actions, perceptions and conceptions. These patterns and structures we are dealing with here are known as **image schemas**. Image schemas are relatively abstract patterns or mental structures that arise directly from our daily interaction with and observation of the world around us. Such patterns emerge as meaningful structures mainly at the level of our bodily movements through space, our manipulation of objects, and our perceptual interactions. The notion "image" in "image schemas" is similar to the use of this term in psychology, in which "imagistic" experience relates to and derives from our experience of the external world. The term "schemas" in "image schemas" implies that image schemas are not rich or detailed concepts, but rather abstract concepts consisting of patterns coming from repeated instances of bodily experience.

Image schemas are so fundamental to our way of thinking that we are not consciously aware of them. For example, gravity ensures that unsupported objects fall to the ground; given the asymmetry of the human vertical axis, we have to stoop to pick up fallen objects, look in one direction (downwards) for fallen objects, and in another (upwards) for rising objects. This aspect of our experience gives rise to the UP-DOWN image schema. Another important example is the **CONTAINER schema**. Our encounter with containment and boundedness is one of the most pervasive features of our bodily experience. The CONTAINER schema comprises three parts: the interior, the exterior and the boundary. We constantly experience physical or metaphoric containment in our surroundings. The following utterance, quoted from Lakoff and Johnson (1987), is a general description of an ordinary morning, demonstrating how frequently we are involved in the CONTAINER schema:

You wake *out of* a deep sleep and peer *out from* beneath the covers *into* your room. You gradually emerge *out of* your stupor, pull yourself *out from* under the covers, climb into your robe, stretch *out* your limbs, and walk *in* a daze *out* of the bedroom and *into* the bathroom. You look *in* the mirror and see your face staring *out* at you. You reach *into* the medicine cabinet, take *out* the toothpaste, squeeze *out* some toothpaste, put the toothbrush *into* your mouth, brush your teeth *in* a hurry, and rinse *out* your mouth.

(Lakoff & Johnson, 1987: 271)

In this utterance, many everyday objects and experiences are understood in terms of expressions of *in* and *out* as specific instances of schematic concept CONTAINER. The "containers" not only include these obvious physical containers such as *bedrooms*, *medicine cabinets* and *toothpaste tubes*, but also include some less obvious "containers" like *bed-covers* and *clothing*, or some metaphoric "containers" like *sleep*, *stupor* and *daze*.

Image schemas have a small number of parts and relations, from which numerous perceptions, images and events are able to be structured. A good example that shows what is meant by "parts" and "relations" is the **PATH schema**. This image schema consists of three

Figure 11.2 The PATH image schema

"parts" (a source point A, a terminal point B, and a path moving from A to B) and a relation (specified as a force vector moving from A to B), as shown in Figure 11.2.

However, in practice, the PATH schema also exhibits internal complexity. Different components of the PATH can be highlighted by using different lexical items:

(1) a. **SOURCE**:

Tom left [England].

b. **GOAL**:

Tom travelled [to France].

c. **SOURCE-GOAL**:

Tom travelled [from England] [to France].

d. **PATH-GOAL**:

Tom travelled [through the Chunnel] [to France].

e. **SOURCE-PATH-GOAL**:

John travelled [from English] [through the Chunnel] [to France].

Apart from these image schemas having been discussed above, there are many other important image schemas: BALANCE, PROCESS, PART-WHOLE, BLOCKAGE, FULL-EMPTY, LINK, COMPULSION, CENTRE-PERIPHERY, FORCE, etc. These image schemas are not generally experienced in an isolated or self-contained fashion, but are interwoven and superimposed upon one another, which can transform from one image schema into another. They are held to pervade not only the fabric of our experience, but also the fabric of our conscious understanding.

11.6　Construal

Have you ever heard of the famous saying of Shakespeare: "There are a thousand Hamlets in a thousand people's eyes"? What does it mean? It certainly implies that different people may use different ways to describe the same thing. To be sure, cognitive linguistics generally holds that there is no direct mapping between the external world and language form. That is to say, the same situation can be interpreted in alternate ways. For example, the same group of stars in the sky can be described in various ways: as *specks of lights in the sky*, *a cluster of stars*, *a constellation*, or a *Big Dipper*, etc. The term that has come to be used for different ways of viewing a particular thing or situation is **construal**. The notion *construal* not only relates to the way a language user chooses to "package" and "present" an experience, but also relates to the ways that an utterance is construed or interpreted by the hearers. For example, in describing the same experience "Jack hid Tom's keys", we can use the active form *Jack hid Tom's keys*, which focuses on the AGENT (Jack) of the action; when we use the passive form *Tom's keys were stolen by Jack*, we highlight the PATIENT (Tom's keys).

In most cases, when we utter a sentence, we unconsciously structure every aspect of the experience we intend to convey. The following are cases in point.

(2) a. Oh, Jesus, John is so thrifty!

　　b. Oh, Jesus, John is so stingy!

In examples (2a) and (2b), both "thrifty" and "stingy" are applied to express the same proposition of "John is spending as little money as possible", but in fact they convey different information: (2a) presupposes that spending as little money as possible is good, while (2b) presupposes a completely opposite position, that is, spending as little money as possible is not good.

One important factor involved in alternate construals has to do with **perspective** or **viewing arrangement**, that is, the overall relationship between the "viewer" and the situation being "viewed". For example, if we say:

(3) a. The path falls steeply into the valley.

　　b. The path climbs steeply out of the valley.

(4) a. Your camera is upstairs, in the bedroom, in the closet, on the shelf.

　　b. Your camera is on the shelf, in the closet, in the bedroom, upstairs.

Although sentences in each group describe "the same situation", they never express the same thing, because different structures spell different meanings. The difference between them has to do with perspective or viewing arrangement. In (3a), the viewpoint is that of someone looking down into the valley, while in (3b) it is that of someone looking up from the valley floor. The sentences (4a) and (4b) contain the same elements and the same objective situation. The difference between them is that the first expression "zooms in" from the largest area to successively smaller ones, while the second expression starts from the smallest area and "zooms out".

11.7   Iconicity

At the beginning of the 20th century, the founder of modern linguistics, Ferdinand de Saussure pointed out that the form of most words is linked to what they refer to only by convention; in other words, the relationship between form and meaning is in fact **arbitrary**. For example, the word for the animal dog in English is called "dog", in Chinese as "gou", but "yilu" in Japanese; it barks *wow wow* in English but *wang wang* in Chinese. This intuition has truly dominated linguistic study for a long time. More recently, the idea of "arbitrariness" has come under increasing criticism. Contrary to the Saussurean idea, considerable linguistic research in the twentieth century has shown that **iconicity** operates at every level of language (phonology, morphology, syntax) and practically in every known language. The iconicity of language means that the structure of language reflects in some way the structure of experience, that is, the language mimes the world. The structure of language is therefore explained by the structure of experience to the extent that the two match.

On the syntactic level, the iconicity of language manifests itself especially as iconicity of order, iconicity of distance, and iconicity of complexity.

i) Iconicity of order

Iconicity of order refers to the order of elements in language parallels that in physical experience or the order of knowledge. Word-order iconicity is found in the ordering of events in narrative sequences, which tends to reflect **closeness in time**. This is especially evident in coordinate structures:

(5) Veni, vidi, vici. (I came, I saw, I conquered.)

(6) a. He opened the bottle and poured himself a glass of wine.

  b. *He poured himself a glass of wine, and opened the bottle.

(7) a. He jumped onto his horse and rode out into the sunset.

  b. *He rode out into the sunset and jumped onto his horse.

As shown in (5) — (7), the sequence of the (5), (6a) and (7a) corresponds to the natural temporal order of events. In contrast, (6b) and (7b) are odd, to say the least, because they do not comply with natural order. As far as the rules of syntax proper are concerned, nothing is wrong with (6b) and (7b). However, the sentences are unacceptable because the order in which the clauses are arranged violates the principle of iconicity of order.

Another example of iconic ordering involves the concept of **closeness to the speaker**. What is nearest to the speaker in a physical or metaphorical sense is always mentioned first. Thus we say *here and there*, *this and that*, *now and then*, *sooner or* later, etc. The motivation for putting *here*, *this*, *now* and *sooner* in first position is mainly because they are closer to the speaker than *there*, *that*, *then*, and *later*.

ii) Iconicity of distance

Iconicity of distance means that the linguistic distance between expressions corresponds to the conceptual distance between the ideas they represent. For example, lexical causatives (e. g. *kill*) tend to convey a more direct causation than periphrastic causatives (e. g. *cause to die*).

(8) a. The farmer killed the animal.

b. The farmer caused the animal to die.

While (8a) emphasizes the happening of causing and dying at the same place and in the same time, (8b) does not necessarily mean that. (8a) can be represented as "One of whom causes the event in question, the other of whom dies in that event"; and (8b) can be represented as "He causes something to come about, namely that the animal dies". Thus, we see that where cause and result are formally separated, conceptual distance is greater than they are not.

Iconicity of distance can explain the simple adjacency of head and modifier. The principle of iconicity of order implies that the modifiers that are closest to the head in content are generally placed closest to it as well, as illustrated in (9):

(9) a. those three nice little white wooden dolls

b. * those wooden three nice little white dolls

c. * those nice three little white wooden dolls

d. * three those wooden nice little white dolls

In (9), only the first sentence follows the principle of distance iconicity. We can see that the qualifying adjectives appear closer to the noun than the quantifying modifiers. Further, absolute objective qualities like *wooden* and *white* are closest to the noun, whereby those qualities involving substance (*wooden*) are expressed closest to the noun. Relative objective qualities (size, e. g. *little*) are expressed farther away from the noun, and subjective qualities like *nice* are expressed still farther. Farthest away from the noun is the determiner because it serves only to pick out the referent.

iii) Iconicity of complexity

Iconicity of complexity suggests that more complex meanings are expressed by more complex forms. For example, in English, the derivatives which take more information are usually more complex than the forms they derive from, such as *act* → *act-ive* → *act-*

iv-ate→ act-iv-at-ion. On the syntactic level, conceptual complexity and structural complexity tend to go hand in hand. This principle of iconicity can be used as well to explain why the description of a multi-event is longer than that of a single event. Consider the following example:

  (10) a. Mary cleaned the floor.

    b. Mary cleaned the floor, and then watered the flowers.

    c. Mary cleaned the floor, watered the flowers, and then walked to the kitchen.

11. 8 Summary

In this chapter we have outlined some basic concepts in cognitive linguistics. Cognitive linguistics is described as a movement or an enterprise rather than a specific theory, which is concerned with the relationship between human language, the mind and socio-physical experience. We have discussed some key concepts in cognitive linguistics: categories and categorization, image schemas, conceptual metaphors and metonymies, construal and iconicity. All of these concepts indicate that language and thought are inextricably intertwined. Thus we say that natural language is a product of the human mind, based on the same organizing principles that operate in other cognitive domains.

Self-study Activities

1. Define the following terms in brief.

 (1) cognitive linguistics (2) categorization (3) category

 (4) prototype (5) construal (6) conceptual metaphor

 (7) conceptual metonymy (8) image schema (9) iconicity

2. What are the distinctions between the classical theory and prototype theory of categorization?

3. Distinguish conceptual metaphor from linguistic metaphor.

4. What are the differences between conceptual metaphor and conceptual metonymy?

5. Give at least 10 linguistic metaphors for the conceptual metaphor LOVE IS A JOURNEY.

Sources and Suggestions for Further Reading

Croft, W. & Cruse, D. A. 2004. *Cognitive Linguistics.* Cambridge: Cambridge University Press.

Fauconnier, G. 1997. *Mappings in Thought and Language.* Cambridge: Cambridge University Press.

Haiman, J. (ed.)1985. *Iconicity in Syntax.* Amsterdam: John Benjamins.

Heine, B. 1997. *Cognitive Foundation of Grammar.* Oxford: Oxford University Press.

Hopper, P. J. & Traugott, E. C. 2001. *Grammaticalization.* Beijing: Foreign Language Teaching and Research Press.

Johnson, M. 1987. *The Body in the Mind.* Chicago: The University of Chicago Press.

Kövecses, Z. 2002. *Metaphor: A Practical Introduction.* Oxford: Oxford University Press.

Lakoff, G. 1987. *Women, Fire and Dangerous Things.* Chicago: The University of Chicago Press.

Lakoff, G. & Johnson, M. 1980. *Metaphors We Live By.* Chicago: The University of Chicago Press.

Langacker, R. W. 1987. *Foundations of Cognitive Grammar Vol. I: Theoretical Prerequisites.* Stanford: Stanford University Press.

Langacker, R. W. 1991. *Foundations of Cognitive Grammar Vol. II: Descriptive Application.* Stanford: Stanford University Press.

Lee, D. 2001. *Cognitive Linguistics: An Introduction.* Oxford: Oxford University Press.

Talmy, L. 2000. *Toward a Cognitive Semantics* (2 Vols.) Cambridge, Mass. : The MIT Press.

Taylor, J. 2001. *Linguistic Categorization* (2 nd ed.) . Beijing: Foreign Language Teaching and Research Press.

Ungerer, F. & Schmid, H. J. 2008. *An Introduction to Cognitive Linguistics.* Beijing: Foreign Language Teaching and Research Press.

Chapter 12   Applied Linguistics

12. 1   Introduction

The word "applied" in the title might have made you think of something like "linguistics applied". Yes, indeed, as a branch of linguistics, the primary concern of **applied linguistics** is to apply linguistic theories, methods and findings to solve problems or improve situations involving language and its users and uses. The emphasis on application distinguishes it from the study of language in the abstract, that is, general or theoretical linguistics which covers the branches of linguistics that we learned through Chapters 2 to 5.

The history of applied linguistics can be traced back to the studies of grammar and rhetorics in ancient Greece, China and India thousands of years ago, where scholars were engaged in the analysis of language as well as its practical application in the realms of language teaching and use in the real world. The term applied linguistics, which originally arose in relation to general linguistics, can be traced back to 19 th century Europe, when linguistics was gaining recognition as an autonomous and scientific discipline distinct from philology, the humanistic study of the areas of language, culture, and literature. Given such a long history of development, the coverage of the discipline has never been, nor will ever be, unanimously defined.

In the widest definition, it may include all of what Charles Frederick Voegelin (a North American linguist, 1906—1986) called "hyphenated linguistics", that is, everything but language theory, history, and description. That will cover the studies we learned through Chapters 6 to 12. In addition to those, there are many more, such as Language Acquisition, Language Teaching, **Lexicography** (dealing with the art of dictionary making), Translation, **Speech Pathology** (concerned with the diagnosis and treatment of language disability), and Forensic Linguistics. However, applied linguists do agree that the most well-developed branch of applied linguistics is the study of second and foreign language learning and teaching, and sometimes the term is used as if this were the only field involved. In this chapter our discussion will be confined to topics and findings in this field which can help readers to be more efficient foreign language learners or theoretically well-prepared foreign language teachers. It is our hope that upon finishing this chapter you are able to approach the following questions like an expert in foreign language learning and teaching:

1) What are the characteristics of "good language learners"?

2) How should second language (L2) learners' errors be treated?

3) How do good L2 teachers teach?

4) How can we tell whether a language test is good or not?

12. 2　Some basic concepts

12. 2. 1　Second vs. foreign language

In a broad sense, the term **second language** refers to any language learned after one has learnt one's native language or mother tongue, also called first language. However, it, in contrast with **foreign language**, refers more narrowly to a language that plays a major role in a particular country or region though it may not be the first language of many people who use it. For example, the learning of English by Chinese immigrants in the US is a case of second (not foreign) language learning. English is also a second language for many people in countries like India, Singapore and the Philippines, because English fulfils many important functions in those countries, serving as a medium of instruction in schools and of communication in government and media.

A foreign language is, by definition, one that is not the mother tongue of large numbers of people in a particular country or region; it is not used as a medium of instruction in schools, nor is it widely used as a medium of communication in government, media, etc. Foreign languages are typically taught as school subjects for the purpose of communicating with foreigners or for reading printed materials in the language. For instance, English is always learned as a foreign language in China.

12. 2. 2　Second language acquisition vs. foreign language learning

This contrast between **language learning** and **language acquisition** is widely held in applied linguistics. Language learning refers to a conscious process involving the study of explicit rules of language. It, in a broad sense, includes both formal learning in the classroom stimulated by teaching and natural, informal learning without instruction from any teacher. Language acquisition is said to be a subconscious process of rule internalization resulting from exposure to comprehensible input when the learner's attention is on meaning rather than form, and it is not dependent on the teaching of grammatical rules.

A person's first language is basically acquired, while in the development of second or foreign language, both learning and acquisition are involved. Many people believe that learning is often typical of classroom learning in a foreign language context, with acquisition very likely to be more significant in a second language context. However, "second language acquisition" (SLA) has become established as the preferred term for the academic discipline dealing with second or foreign language learning and teaching, with "second language" used as a cover term both for second language and foreign language, in that both are learned when the first language system is already in place. In the coming sections, following the practice of most scholars of SLA, "learning" and "acquisition" are used interchangeably unless we are directly addressing Krashen's work.

12.3　Second language acquisition

12.3.1　Learner factors

As L2 learners, you must have noticed this: even in the same learning situation, some learners learn faster and better than others, some may be better in reading but poorer in writing than others, and some may do better in pronunciation or speaking but may be poorer in grammar. Then, how do learners vary enormously in learning a language? Or what are the factors responsible for individual differences in L2 learning? Other things almost being equal, what make the differences between individual learners in such factors as age, intelligence, motivation, memory, and so forth? Here, we take a look at some of the key individual learner differences that may affect the process of L2 learning.

Let's begin with the question of age in relation to L2 learning. Although many people tend to believe that young children seem to learn a second language more easily than adults and are thus in favor of an early start in L2 learning, scientific studies do not provide solid support for that position. Research shows that language learning may occur at any age from the early years to adult life. No age or stage stands out as optimal or critical for all aspects of L2 learning. Each stage of development may have certain advantages and disadvantages. In certain respects, children and adults at different ages, differ psychologically in their approaches to L2 learning. It appears that young children acquire L2 more readily and intuitively in social and communicative situations while older learners tend to learn more readily by means of cognitive and academic approaches.

In our everyday experience of language teaching and learning, we often find that some language learners appear to have a gift for languages while others do not. In SLA, such a gift is called **language aptitude**, which refers to the natural ability to learn a language, not including intelligence, motivation, interest, etc. It is thought to be a combination of various abilities, such as the ability to imitate sounds not heard before, the ability to identify and remember sound patterns in a new language, the ability to recognize the different grammatical functions of words in sentences and to infer grammatical rules, and the ability to remember words, rules etc. in a new language. All other factors being equal, a learner with high language aptitude can learn more quickly and easily than one with low language aptitude. To measure a person's aptitude for L2 learning and to identify those learners who are most likely to succeed, there are **language aptitude tests**, and two well-known ones are The Modern Language Aptitude Test and The Pimsleur Language Aptitude Battery.

Another factor is **motivation**. In general, motivation means the driving force in any situation that leads to action; in SLA, motivation refers to a combination of the learner's attitudes, desires, and willingness to expend effort in order to learn the second language. There is a widely drawn distinction between intrinsic motivation and extrinsic motivation. The former is enjoyment of language learning itself, while the latter is driven by external factors such as parental pressure, societal expectations, more practical concerns such as getting a job or passing an examination, and other sources of rewards and punishments. Motivation is generally considered to be one of the primary causes of success and failure in L2 learning. Some scholars regard it as the second of the "big two" individual factors, accounting for only slightly less of the variance in learners' achievement scores than language aptitude. Research has repeatedly proven that intrinsic motivation contributes strongly to L2 learning. No doubt, the study of learners' motivation is not only of importance for understanding language learning but also of the potential for maximizing its success.

In addition, the feelings that learners have about the target language, called **language attitude**, may also affect L2 learning. The attitude that speakers have towards their own language or the language (s) of others can be either positive or negative. Some people may particularly value a foreign language or think that a language is especially easy to learn, while some may not. Positive attitudes towards a L2 may evoke greater interest and more effort to learn. And knowing about attitudes is an important aspect of evaluating the likely success of a language teaching programme.

The so-called "good language learner" studies of the 1970s, investigating some of the qualities that characterize successful language learners, reveal that these learners are characterized above all by strategies for active involvement: for instance, they repeat silently to themselves what the teacher or other students say; they think out their own answers to questions which the teacher puts to other students; they pay close attention to the meaning of the language they are practicing; and they seek opportunities to use the language outside class, for example by reading or seeking personal contacts. Subsequent research has confirmed that successful learners generally use a greater number of active **learning strategies**. Learning strategies are defined as behaviors or actions which learners use to make language learning more successful, self-directed and enjoyable. In general, they are the ways in which learners attempt to work out the meanings and uses of words, grammatical rules, and other aspects of the language they are learning. They are generally viewed as conscious and problem-oriented, that is, learners deploy them to overcome some learning problem. Five broad categories of learning strategies have been identified:

i) Cognitive strategies, e. g. , analyzing the target language, comparing what is newly encountered with what is already known in either the L1 or the L2, and working out techniques for memorizing vocabulary;

ii) Metacognitive strategies, e. g. being aware of one's own learning, making an organized plan, and monitoring one's progress;

iii) Affective strategies, e. g. ways to deal with frustration and increase motivation;

iv) Social strategies, e. g. making friends with native speakers of the target language or working with peers in a classroom setting;

v) Resource management strategies, e. g. setting aside a regular time and place for language study.

To sum up, theoretically, researchers of learner factors have been motivated by the wish to contribute to SLA theory by specifying the contribution that learners can make to L2 learning and explaining why some learners succeed more than others, but their research also has an "applied" side. It has served as a basis for matching learners of different aptitude to different types of instruction so as to maximize learning. What is more important is that it has been used to identify the characteristics of good language learners as a basis for learner training.

12. 3. 2 Learner training

By learner training we mean the procedures or activities in language teaching that seek to 1) raise learners' awareness of what is involved in the processes of L2 learning, 2) help learners become more involved in and responsible for their own learning and 3) help learners develop and strengthen their language learning strategies.

Of the three, strategy training is of the greatest importance, where learners are trained in the use of the learning strategies leading to successful learning in order to improve the trainee's effectiveness in L2 learning. The following approaches are widely used in strategy training:

i) Explicit or direct training, where learners are given information about the value and purpose of particular strategies, taught how to use them, and how to monitor their own use of the strategies.

ii) Embedded strategy training, where the strategies to be taught are not taught explicitly but are embedded in the regular content of an academic subject area, such as reading, maths or science.

iii) Combination strategy training, where explicit strategy training is followed by embedded training.

12. 3. 3 Learner language

In SLA, **learner language** refers to the language that a L2 learner produces when he attempts to express meanings, either in speaking or writing, in the language being learned. You do not have to be very observant to find that there are often many expressions in learner language that do not go in agreement with native speakers' use or are against the grammar of the target language. What are the causes of the mistakes by L2 learners? What do those mistakes tell about L2 learning? Questions like those have caught great attention of researchers in SLA.

i) Error analysis

In the 1960s, a branch of applied linguistics, called **Error Analysis**, developed, which carried out systematic observation of learner language, studying and analyzing the **errors** made by L2 learners. When a second language learner uses a linguistic item (e. g. a word, a grammatical item, etc.) in a way which fluent or native speakers of the language regard as showing faulty or incomplete learning, he is considered to have made an error. A distinction is sometimes made between an error, which results from incomplete knowledge, and a **mistake** which is made by a learner in writing or speaking, caused by lack of attention, fatigue, carelessness, etc.

Error analysis demonstrates that many learner errors are not due to the learner's mother tongue interference but reflect universal learning strategies. Errors are generally classified into interlingual errors and intralingual ones. The former are errors caused by the learner's native language. They result from the effect of the learner's mother tongue on the learning of L2, known as **language transfer**. When both the native language and the target language have the same form, language transfer may make learning easier. In this case, **positive transfer** occurs. However, when the learner's use of a native-language pattern or rule leads to an inappropriate form or an error in the target language, **negative transfer**, also known as **mother tongue interference**, occurs. For example, a Chinese English learner may say a sentence like *There are very many people support him*, when he follows the Chinese pattern *You henduo ren zhichi ta* (naturally, *There are many people supporting him*, or just, *Many people support him*).

An intralingual error is one which results from faulty or partial learning of the target language, rather than from language transfer. Intralingual errors may be caused by the influence of one target language item upon another. The following are some of the well-known subcategories of intralingual errors:

i) Overgeneralizations, errors caused by extension of target language rules beyond their accepted uses, generally by making words or structures follow a more regular pattern. For example, a learner may use *mans* instead of *men* for the plural of *man*.

ⅱ) Communication-based errors, errors resulting from improper application of strategies of communication.

ⅲ) Errors of avoidance, errors resulting from failure to use certain target language structures because they are thought to be too difficult.

Error analysts believe L2 learners should not be blindly blamed or punished for the errors they commit in L2 learning. Rather, error analysis should be carried out so as 1) to identify strategies which learners use in language learning, 2) to identify the causes of learner errors, and 3) to obtain information on common difficulties in language learning. In brief, errors are significant in the process of language teaching and learning.

ⅱ) **Interlanguage**

In the late 1960s, an alternative view on learner language began to take shape. Learner language is no longer viewed as inferior or incomplete form of the target language, but as a natural language system on its own, called **interlanguage**. The **Interlanguage Hypothesis** holds that language learners possess a grammatical system that is different from both the first language and the target language but is nevertheless a natural language. In other words, interlanguage differs systematically from both the native language and the target language. In this view, SLA is similar in many ways to a child's acquisition of a mother tongue, and errors are interpreted as attempts by L2 learners to create their own explanations of how structures in the new language are patterned.

The notion of interlanguage has been central to the development of the field of research on L2 acquisition and continues to exert a strong influence on both the development of SLA theory and the nature of the central issues in that field, such as the development of learner language, the psycholinguistic processes that shape learner language, judgments made by learners about the identity or similarity of structures across linguistic systems (called **interlingual identification**), and the troubling process in which " incorrect " linguistic features become a permanent part of L2 learners' interlanguage (known as **fossilization**).

12. 4　Second language teaching

12. 4. 1　The teacher's role

Traditionally, L2 teaching is viewed as a one-way process in which information, skills, knowledge, etc. are transmitted from the teacher to the learner. In this kind of practice, known as **transmission mode of teaching**, the teacher is put at the center, with the learner playing a passive role, like an empty container waiting to be filled. Very likely, in this kind of teaching style, instruction is closely managed and controlled by the teacher, where students often respond in unison to teacher's questions.

By contrast, contemporary language-teaching approaches seek to give learners an active role in learning, hence they are said to be less teacher-centered and more student-centered than traditional ones. Research on SLA has repeatedly demonstrated that L2 learning is dependent upon the nature and will of the learners and that attention to the nature of learners should be central to all aspects of language teaching, including planning teaching, and evaluation. Learner-centeredness may be reflected by recognizing 1) learners' prior knowledge, 2) learners' needs, goals and wishes, 3) learners' learning styles and learning preferences and 4) learners' views of teaching and of the nature of classroom tasks. Learner-centered teaching, emphasizing the active role of students in learning, tries to give learners more control over what and how they learn and encourage learners to take more responsibility for their own learning.

In learner-centered teaching, teachers serve as a guide and companion as well as a motivator, counselor and analyst of needs. Their knowledge of learning theory and educational practice allows them to plan flexible learning experiences and to respond sensitively to learners of differing language ability levels and varying backgrounds, interests and needs.

12. 4. 2　Methods of second language teaching

The method links theory and practice. It is an application of views on how a language is best taught and learned and a particular theory of language and of language learning. In what follows, we will briefly discuss four methods that are significant to L2 teaching.

i) Grammar-translation method

Until the middle of the twentieth century, the **grammar-translation method** as the traditional method was the predominant method for language teaching in most educational contexts. Language is viewed as an academic discipline rather than a means for conducting everyday social interactions. Priority goes to the written language, with comprehension achieved through translation from the target language into the mother tongue, and competence developed through translation from the mother tongue into the target language. The grammar system of L2 is mastered through grammatical analysis of linguistic expressions, other form-focused exercises, and memorization of lexical items. Oral skills are fostered through the use of dictations, rote-learning of texts, and reading aloud. The teacher's role is that of an expert linguist, with the learner as a recipient of knowledge.

In this method, achievement is measured in terms of the accurate use of grammar and vocabulary rather than effective communication. As a result, learners may read well and perform well in written tests, but can hardly speak or listen. The limited practicality of this method for communicating in everyday situations created dissatisfaction toward the end of the nineteenth century among language teachers in Europe.

ii) The direct method

At the end of the 19 th century, **the direct method** came about as a reaction to the grammar-translation method and was the first oral-based method to become widely adopted. This method is premised on the belief that, a total immersion in the target language is conducive to rapid progress in communicating. The teacher's role is to supply contextual support for the learners, without turning to the learners' mother tongue. Listening and speaking skills precede reading and writing. Grammar learning is inductive and restricted in scope to forms that are commonly used in the spoken language.

In this method, interaction is encouraged through the learning of oral responses in dialogues, and much of this is mimicry and responses are sometimes learned inflexibly. Not given enough attention, learners' reading and writing skills are likely to be weak as a result of lack of breadth of vocabulary gained from reading. With grammar largely ignored on purpose, accuracy of L2 can hardly be guaranteed. In particular, the absence of active and overt grammar teaching makes the method hardly agreeable for adult learners who tend to use their cognitive learning strategies to facilitate their approaching the target language rules.

iii) The audiolingual method

In the middle of the twentieth century, **the audiolingual method** came into being as a result of experimentation in psychology. This method views learning as being brought about by positive reinforcement of correct behavior or utterances (in the case of language learning), with the correctness being instilled by repetition or drilling. It also draws on the work by scholars such as Leonard Bloomfield (American structural linguists, 1887—1949) in structural linguistics, which is concerned with compiling descriptive rather than prescriptive grammars of languages.

The audiolingual method focuses primarily on oral skills, with the teacher modeling utterances. Learners are drilled to produce correct responses with a strong emphasis on habit formation. In their opinion errors occur when the learner fails to respond correctly to a particular stimulus in the second language. Since an error may serve as a negative stimulus which reinforces "bad habits", it should not be allowed to occur. The utterances are organized into structures commonly used to realize speech acts in daily situations, with the learners' attention being drawn (through **contrastive analysis**) to differences between the target language and the mother tongue, so as to minimize confusion and error. The mechanical learning entailed in the audiolingual method led to the popularity of language laboratories, which afforded opportunities for both teacher-led and independent study.

The audiolingual method is most severely criticized for the behaviorist theory of language learning. Mainstream research in language acquisition rejects the idea that language learning is just a process of habit formation through stimulus-response learning. Instead, it has been repeatedly emphasized that language learning is more complex and involves analysis and generalization of rules on the basis of limited exposure to language.

iv) The communicative approach

At roughly the same time as the development of the direct approach, there emerged a far more durable new method known as the **communicative approach** or **Communicative Language Teaching**. Toward the end of the twentieth century, the communicative approach won great attention and has remained the dominant orthodoxy in progressive language teaching. However, in reality, this term, instead of being the name of a single, specific method, is used as an umbrella term for a range of teaching methods united by common principles or views, which include: 1) language is essentially viewed as social practice, and communication as social interaction and therefore dynamic and influenced by the cultural context, rather than being a fixed linguistic system existing in a vacuum; 2) the goal of language teaching is to cultivate the learner's competence to communicate in the target language; 3) language learning is best brought about by involving learners actively in communication related to real-life contexts; 4) the teacher plays the role of a facilitator and motivator, as well as source of knowledge. The communicative approach draws on sociolinguist Dell Hymes's concept of communicative competence which includes not only the knowledge about the language (Chomsky's linguistic competence) but also the ability to use the language appropriately in various social circumstances. Achievement is thus to be assessed not in terms of accurate grammar and pronunciation for their own sake, but by the ability to do things with the target language, appropriately, fluently and effectively.

Among all the versions of the communicative approach, **task-based teaching (method)**, also known as **task-based instruction**, has gained the most attention. Task-based teaching, based on the use of communicative and interactive tasks as the central units for the planning and delivery of instruction, was promoted as a strong form of the communicative approach in that it emphasizes holistic language, not like the weak forms which focus on the mastery of discrete linguistic items, although in realistic contexts of use. The task-based teaching method has a strong element of group-work and autonomous activities, and thus well embodies the communicative views of language learning that stress the development of learners' communicative competence.

Before we move on to the next topic, it should be pointed out that no method is superior to the others in every aspect. A common sense truth goes here: No method is perfect, nor is any method totally short of merits. The best method should be the one that fits.

12.5   Language testing

12.5.1   Types of language tests

The overall description of a test can be conducted in terms of the purpose it serves and its objectivity or subjectivity. The following are some of the key types of language tests.

1) Subjective vs. objective tests

A test, scored according to the personal judgment of the marker, is a **subjective test**, for instance, an essay examination. By contrast, a test, if scored without the use of the marker's personal judgment, is an **objective test**. In a same test, it is possible that some test items, such as translations and writings, are subjectively scored and some, such as true-false and multiple-choice items, are objectively marked.

2) Summative vs. formative tests

A **summative test** is given at the end of a course of instruction, which measures or "sums up" how much a student has learned from the course. However, a **formative test** is given during a course of instruction, which informs both the student and the teacher how well the student is doing. A formative test includes only topics that have been taught, and shows whether the student needs extra work or attention. It is usually a pass or fail test. If a student fails, he/she will do more study and take the test again.

3) Criterion-referenced vs. norm-referenced tests

If a test is designed to measure a student's performance according to a particular standard or criterion which has been agreed upon, it is a **criterion-referenced test**, such as **IELTS**. The student must reach this level of performance to pass the test, and his score is therefore interpreted with reference to the criterion score, rather than to the scores of other students. By contrast, a **norm-referenced test** is designed to measure how a particular student or group of students perform in comparison with the performance of another student or group of students whose scores are given as the norm, such as The College English Test Band 4 and Band 6 in China.

4) Achievement vs. proficiency tests

Both are designed to measure how much of a language the learner has learned. But the **achievement test** is usually designed to measure how much of language learners have successfully learned with specific reference to a particular course, textbook, or programme of instruction, thus a type of criterion-referenced test, such as the unit tests in China's middle schools. Its results are often used to make advancement or graduation decisions regarding learners or judge the effectiveness of a programme, which may lead to curricular changes. However, a **proficiency test** is not linked to a particular course of instruction, but is designed to measure the learner's general level of language mastery and is thus a type of norm-referenced test, such as the American TOEFL that is used to measure the English language proficiency of international students who wish to study in the USA or other English-speaking countries.

5) **Diagnostic vs. non-diagnostic tests**

If a test is designed to provide information about L2 learners' strengths and weaknesses, it is a diagnostic test; otherwise, it is a non-diagnostic test. For example, a diagnostic pronunciation test may be used to measure the takers' pronunciation of English sounds. It would show which sounds the learners are and are not able to pronounce or whether their pronunciation is intelligible or not. Diagnostic tests may also be used to find out how much L2 learners know before beginning a language course so as to better provide an efficient and effective course of instruction.

It should be noticed that the above categories may overlap. For example, TOEFL can be referred to both as a proficiency test and as a norm-referenced test.

12. 5. 2   Criteria of good tests

The most frequently used criteria against which language tests, actually tests in general, are evaluated are **reliability** and **validity**.

Reliability is a measure of the degree to which a test gives consistent results. In other words, a test is said to be reliable if it gives the same results when it is given on different occasions or when it is used by different people. Validity is the degree to which a test measures what it is supposed to measure, or can be used successfully for the purposes for which it is intended.

To know the reliability and validity of a test, one has to do a lot statistical analysis of the test takers' performance in the test. Technically, a number of sophisticated statistical procedures will be applied, which will take too much space to be elaborated here.

12. 6   Summary

Applied linguistics is an interdisciplinary, empirical science which is fieldwork-based and data-driven. Its task is to mediate between linguistics and language use. It not only provides principles and basic methodologies for language teachers, but provides feedback to linguistics by summing up the experience from the practical areas such as language teaching.

Linguists and applied linguists argue that language teachers need to learn about the theories and research findings generated by linguists and applied linguists. This is to say, armed with this knowledge about language, teachers will, among other things, be able to understand and diagnose student problems better, provide better explanations and representations for aspects of language, and have a clearer idea of what they are teaching. Likewise, it will also be beneficial for L2 learners to know some knowledge about applied linguistics, especially the findings of second language acquisition. Hopefully, upon finishing this last chapter of the book, you have become or are becoming a more effective learner of the second language that you are working on.

Self-study Activities

1. What advantages and disadvantages does the grammar-translation method have, compared with the communicative approach of language teaching?

2. You are having or have had the course called "Intensive Reading". What approaches does or did your teacher use? Justify your answer with detailed analysis.

3. Can the Test for English Majors (Grade 4) and the College Entrance Test of English be grouped into the same category of test? Why or why not?

4. If you were to design an English test for the second-year senior middle school students, what factors would you take into consideration to make it a good one?

Sources and Suggestions for Further Reading

Alderson, J. C., Clapham, C. and Wall, D. 1995. *Language Test Construction and Evaluation.* Cambridge: Cambridge University Press.

Cook, G. 2003. *Applied Linguistics.* Oxford: Oxford University Press.

Crystal, D. 2008. *A Dictionary of Linguistics and Phonetics* (6th ed.). Oxford: Blackwell Publishing Ltd.

Davies, A. 2007. *An Introduction to Applied Linguistics: From Practice to Theory* (2nd ed.) Edinburgh: Edinburgh University Press.

Davies, A. and Elder, C. 2004. *The Handbook of Applied Linguistics.* Oxford: Blackwell Publishing Ltd.

Ellis, R. 1994. *The Study of Second Language Acquisition.* Oxford: Oxford University Press.

Krashen, S. D. 1981. *Second Language Acquisition and Second Language Learning.* Oxford: Pergamon.

Scovel, T. 2004. *Learning New Languages: A Guide to Second Language Acquisition.*

Index

A

Answers to self-study activities

Chapter 1   Preliminaries

1. (1) language: a system of arbitrary vocal symbols used for human communication.

(2) linguistics: the scientific or systematic study of language.

(3) arbitrariness: the absence of similarity between the form of a linguistic sign and what it relates to in reality, e. g. the word "dog" does not like a dog.

(4) duality: the term refers to the two levels of language structure: One is that minimal meaningless units are combined into larger, meaningful units. The other is that minimal meaningful units can be combined into longer, more complex expressions.

(5) phonetics: the study of linguistic speech sounds, including how they are produced, how they are perceived and their physical properties.

(6) phonology: the study of the abstract systems underlying the sounds of language.

(7) syntax: the term refers to either the structure of sentences or the study of sentence structures.

(8) semantics: the study of linguistic meaning.

(9) pragmatics: a branch of linguistics that studies language in use.

(10) sociolinguistics: the study of language and society: how social factors influence the structure and use of language.

(11) psycholinguistics: the study of language and mind: the mental structures and processes which are involved in the acquisition, comprehension and production of language.

(12) stylistics: the study of how literary effects are related to linguistics.

(13) discourse analysis: the study of how sentences in spoken and written language form larger meaningful units such as paragraphs, conversations, and interviews.

(14) corpus linguistics: linguistic description based on the extensive accumulation of actually occurring language data and its analysis by the computer.

2. No. It is true that many speeches communicate through a specific system of communication. Humans also use systems other than their language to relate to each others and to send messages (body language, sign language, code, and facial expression) . Both use the sound system. But the major difference between human and animals is that human language is not just a response to external or even internal emotional stimuli like the sounds and the gestures of animals. Human languages have the features of productivity and creativity. The messages sent by animals are very limited in number or finite. Their sound combination is not varied, either.

3. Omitted.

4. Ferdinand de Saussure (1857—1913) was a Swiss linguist who occupies an important place in the history of linguistics. He was the pivotal figure in the transition from the 19th to 20th century when the emphasis of linguistic study wad shifted from language change to language description, and is generally considered the founder of modern linguistics. His book *Course in General Linguistics* (1915) exerted a major influence on the course of linguistics, particularly in Europe. It was posthumously published in 1916. It is considered Saussure's most influential work. His ideas in this book leave a monumental impact. De Saussure's crucial achievement is his explicit and reiterated statement that all language items are essentially interlinked. In the book *Course in General Linguistics*, his distinctions of synchronic vs. diachronic and langue vs. parole have played a significant role in modern linguistic studies. His insistence that language is a carefully built structure of interwoven elements initiated the era of structural linguistics.

5. Historical linguistics (also called Diachronic Linguistics) is a branch of linguistics which concerns the study of phonological, grammatical, and semantic changes, the reconstruction of earlier stages of languages, and the discovery and application of the methods by which genetic relationships among languages can be demonstrated. It flourished in the 19th century that more scientific methods of language comparison and sufficient data on the early Indo-European languages are combined to establish the principles now used by historical linguists. The 19th century concern with reconstructing Proto-Indo-European, and making hypotheses about the way it split into various modern languages, was encouraged by the general intellectual climate of the times. In 1859, Darwin published his famous *Origin of Species*, putting forward the theory of evolution. It seemed natural to attempt to chart the evolution of language alongside the evolution of species. This emphasis on language change eventually led to a major theoretical advance. In the last quarter of the century, a young group of scholars nicknamed the "Young Grammarians" claimed that language change is regular. It was an important step forward for linguists to realize that language changes were not just optional tendencies, but definite and clearly *stateable* "laws".

6. No, we cannot teach a dog language, but we can condition the dog to certain stimuli to respond in some way so that this reflex becomes conditional. To dogs, these words are not a language, but a combination of sounds only. For example, the human's utterance such as "*sit up*" is just a stimulus to dogs the same as using the stimulus of food, and the dog can automatically respond by sitting immediately after some training, which is involuntary reaction to stimuli. In brief, language is human specific, and the possession of language, perhaps more than any other attribute, distinguishes humans from other animals, so dogs can not learn and use language. When animals vocally imitate or react to human utterances, it does not mean they possess language. For example, "Talking" birds imitate sounds but can neither segment these sounds into smaller units, nor understand what they are imitating, nor produce new utterances to convey their thoughts. Just as Norman Geschwind (1979) says "The nervous systems of all animals have a number of basic functions in common, most notably the control of movement and the analysis of sensation. What distinguishes the human brain is the variety of more specialized activities it is capable of learning. The preeminent example is language".

Chapter 2 Phonetics and Phonology

1. (1) Labiodental (s); (2) Alveolar (s); (3) Palatal (s); (4) Dental (s); (5) Velar (s)

2. (1) Nasal (s); (2) Plosive (s); (3) Affricate (s); (4) Approximant (s); (5) Fricative (s)

3. (1) /w/, a consonant, all the other four are vowels.

(2) /b/, a voiced consonant, all the others are voiceless.

(3) /l/, an oral sound, all the others are nasals.

4. Omitted.

Chapter 3   Morphology

1. (1) morphology: the study of the internal structure, forms and classes of words.

   (2) Bound morpheme: a morpheme that cannot stand alone as a word, e. g. *-ment* (as in astonishment), and *-er* (as in worker) .

   (3) free morpheme: a morpheme that can stand alone or independently as a word.

   (4) prefix: a prefix is an affix attached before a root or a stem, like *re-*, *un-* and *in-* in *re*make, *un*kind and *in*accurate.

   (5) suffix: a suffix is an affix attached after a root or a stem, like *-ly*, *-er*, *-ist*, *-s*, *-ing* and *-ed* in kind*ly*, wait*er*, social*ist*, book*s*, walk*ing* and jump*ed*.

   (6) infix: an infix is an affix inserted inside the root itself, such as bloody in kanga-*bloody*-roo.

   (7) morph: a morph is the phonological (spoken) or orthographic (written) form which realizes morpheme and it is the minimal meaning carrier.

   (8) allomorph: the morphs representing the same morpheme are called allomorphs of that morpheme, e. g. *-s*, *-es*, and *-en* are all allomorphs of the plural morpheme.

   (9) inflection: the morphological process which adjusts words by grammatical modification, e. g. in *The buses came*, *bus* is inflected for plurality and *came* for past tense.

   (10) derivation: the process of creating separate but morphologically related words, which is done by adding derivational affixes to other words or morphemes.

   (11) compounding: the way of building new words by combining two or more words together.

   (12) conversion: (also *zero derivation*) the derivation of a new word by changing its word class without altering its morphological structure, e. g. the change of *water* as a noun in *the water* to a verb in *to water*.

   (13) backformation: an abnormal type of word-formation where a shorter word is derived by deleting an imagined affix from a longer form that already exists in the language, e. g. *donate* from *donation*.

   (14) acronym: words that are composed of the first letter of a series of words and are pronounced as single words. Examples: *NATO*, *radar* and *yuppy*.

   (15) initialism: a new word that is composed of the first letters of a series of words

and pronounced by saying each letter in them, such as USA (the United States of America).

2. Omitted.

3. (1) NATO: North Atlantic Treaty Organization

(2) WWW: World Wide Web

(3) SOS: Save Our Souls

(4) TOEFL: Test of English as a Foreign Language

(5) UN: the United Nations

(6) GMT: Greenwich Mean Time

(7) NSC: National Security Council

(8) a.m: ante meridiem

(9) VIP: very important person

(10) IBM: International Business Machines

(11) UNESCO: United Nations Educational Scientific and Cultural Organization

(12) asap: as soon as possible

(13) dink: double income no kids

(14) FAQ: Food and Agriculture Organization

(15) VAT: valued added tax

(16) laser: light amplification by stimulated emission of radiation

(17) radar: radio detecting and ranging

4. brunch = breakfast + lunch   heliport = helicopter + port

motel = motor + hotel   smog = smoke + fog

talkathon = talkative + marathon   chunnel = channel + tunnel

mingy = mean + stingy   guesstimate = guess + estimate

comsat = communication + satellite   breathalyser = breath + analyzer

stagflation = stagnation + inflation   chortle = chuckle + snort

hi-fi = high + fidelity

5. The following sentences are all examples of conversions from noun to verb. Conversion is the formation of new words by changing their word class without altering their morphological structures.

(a) We punk-rocked the night away.

The word punk-rock is used as a verb here and means that we spent the night in playing and listening to punk-rock music.

(b) She dog-teamed her way across the arctic.

Dog-team is used in this sentence to mean that she crossed the arctic on a vehicle pulled by a team of dogs.

(c) We MG'd to Perth.

MG, short for Morris Garage, is a famous English brand for cars. Here, it means that we drove to Perth in the MG car.

(d) We Concorded to London.

Concord is the leading brand of American jazz record company. "Concorded to London" means that we were listening to the Concord music all the way to London.

(e) He Maradona'd the ball into the net.

Diego Armando Maradona is an outstanding Argentine soccer player who led the Argentine soccer team to win the World Cup twice. Later his last name became a word in the vocabulary of soccer English. So this sentence means that he shot the ball into the net successfully.

(f) I microwaved the parsnips.

I used the microwave to heat the parsnips.

(g) She Robinson Crusoed in the Galapagos.

Robinson Crusoe is a character in the novel *Robinson Crusoe* written by Daniel Defoe. In this novel, Robinson survived from a sinking boat and was drifted to a waste island. He lived there alone for many years and transformed the island into a civilized one all by himself. In this sentence, the name Robinson Crusoe is used as a verb to convey that she boated in the Galapagos like Robinson Crusoe, without the help of other people or advanced technology.

(h) We'll have to Ajax the sink.

Ajax is the name of an explosion. "to Ajax the sink" means to bomb the sink.

(i) He Windolened the windows.

Windolen is originally a brand of cleaning agent used to clean windows. Here it means that he used the Windolen to clean the windows.

(j) You should Clairol your hair.

Clairol is a brand of shampoo. Here it means that you should wash your hair with Clairol.

6. Omitted.

Chapter 4   Syntax

1. (1) syntax: the study of the rules and patterns by which sentences are combined.

   (2) recursion: syntax is about the infinite uses of finite means: finite in that in most languages the number of basic words is relatively limited and more importantly syntax rules and patterns are finite; infinite because there is no longest sentence and syntax rules can be applied to their own output in a repeated way to create unlimited number of structures. Such infiniteness is labeled "recursion" or "recursiveness".

   (3) PS rules: it is an abbreviation for "phrase structure rules", which refers to the rules for building a constituent structure.

   (4) movement: in syntax, it is a rule that plays a role in deriving a surface structure by the reordering of constituents.

   (5) I-language: it is an abbreviation for "internalized language", which is the knowledge of language or knowledge of rules that govern the formation of structures.

   (6) Universal Grammar: the grammar of human language that is genetically determined and internal to the human brain/mind.

   (7) metafuntions: in systemic functional grammar, language is a social rather than an individual phenomenon. Language is a system for making meanings. All languages are organized around three modes of meaning (also called three meta-functions): the ideational, interpersonal and textual meaning which are realized by different lexical-grammatical systems.

   (8) transitivity: transitivity specifies different types of processes and the participants involved, which mainly subsumes material process, mental process, relational process, behavioral process, verbal processes and existential process.

2. (1) Nutritious food and drink

   Helpful hint: The ambiguity results from the modification of the adjective "nutritious". It can modify either "food" or "food and drink", as is shown:

   [[Nutritious food] and [drink]]

   [[Nutritious] [food and drink]]

   (2) Student film club

   Cf. the explanation of (1).

(3) Visiting professors can be boring.

Helpful hint: (a) Professors who visit can be boring. (b) [The act of] visiting professors can be boring.

(4) Dick finally decided on the boat.

Helpful hint: (a) Dick finally made the decision to buy the boat. (b) While on the boat Dick made a final decision (about something).

(5) They said she would go yesterday.

Helpful hint: (a) They said, she would go yesterday. (b) They, said she, would go yesterday. (c) They said yesterday, she would go.

3. (1) To help you is my honor.

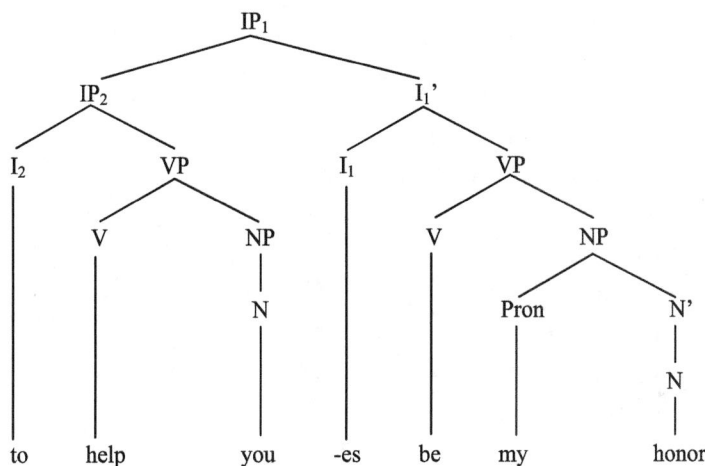

Since English V cannot be moved out of VP, the affix – es has to be attached to V by affix-hopping operation, that is, the affix is lowered onto the relevant verb. Otherwise, the affix is spelled out as an inflected form of DO, or Do-Support. For instance, "John likes you" vs. "John does like you".

（2）We would like you to stay.

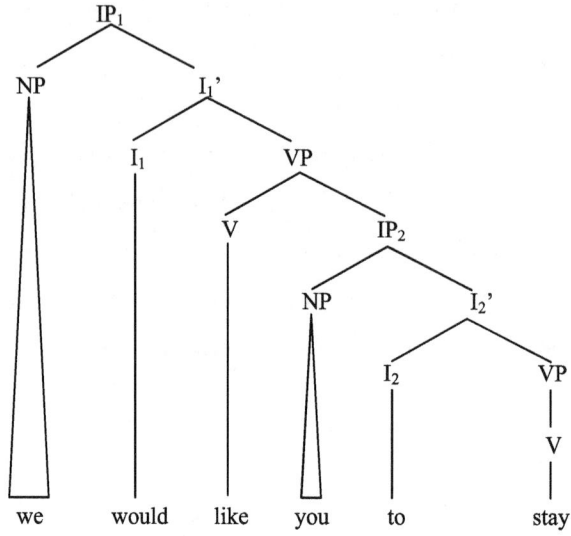

```
                        IP₁
               NP                I₁'
                           I₁          VP
                                   V          IP₂
                                         NP          I₂'
                                                 I₂       VP
                                                              V

               we      would  like   you    to          stay
```

（3）We know that he enjoys syntax.

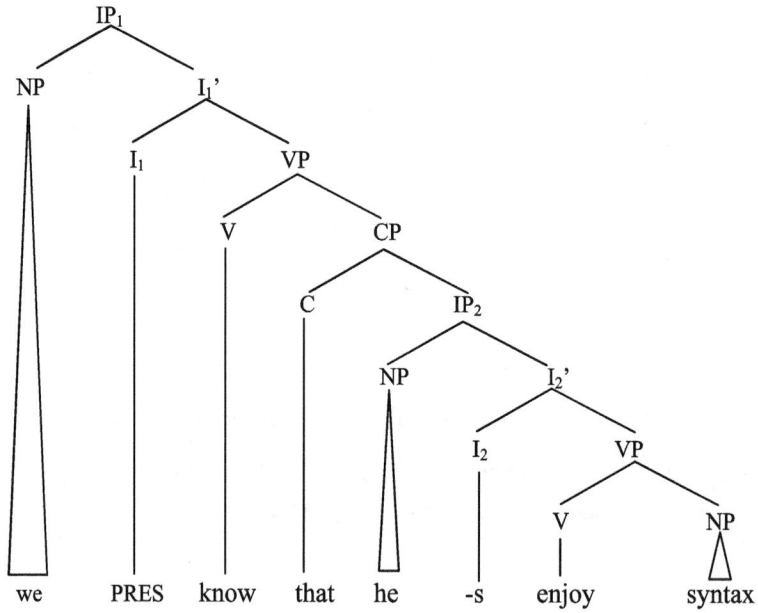

```
                     IP₁
             NP              I₁'
                       I₁          VP
                               V          CP
                                     C          IP₂
                                           NP          I₂'
                                                   I₂        VP
                                                          V        NP

             we    PRES   know   that   he    -s    enjoy     syntax
```

(4) He wants to try to help others.

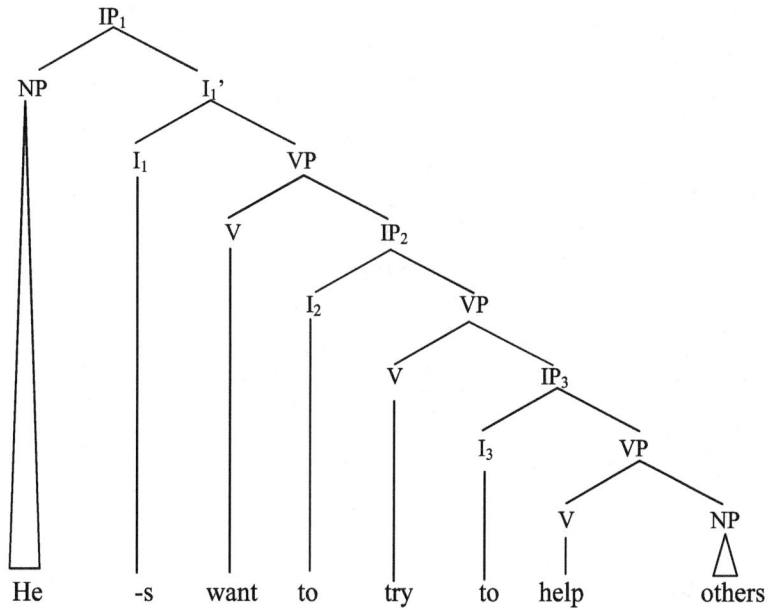

```
                        IP₁
                 ┌───────┴───────┐
                NP              I₁'
                 │         ┌──────┴──────┐
                 │        I₁            VP
                 │         │      ┌──────┴──────┐
                 │         │      V           IP₂
                 │         │      │      ┌──────┴──────┐
                 │         │      │     I₂           VP
                 │         │      │      │      ┌──────┴──────┐
                 │         │      │      │      V           IP₃
                 │         │      │      │      │      ┌──────┴──────┐
                 │         │      │      │      │     I₃            VP
                 │         │      │      │      │      │       ┌─────┴─────┐
                 │         │      │      │      │      │       V          NP
                 │         │      │      │      │      │       │           △
                He        -s   want    to    try     to    help       others
```

(5) That Julie admired Romeo surprised us.

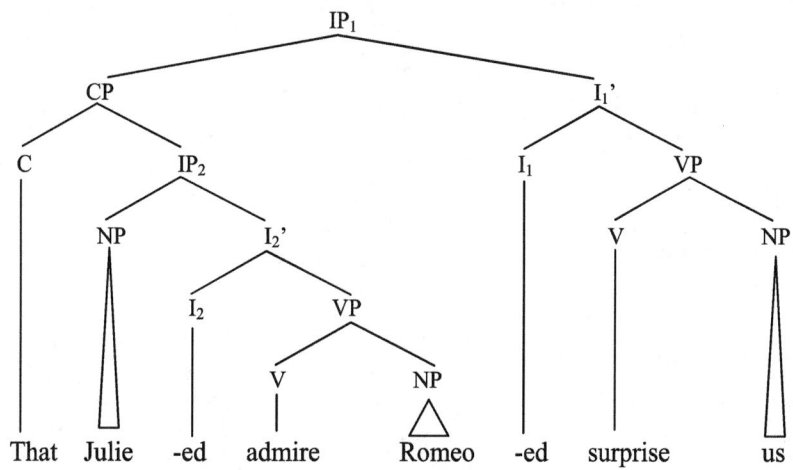

```
                                IP₁
                ┌────────────────┴────────────────┐
               CP                                I₁'
        ┌───────┴───────┐                 ┌────────┴────────┐
        C             IP₂               I₁                 VP
        │       ┌──────┴──────┐          │           ┌──────┴──────┐
        │      NP            I₂'         │           V           NP
        │       △       ┌─────┴─────┐    │           │            △
        │       │      I₂          VP    │           │            │
        │       │       │     ┌─────┴──┐ │           │            │
        │       │       │     V       NP │           │            │
        │       │       │     │        △ │           │            │
      That    Julie    -ed  admire  Romeo  -ed    surprise       us
```

4. (1) Which foreign language can you speak?

Wh-movement and head movement are involved.

```
                        CP
              ┌─────────┴─────────┐
             NP                   C'
            ╱│╲            ┌───────┴───────┐
           ╱ │ ╲           C              IP
          ╱  │  ╲          │        ┌──────┴──────┐
         ╱   │   ╲         │       NP            I'
        ╱    │    ╲        │       ╱│          ┌──┴──┐
       ╱     │     ╲       │      ╱ │          I     VP
      ╱      │      ╲      │     ╱  │          │   ┌──┴──┐
                                              V     NP
                                              │      △
 Which foreign languageⱼ  canᵢ  you   tᵢ   speak    tⱼ
```

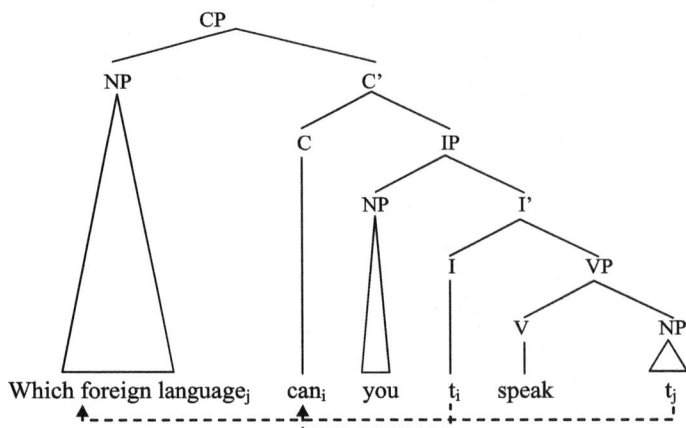

(2) Did Rosie look wonderful?

Head movement is involved.

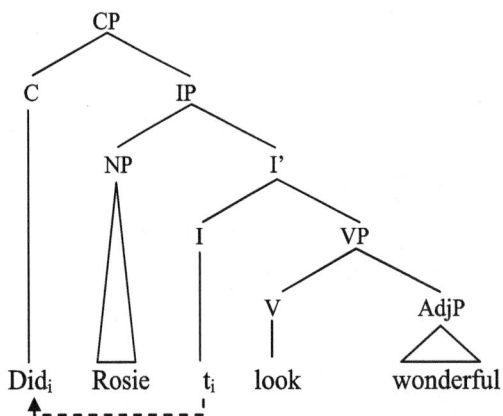

```
                CP
          ┌─────┴─────┐
          C          IP
          │     ┌─────┴─────┐
          │    NP           I'
          │    ╱│       ┌────┴────┐
          │   ╱ │       I        VP
          │  ╱  │       │      ┌──┴──┐
          │ ╱   │       │      V   AdjP
                        │      │     △
        Didᵢ  Rosie    tᵢ    look  wonderful
```

(3) He forgot where she lived.

Wh-movement is involved.

```
                    IP₁
           NP               I₁'
                        I₁         VP
                                V        CP
                                   Wh-phrase      C'
                                             C        IP₂
                                                 NP         I₂'
                                                        I₂        VP
                                                                     V'
                                                                 V        PP
          He      -ed    forgot   whereᵢ    she    -ed    live        tᵢ
```

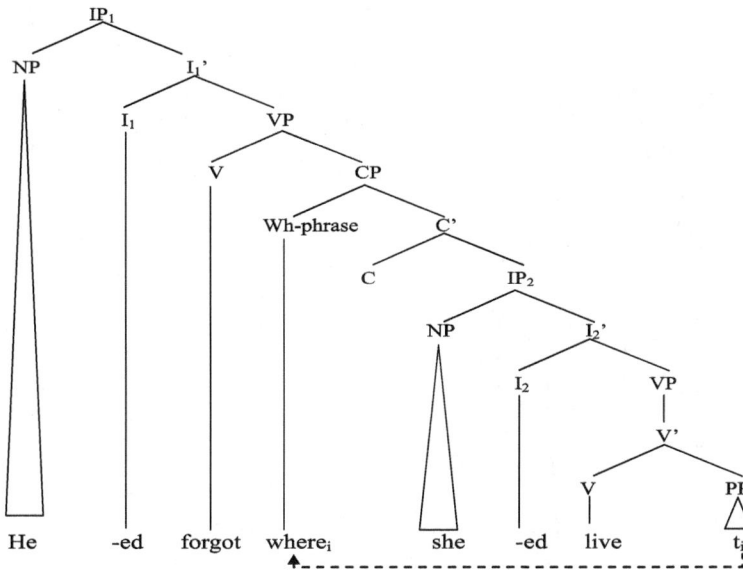

(4) Was anyone arrested?

Head movement and NP movement are involved.

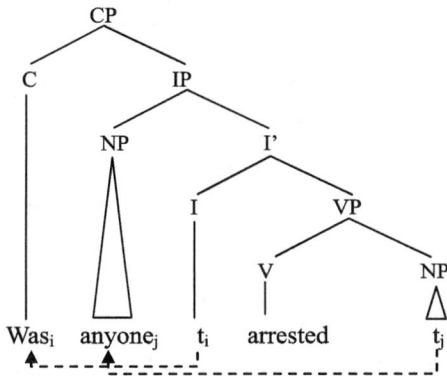

```
                CP
          C            IP
                   NP        I'
                          I        VP
                                V        NP
        Wasᵢ   anyoneⱼ   tᵢ   arrested    tⱼ
```

(5) I don't know which exams he has failed.

Wh-movement is involved.

IP₁ — NP, I₁'
I₁' — I₁, NegP
NegP — Neg, VP
VP — V, CP
CP — Wh-phrase, C'
C' — C, IP₂
IP₂ — NP, I₂'
I₂' — I₂, VP
VP — V, NP

I   do   not   know   which exams$_i$ he   has   failed   t$_i$

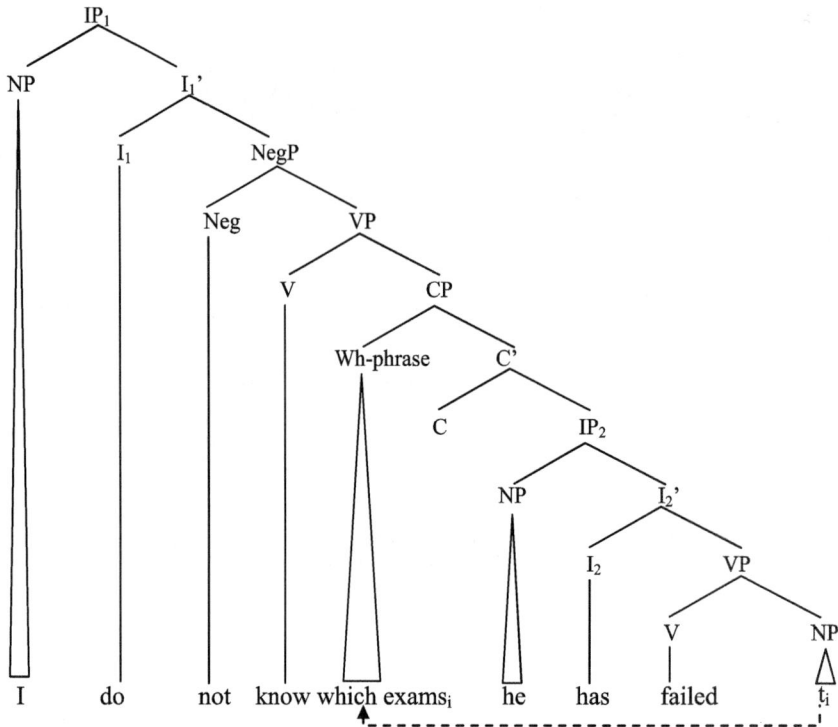

5. (1) <u>What kids need</u> is love and support.

        Theme   Rheme

        Given   New

(2) <u>Under the hill</u> lived an old man.

        Theme   Rheme

        Given   New

(3) <u>When lead is added to petrol</u>, it improves the car's performance.

            Theme   Rheme

            Given   New

(4) <u>What tremendously easy questions</u> you ask.

          Theme   Rheme

          New   Given

(5) (—Who broke the window?)

—<u>My brother</u> broke the window.

        Theme   Rheme

        New   Given

6. Omitted.

Chapter 5 Semantics

1. (1) Yes;   (2) Yes;   (3) No;   (4) No;   (5) Yes

2. (1) presuppose;   (2) entail;   (3) presuppose;   (4) entail;
   (5) presuppose

3. a. Meaning 1: She can't give birth to children.

   Meaning 2: She can't tolerate children.

   b. Meaning 1: I saw him and he was walking by the bank of the river.

   Meaning 2: I saw him and he was walking by the financial institution.

   Meaning 3: I was walking by the bank of the river when I saw him.

   Meaning 4: I was walking by the financial institution when I saw him.

4. a. I, her   b. this   c. last year   d. these

5. a. The speaker will go to that restaurant and have a dinner there.

   b. Mr. Smith is not good at study.

Chapter 6 Pragmatics

1. Entailment is the relation existing between propositions. Presupposition is what the speaker assumes to be the case prior to making an utterance. Entailment, which is not a pragmatic concept, is what logically follows from what is asserted in the utterance. Speakers have presuppositions while sentences, not speakers, have entailments. Presupposition can survive negation, while entailment cannot. Presuppositions are defeasible or cancelable in certain context. Generally speaking, entailment is not a pragmatic concept (i. e. having to do with the speaker meaning), but it is considered a purely logical concept.

2. According to the CP, we can assume that the two participants in the communication are cooperative. In this example, the maxim of relevance is responsible. It is only on the basis of assuming that B's utterance is relevant that we can understand it as providing a partial answer to A's question. The only way we can reconcile the assumption that B is cooperative with the content of B's utterance is to assume that B is not in a position to provide the full information, that is, the exact time as requested by A. B thinks that the milkman's coming might provide A with the way to derive a partial answer. Hence A may infer that B intends to use the milkman's coming as a reference point for time.

3. (1) T; (2) F; (3) T; (4) F; (5) F

4. (1) Context is regarded as constituted by all kinds of knowledge assumed to be shared by the speaker and the hearer.

(2) Locutionary act refers to the utterance of a sentence with ostensible sense and reference.

(3) Illocutionary act is the real, intended meaning in the making of an utterance, such as commanding, offering, promising, etc.

5. (1) You'd better close the window/door.

(2) You should answer the phone.

(3) Some but not all the students went to the lab.

Chapter 7　Discourse Analysis

1. (1) discourse: the study of language above the sentence or above the clause. More specifically, it is a continuous stretch of language larger than a sentence, often constituting a coherent unit such as a sermon, argument, joke, or narrative.

(2) discourse analysis: discourse analysis, also known as discourse linguistics and discourse studies, or text analysis, is an area of linguistics that primarily deals with the analysis of language "beyond the sentence", a study of how sentences in spoken and written language form larger meaningful units such as paragraphs, conversations, interviews, etc.

(3) information structure: information structure is the most common term for those aspects of a sentence's meaning that have to do with the way in which the addressee integrates the information into already existing information. Put more simply, information structure is the domain of language structure and language study that is concerned with notions such as given and new information, topic, comment, presupposition, and focus, etc.

(4) given information: the information that is assumed by the speaker to be known to, assumed by, or inferable by the addressee at the time of the speaker's utterance.

(5) new information: the information that is assumed by the speaker not to be known to or assumed by the addressee, or previously established in the discourse.

(6) topic: a topic is a noun phrase that expresses what a sentence is about, and to which the rest of the sentence is related as a comment.

(7) focus: focus refers to that portion of an utterance that represents new information, i. e, just that portion which augments or updates the hearer's view of the common ground.

(8) cohesion: cohesion occurs when the interpretation of some element in the discourse is dependent on that of another. It concerns with the grammatical and/or lexical relationships between the different elements of a discourse.

(9) coherence: coherence is what makes a text semantically meaningful in the mind of the writer and reader.

(10) discourse marker: Discourse markers are linguistic expressions used to signal the relation of an utterance to its immediate context, with the primary function of bringing to the listener's attention a particular kind of linkage of the upcoming utterance with the immediate discourse context.

(11) multimodal discourse analysis: multimodal discourse analysis (MDA) is an emerging paradigm in discourse studies which extends the study of language per se to the study of language in combination with other resources, such as images, scientific symbolism, gesture, action, music and sound.

(12) critical discourse analysis: critical discourse analysis (CDA) is a field that is concerned with studying and analyzing written and spoken texts to reveal the discursive sources of power, dominance, inequality and bias. It examines how these discursive sources are maintained and reproduced within specific social, political and historical contexts.

2. Cohesion and coherence may seem almost interchangeable. However, there is an important difference between them. Cohesion refers to the linguistic devices by which the speaker can signal the experiential and interpersonal coherence of the text, and is thus a textual phenomenon. In this regard, we can point to features of the text which serve a cohesive function. Coherence, on the other hand, is in the mind of the writer and reader. Thus it is a mental phenomenon and cannot be identified or quantified in the same way as cohesion. Cohesion and coherence are in most cases linked, in that a text which exploits the cohesive resources of the language effectively should normally be perceived as coherent. However, all language users generally predisposed to construct coherence even from language with few recognizable cohesive signals, if they have reason to believe that it is intended to be coherent.

3. In this text the word *Brazil* is a hyponym of the word *country*, to put it in another

way, the word *country* is *a* superordinate of the word *Brazil*. The text is composed of two clauses which are linked through a conjunction *and*. Reference, conjunction and lexical cohesion are the major cohesive devices in this text. 1) Anaphoric reference: the pronoun *her* refers back to the word *Brazil*. 2) Conjunction: *and* is used to link two clauses, which shows the logical relation of these two clauses, that is, cause and effect. 3) Lexical cohesion: in this discourse, reiteration takes place through occurrence of a different lexical item *country* that is systematically related to the first one *Brazil*. More specifically, the word *Brazil* in the first clause serves as a hyponym of the word *country* in the following clause.

4. The difference lies in the arrangement of hyponym and superordinate in these two texts. In the former text, *Brazil*, a hyponym of the word *country*, is arranged ahead of its superordinate *country*, which serves as the topic of the clause in succession, while the superordinate is arranged ahead of its hyponym in the latter one. The text in exercise 3 is supposed to be coherently better than that in exercise 4, because in the former text, reiteration is successfully achieved through a good arrangement of hyponym and superordinate in the discourse. In contrast, in the latter text, reiteration cannot be achieved in terms of the hyponym and superordinate.

5. (1) anaphoric reference
   (2) ellipsis
   (3) demonstrative reference
   (4) ellipsis of noun and verb
   (5) verbal substitution
   (6) nominal substitution
   (7) cataphoric reference
   (8) repetition
   (9) superordinate
   (10) repetition and collocation

Chapter 8　Sociolinguistics

1. (1) sociolinguistics: the study of language in its social contexts, or the study of how social factors influence the structure and use of language.
   (2) code switching: in a narrow sense, it refers to the use of two or more languages (or dialects) within a sentence or discourse. Code-switching can be divided into

metaphorical code-switching and situational code-switching.

(3) dialects: language contains rich varieties functioning in different regions, at different times, for different social classes, and favored by different individuals. Such sub-varieties of a single language are called dialects. Dialects include regional or geographical dialects, temporal dialects, social dialects, idiolects, etc.

(4) registers: varieties of language (e. g. novels, lectures, and baby talk) classified according to use and characterized by participants, their relationships, the setting, the level of formality, the subject matter, etc.

(5) Diglossia: a relatively stable situation where two closely related languages are used side by side in a speech community, each with a clearly defined role, one for high (H) functions in public life and one for low (L) functions in domestic life.

2. When the marital status of a woman addressee is not known, use *Ms.* (e. g. *Dear Ms. Smith*); When the gender of an addressee is not known, use the full name (e. g. *Dear Sana Damasi*); When writing to organizations, or to persons whose names are not known, use the following greetings: *Dear Sir/Madam*; *Dear Colleague* (to a person who is of the same profession as the writer, and usually used when you are sending a circular to many people) . Generally speaking, these greetings take into consideration the relationship between language and gender as well as the notion of register. With the rise of women's status in workplace and their sense of social equality, one needs to use sexism-free language especially in public encounters with superior strangers. Recognition of women's independence is expected rather than the taken-for-granted *Miss or Mrs.* distinction; gender-free address is preferred to the male-only stereotype *Dear Sir.* Meanwhile, business letters require a formal and professional style.

3. Sometimes a child will grow up in a household in which each parent speaks a different language; in that case, the child becomes bilingual by learning to speak to each parent's language. Children can also become bilingual if some other significant person in their life (such as a grandparent or caretaker) speaks to them consistently in another language. The second-generation immigrants, the children of the adult immigrants, are likely to be bilingual, speaking their parents' language at home and another at school. In short, a young child who is regularly exposed to two languages

from an early age will most likely become a fluent native speaker of both languages.

4. The mother, as an adult immigrant to the U. S. , may hardly become fluent in English. She speaks ungrammatical and broken English with Chinese characteristics, for all-purpose and wide use, unlike pidgin English which is used in fairly restricted social domains and for limited social or interpersonal functions. Besides, a pidgin is characterized by a small vocabulary and a reduction of many grammatical features. Hence, the mother's strange-sounding English is a sort of Chinglish.

Chapter 9   Stylistics

1. Roughly speaking, the two passages express the same meaning, but they differ in style: Passage 1 is dominant in verbal predicates, whereas all the corresponding actions are expressed in nominalized expressions in passage 2. In this sense, we may conclude that while passage 1 presents a dynamic description, passage 2 encodes such actions into static nominalized expressions.

2. (1) This poem is characterized with colloquial Black English expressions. First, the copula "be" is absent throughout the poem, e. g. "When I born, I black" (= When I *was* born, I *was* black) . Second, some colloquial words and expressions typical of Black English are used in the poem, such as "fella" for "fellow", "couple things" for "a couple of things" . As a whole, the poem expresses the black people's protest against their long being wrongly labeled as "coloured" .

   (2) This passage is excerpted from the Charter of the United Nations, which is characterized with the linguistic features of a forensic text, including the dense use of Latinate words, i. e. *establish*, *authority*, *international*, *administration*, *supervision*, *territory*, *subsequent*, *individual*, *agreements*, *refer* (*to*) , and formal expressions such as *thereunder* and *hereafter*, which are generally restricted to legal documents.

3. (1) In this sentence, the figure of speech of hyperbole is used to exaggerate the effect of laughing.

   (2) The figure of speech of metonymy is involved here in that "the grey hair" is used to stand for the senior citizens, i. e. old people.

   (3) In this sentence, the word "cradle" is used metaphorically for the "origin" or "departure" .

(4) The oxymoronic expression "disorderly chaos" is used here to describe the professor's desk, which at first sight seems to be chaotic but in fact is in good order.

(5) This sentence is a paradox, which is a seemingly self-contradictory and absurd statement but actually a twisted truth, the real meaning of which the reader can only arrive at upon further thinking.

(6) In this sentence, the word "threshold" is used metaphorically for the frontier of Russia. This makes the description more concrete.

(7) In this sentence, the adjective "delightful" is used ironically to mean "unpleasant, inconvenient, humiliating, etc".

(8) This sentence is an antithesis, in which contrasting expressions "teach English so poorly" and "teach grammar so well" are deliberately arranged in balanced structural form to achieve emphasis.

(9) In this sentence, the verbal expressions "rolled off" and "creeping" are used metaphorically in that the abstract nouns "rank and fashion" and "trade" are all used as if they are some concrete, animate entities which can move by themselves. This makes the description more vivid.

(10) In this sentence, the nominal expression "man's final release from earthly struggles" is used as a euphemism for "death", which seems to make the unpleasant topic light-toned.

Chapter 10　Psycholinguistics

1. (1) psycholinguistics: Psycholinguistics is a new science which attempts to study language as a psychological process, a study of great theoretical and practical significance. It takes the human language and its psychological processes as its subject area. Its aim is to find out the structures and processes that underlie human being's ability to learn, to speak and to understand language.

(2) linguistic determinism: Linguistic determinism is the idea that language and its structures limit and determine human knowledge or thought. Determinism itself refers to the viewpoint that all events are caused by previous events, and linguistic determinism can be used broadly to refer to a number of specific views.

(3) linguistic relativity: The linguistic relativity principle is the idea that the varying

cultural concepts and categories inherent in different languages affect the cognitive classification of the experienced world in such a way that speakers of different languages think and behave differently because of it. Popularly, the distinction is between a weak and a strong version (ⅰ) weak: "language limits thought" and (ⅱ) strong: "language determines thought".

(4) The Sapir-Whorf Hypothesis: The Sapir-Whorf theory, named after the American linguists Edward Sapir and Benjamin Lee Whorf, is a very influential but controversial theory concerning the relationship between language, thought and culture. What this hypothesis suggests is like this: our language helps mould our way of thinking and, consequently, different languages may probably express our unique ways of understanding the world. Following this argument, two important points could be captured in this theory. On the one hand, language may determine our thinking patterns; on the other, similarity between languages is relative, the greater their structural differentiation is, the more diverse their conceptualization of the world will be. For this reason, this hypothesis has alternatively been referred to as Linguistic Determinism and Linguistic Relativity. Nowadays, few people would possibly tend to accept the original form of this theory completely. Consequently, two versions of the Sapir-Whorf Hypothesis have been developed, a strong version and a weak version. The strong version of the theory refers to the claim the original hypothesis suggests, emphasizing the decisive role of language as the shaper of our thinking patterns. The weak version of this hypothesis, however, is a modified type of its original theory, suggesting that there is a correlation between language, culture and thought, but the cross-cultural differences thus produced in our ways of thinking are relative, rather than categorical.

(5) undergeneralization: When a child uses a word (or a linguistic construct) in a more limited way than adults do, this phenomenon is called undergeneralization.

(6) overgeneralization: In language acquisition, children tend to have a wider use of a grammatical feature or concept than adult norms permit. This phenomenon is called overgneralization.

(7) conceptualization: It is a process of language production during which an infant adjusts the range of senses attached to a word until it resembles the range of an adult.

(8) language comprehension: It is one of the central topics in psycholinguistics. It is concerned about the retrieval of language information. It includes sound comprehension, word comprehension, sentence comprehension and text comprehension.

2. (1) T; (2) T; (3) F; (4) F; (5) F

3. It's a fact that children have been found easy to commit various mistakes of overgeneralization. However, it does not follow that overgeneralization can only be found in children's speech. Adults are not immune to the problem of this type. Why? On the one hand, each of us has to think about new experiences in terms of old experiences. We recognize most easily those qualities in a person or thing which we have seen before. On the other hand, our automatic thoughts are based on our memories of past experiences, we might expect that many of those thoughts will tend to be generalizations that distort our perception of what we see. And that is the case.

4. The four expressions share the same grammatical pattern: "A $Noun_1$ + without + $Noun_2$". In terms of language comprehension, it's easy to apprehend the shared structure. However, it's not equally easy to understand each of the four. This implies that language comprehension takes places at different levels at which different language users tend to stop in the process of understanding, due to different experiences. "A room without light" is so plain that no problem will occur in comprehension. "A river without lighthouse" needs some specific experiences or observations for complete comprehension. "A professor without skill" does not make sense unless the hearer has his own sensual evaluation because this expression is rather than a descriptive fact. "A stick without length" is a pseudo-expression which defies the view that language comprehension can be image-based.

5. The four quotes are typical instances of Bushism: the way George W. Bush speaks ungrammatically. Bush has displayed a special type of spoonerism by saying "I arrived in President" as in (1). Instead, he should have said "I arrived as President". This error indicates that even adult's speech may be influenced by habitual use of words. Another problem in this instance is that the use of "during" suggests a non-native speaker's language competence.

　　In (2), Bush said "I talk to families who die", he has been influenced by someone else's words— "I talked to those who've lost their lives". This indicates that Bush has not really comprehended the correct expression. In psycholinguistics,

Bush's use of language harbors comprehension barriers.

In (3), Bush said it as if he meant it or as if he made no mistake in saying so. Bush failed to monitor his speech and failed to correct himself there on the spot. Language production needs monitoring mechanism, but it is not always the case as is shown by Bush.

In (4), "Rarely is the question asked: Is our children learning?", the second "is" indicates that undergeneralization happens even in an adult's speech. Just because the first "is" is used, Bush use "is" again to make "children" in agreement with a singular noun. In psycholinguistics, children tend to undergeneralize in their speech. For example, children tend to treat a group as a single, dogs as a definite dog, etc. Interestingly, people think that Bush deliberately uses "Is our children learning" to prove a fact that such kind of question is "rarely asked". This quote— "Rarely is the question asked: Is our children learning?" —has the same effect in terms of psycholinguistics as that— "Are our president learning".

Chapter 11   Cognitive Linguistics

1. (1) cognitive linguistics: it is a modern school of linguistic thought and practice, which is concerned with investigating the relationship between human language, the mind and socio-physical experience.

   (2) categorization: The mental process of classification is called categorization.

   (3) category: the product of categorization.

   (4) prototype: the central member of a category in the prototype theory.

   (5) conceptual metaphor: within the domain of cognitive linguistics, metaphor is defined as understanding one conceptual domain in terms of another conceptual domain, which can be schematized as: CONCEPTUAL DOMAIN (A) IS CONCEPTUAL DOMAIN (B).

   (6) conceptual metonymy: metonymy can be defined as a cognitive process in which one conceptual entity provides mental access to another conceptual entity within the same domain.

   (7) construal: The term construal not only relates to the way a language user chooses to "package" and "present" an experience, but also relates to the ways that an utterance is construed or interpreted by the hearers.

   (8) image schema: Image schemas are relatively abstract patterns or mental

structures that arise directly from our daily interaction with and observation of the world around us.

(9) iconicity: the structure of language reflects in some way the structure of experience, that is, the language mimes the world.

2. The classical theory has the following viewpoints: 1) Categories are defined in terms of a set of necessary and jointly sufficient conditions; 2) Features are binary; 3) Categories have clear boundaries; 4) All members of a category have equal status. In contrast, the prototype theory has the following viewpoints: 1) Categories are not defined by virtue of shared criterial features but organized in terms of their family resemblances; 2) The boundary of the category is not clear but fuzzy; 3) Not all members of a category have the same status within a category, which vary according to their prototypicality; 4) Categories are radial, organizing around the prototypes.

3. Conceptual metaphors relate to "ways of thinking", thus are schematic or abstract such as TIME IS MONEY; in contrast, linguistic metaphors are manifestations of the conceptual metaphors, which reveal the existence of conceptual metaphors.

4. Conceptual metonymy reveals the conceptual relation "X stands for Y", while conceptual metaphor reflects the conceptual relation "X is understood in terms of Y". This distinction gives rise to another difference between conceptual metonymy and metaphor: both can be understood as mapping processes, but metonymy is a mapping within one cognitive domain, whereas metaphor is a cross-domain mapping.

5. A. Look *how far* we've *come*. B. We're *at a crossroads*.
C. We'll just have to *go our separate ways*. D. We can't *turn back* now.
E. We're *stuck*. F. It's been a *long, bumpy road*. G. This relationship is a *dead-end street*. H. We're just *spinning our wheels*. I. Our marriage is *on the rocks*. J. We've *gotten off the track*. K. This relationship is *foundering*.

Chapter 12 Applied Linguistics

1. Compare the major features of the two approaches, you can figure out that learners' grammatical knowledge may be better developed by the grammar-translation method which stresses accuracy over fluency, while accuracy may be overlooked in the communicative teaching approach. Check what problems of the grammar-translation method can be solved in the communicative approach, you can tell disadvantages of grammar-translation method.

2. Different teaching methods are used in dealing with different teaching content; there are differences in the concrete teaching of different teachers, who may hold different ideas about language and language teaching and learning. Exemplification is encouraged.

3. No, they can't. Reasons can be given by analyzing the two exams along the basic distinctions in language testing.

4. First of all, what type of test is to be designed should be taken into consideration, for the content of the test items and questions may vary from type to type. Then the potential of the validity and reliability of the test should be considered. Detailed elaboration of the three factors is needed to make a highly valued answer.